Challenges and Opportunities in Education for Refugees in Europe

Studies in Inclusive Education

Series Editor

Roger Slee (*University of South Australia, Australia*)

Editorial Board

VOLUME 37

The titles published in this series are listed at *brill.com/stie*

Challenges and Opportunities in Education for Refugees in Europe

From Research to Good Practices

Edited by

Fabio Dovigo

BRILL

SENSE

LEIDEN | BOSTON

All chapters in this book have undergone peer review.

The Library of Congress Cataloging-in-Publication Data is available online at
http://catalog.loc.gov
LC record available at http://lccn.loc.gov/2018027337

ISSN 2542-9825
ISBN 978-90-04-38320-3 (paperback)
ISBN 978-90-04-38321-0 (hardback)
ISBN 978-90-04-38322-7 (e-book)

This book is printed on acid-free paper and produced in a sustainable manner.

CONTENTS

PREFACE

OPPORTUNITIES AND CHALLENGES OF REFUGEE EDUCATION

The recent wave of migrants arriving in Europe, fleeing war or difficult living conditions, represents both a challenge and a great educational opportunity for European school systems. Even though a large body of literature on the social inclusion of refugees is available today, investigations into refugee children and their education remain relatively underdeveloped, especially in relation to the implementation of school-based interventions and programmes. Current research and good practice in this field have mainly been developed within the boundaries of national educational politics and policies, addressing distinct populations. This fragmentation has stood in the way of a systematic analysis of the question at the European level, which is a necessary condition for advancing successful educational interventions that might do justice to the current size of the phenomenon.

Education is seen as a protective factor for refugee children (Rutter, 2006; Gunton, 2007; Block et al., 2014). Evidence from countries with extensive experience with refugee education show that the ability of schools to provide immediate and appropriate support is pivotal in favouring a smooth accommodation process and ensuring safety, security, and settlement for children (Bash, 2006; Porche et al., 2011). Conversely, inadequate school support often translates into students' absenteeism, disengagement, feelings of disempowerment, poor relationships with peers, and early school leaving. This, in turn, can affect not only the school achievements of refugee children, but also their coping strategies and resilience, undermining future prospects in terms of employment and socio-economic status, and heightening social exclusion (Hek, 2005; Hamilton & Moore, 2004; Taylor & Sidhu, 2012).

The European Union's delay in envisioning and implementing clear-cut policies regarding this issue reflects the prolonged invisibility of asylum-seeker and refugee children within the official educational paths. This void has, to a certain extent, been filled by medical and social services, NGOs, and voluntary associations. However, when responding to the needs of refugee children, such organisations risk framing them as a homogenous group, even though we know that being a refugee is more a "bureaucratic entity" than an experiential one (Kirk & Cassity, 2007; Matthews, 2008; Rutter, 2001). Schools can contribute to reducing that risk by helping to refocus attention on refugee children as whole persons, as well as offering widespread and extensive educational support to them (Arnot & Pinson, 2005). Moreover, while medical and social services may be unfamiliar or be regarded with suspicion, as they are often connected with legal requirements, schools are generally respected and appreciated by refugee families, which consider them as an opportunity for socio-economic mobility (Keddie, 2012; Pugh, Every, & Hattam, 2012). On the one hand, schools in Europe are now working on developing a deeper knowledge of the multiple, complex needs of asylum-seeker and refugee pupils undergoing experiences related to high mobility, displacement, and replacement. On the other, they are actively engaged in complex inter-agency conversations and negotiations with public and private services to define aims, roles, and tasks related to the care of refugee children.

Previous studies highlight that, unlike second-generation migrants, refugee children usually have to deal with barriers related to language, culture and, more generally, different educational systems (McBrien, 2016; Naidoo, 2015; Pastoor, 2017). Language proves to be an especially difficult challenge, as it is essential to assess refugee children's learning and skills in order to place them at the appropriate school level. Children's ages are another important factor affecting refugee students' educational paths, as research shows that the rate of school success is higher for children who are able to attend education in the arrival country starting from kindergarten. However, as we have noted, refugee children should not be considered a homogeneous population, as their educational needs and potentials are highly variable with regard to their country of origin, family's cultural capital, and so on.

The integration of refugee children in education refers to different dimensions, mainly related to school access, performance, and participation. Access to education systems varies greatly depending on national norms and practices. Even though institutions such as the United Nations and European Union recommend that the right to education of refugee children be guaranteed regardless of their legal status, bureaucratic and organisational barriers frequently prevent the actual fulfilment of that right (Dryden-Peterson, 2016; UNHCR, 2016). Moreover, even when schools accept to enrol refugee children, they are often unable to provide the specific support children need in linguistic, educational, and psychological terms. This is compounded by the lack of intercultural training of teachers, many of whom feel unprepared to work with this specific student population. Efforts made by schools to welcome and promote refugee students are especially hindered in countries where students are forcibly enrolled in lower quality schools and classified early into groups based on academic scores and ability. Low school quality and early tracking in turn are reflected in refugee students' school performances, which are generally poorer than those of their classmates, and frequently end up causing grade retention. This is an unsurprising outcome, considering the many challenges refugee children experience while they or their families are trying to settle in the new country, not least the linguistic barriers they have to deal with. Accordingly, it should be considered not an inevitable accident, but an area of improvement for educational institutions committed to ensuring refugee students' full participation by fostering a wider approach to inclusion. This entails offering appropriate support so refugee youths can have a better chance of following valuable curricula at different school levels and completing their educational careers. More generally, it also implies the promotion of an inclusive educational environment where refugee students' attendance and integration can be seen as an opportunity to expand the role of educational institutions as a democratic community.

THE STRUCTURE OF THE BOOK

The book will delve into the multifaceted challenges European schools and services are currently facing by developing shared professional expertise and good practices in the attempt to cope with the recent wave of asylum-seeker and refugee children.

In Chapter 1, Heike de Boer, Benjamin Brass, and Henrik Bruns, is based on empirical research conducted within the mentoring project GeKOS, geared towards refugee children and university students in Germany. The project, implemented in teacher education programs at Koblenz-Landau University since 2015, aims to deal with facets of professionalization in pedagogical work with migrant children. Using narrative network analysis, the chapter delves into the way the GeKOS project has contributed to the children's social and cultural integration. Moreover, it investigates how university students' learning and professionalization processes can be developed through the systematic use of learning journals and case vignettes.

Chapter 2, by Fabio Dovigo, offers an evaluation of the development of refugee education in Italy by examining the existing legal, social and educational framework. The first part of the chapter investigates specific challenges and opportunities that Italian schools currently face. Policies and practices adopted by educational institutions to promote access and integration of refugee students at different school levels are reviewed and commented on. In the second part, the case of a group of schools and health/social services working with refugee families is analysed so as to understand the causes behind persistent difficulties with managing refugee children's education. Finally, the chapter discusses how good practices emerging from multi-agency collaboration could be transformed into an effective and strategic approach to fostering inclusive education for refugees.

Chapter 3 provides an overview of the current situation in Iceland based on data collected from qualitative research carried out by Hermina Gunnþórsdóttir. The report offers an in-depth account of the way school education is perceived by parents of immigrant and refugee children and teachers. Collected interviews show that the role and purpose of education are subjects of continuous negotiation between parents and teachers. Reciprocal expectations and beliefs arising from different cultural backgrounds are the cause of frequent misunderstandings. However, as the analysis highlights, strategies elaborated by schools could help move from a confrontational to a conversational perspective, creating an opportunity to define new and effective forms of home–school collaboration.

In Chapter 4, Tinde Kovacs Cerović, Sanja Grbić, and Dragan Vesić explore the processes of education change at school level accompanying the preparation for and the actual integration of migrant students in Serbia, with the aim to identify key features of the process of inclusion of migrants based on the perspectives of various actors in the education process. The authors provide an analysis of main strengths and areas for improvement of schools by comparing characteristics of the inclusion process in schools differing from each other in several relevant aspects. They finally formulate recommendations for other schools in Serbia and in other countries in a similar situation that start including students with a migrant background.

In Chapter 5, Laure Kloetzer, Miki Aristorenas, and Oula Abu-Amsha discuss a pilot educational project based on Information Technology carried out at the Zaatari Refugee Camp in 2016. The project aimed to train Syrian students in Java programming in order to reconnect them with Higher Education. Throughout the project, several focus groups and interviews were conducted to identify the main barriers Syrian refugee students face nowadays in attending Higher Education. Through a dialogical analysis of data collected over the course of the project, the chapter also highlights what coping mechanisms Syrian refugees use to overcome everyday barriers they face in pursuing their educational paths.

Chapter 6, by Tatjana Atanasoska and Michelle Proyer, collects and discusses contributions from a large number of practitioners currently involved in promoting refugee education in Austria. This broad overview focuses especially on two crucial topics related to the educational path of young people with a refugee background: on the one hand, the issue of learning Austrian German as a second language is explored through the analysis of manifold training experiences offered by educational institutions and third-sector organisations; on the other, initiatives undertaken by the University of Vienna to favour refugee student attendance, native student sensitivity, and prospective teachers' preparation are examined in depth to understand the impact they can have in Higher Education on developing a more comprehensive approach to refugee education.

Finally, in Chapter 7, Wayne Veck, Louise Pagden, and Wayne Veck clarify the social and educational significance of distinguishing assimilation from inclusion for children who, having been uprooted from their homes, continue to confront an unnecessarily cruel world. The chapter examines the pressures on school environment to assimilate children seeking refuge in existing school structures without pausing to consider the ways these children might be included. Two forms of assimilation are analysed: *assimilation into the given* and *assimilation into indifference*. The first is an active process that can see children new to the UK and seeking refuge within it forced both to fit into fixed structures and practices and to conform to established values and social norms. The second is characterised not by what happens to these children but precisely by the absence of activity regarding them, as well as a lack of attention to and concern for them.

REFERENCES

Arnot, M., & Pinson, H. (2005). *The education of Asylum-Seeker and refugee children: A study of LEA and school values, policies and practices.* Cambridge: Faculty of Education, University of Cambridge.

Bash, L. (2006). Identity, boundary and schooling: Perspectives on the experiences and perceptions of refugee children. *Intercultural Education, 16*(4), 351–366.

Block, K., Cross, S., Riggs, E., & Gibbs, L. (2014). Supporting schools to create an inclusive environment for refugee students. *International Journal of Inclusive Education, 18*(12), 1337–1355.

Dryden-Peterson, S. (2016). Refugee education in countries of first asylum: Breaking open the Black box of pre-resettlement experiences. *Theory and Research in Education, 14*(2), 131–148.

Gunton, A. (2007). Refugees in our schools. *Teacher, 187,* 16.

Hamilton, R., & Moore, D. (Eds.). (2004). *Educational interventions for refugee children: Theoretical perspectives and implementing best practice.* London: RoutledgeFalmer.

Hek, R. (2005). *The experiences and needs of refugee and asylum seeking children in the UK: A literature review.* London: Department for Education and Skills.

Keddie, A. (2012). Refugee education and justice issues of representation, redistribution and recognition. *Cambridge Journal of Education, 42*(2), 197–212.

Kirk, J., & Cassity, E. (2007). Minimum standards for quality education for refugee youth. *Youth Studies Australia, 23*(1), 50–56.

Matthews, J. (2008). Schooling and settlement: Refugee education in Australia. *International Studies in Sociology of Education, 18*(1), 31–45.

McBrien, J. (2016). *Refugees and asylum seekers.* In R. Hattam, M. Zembylas, & J. Arthur (Eds.), *The Palgrave international handbook of education for citizenship and social justice.* London: Palgrave Macmillan.

Naidoo, L. (2015). Educating refugee-background students in Australian schools and universities. *Intercultural Education, 26*(3), 210–217.

Pastoor, L. de W. (2017). Reconceptualising refugee education: Exploring the diverse learning contexts of unaccompanied young refugees upon resettlement. *Intercultural Education, 28*(2), 143–164.

Porche, M. V., Fortuna, L. R., Lin, J., & Alegria, M. (2011). Childhood trauma and psychiatric disorders as correlates of school dropout in a national sample of young adults. *Child Development, 82*(3), 982–998.

Pugh, K., Every, D., & Hattam, R. (2012). Inclusive education for students with refugee experience: Whole school reform in a South Australian Primary School. *The Australian Educational Researcher, 39*(2), 125–141.

Rutter, J. (2001). *Supporting refugee children in 21st century Britain: A compendium of essential information.* London: Trentham.

Rutter, J. (2006). *Refugee children in the UK.* Maidenhead: Open University Press.

Taylor, S., & Sidhu, R. K. (2012). Supporting refugee students in schools: What constitutes inclusive education? *International Journal of Inclusive Education, 16*(1), 39–56.

UNHCR. (2016). *Mainstreaming refugees in national education systems.* Retrieved November 30, 2017, from http://www.unhcr.org/560be1493.html

FIGURES AND TABLES

FIGURES

TABLES

HEIKE DE BOER, BENJAMIN BRASS AND HENRIK BRUNS

1. "IT'S SAD AND NICE AT THE SAME TIME"

*Challenges to Professionalization in Pedagogical
Work with Migrant Children*

INTRODUCTION

According to the UNHCR (2015), there were just under 60 million refugees worldwide by the end of 2014 and already over 65 million by the end of 2015. In Germany, the Federal Agency of Migration and Refugees recorded one million asylum seekers in 2015 and 441,899 initial applications, thereof 17,625 in Rhineland-Palatinate (BAMF, 2015).

This is how in Koblenz, a city in the federal state Rhineland-Palatinate, the number of recipients of benefits under the Asylum Seekers Benefits Act tripled between 2012 and 2014 from 272 persons (2012) to 713 persons (2014).[1]

As soon as Koblenz is assigned to a family as their permanent residence, compulsory schooling counts for all their children of six years and older. The children are registered for the closest local elementary school and assigned to adequate classes according to their age. In Germany, children go to elementary school for four years. Children of ten years and older visit secondary schools. The various federal states differ in their practice of integration. A frequent line of distinction is

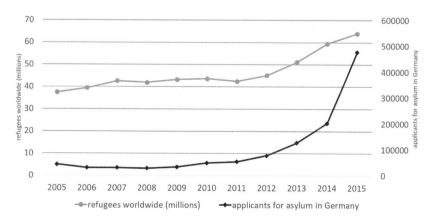

*Figure 1.1. Development of asylum applications in Germany since 2006
in relation to the total number of refugees*

© KONINKLIJKE BRILL NV, LEIDEN, 2018 | DOI:10.1163/9789004383227_001

the question whether a separate school class should be established especially for newly immigrated students or not (von Dewitz et al., 2006). School integration in Rhineland-Palatinate takes place under the principle *integration into the normal school class from the start*, which is supplemented by German immersion courses with 10–15 hours per week (MIFKJF, 2015).

Here, children are included directly into the school context of elementary school classes on the one hand, but are one the other hand not only confronted with the German language and often unfamiliar cultural, legal, and regional circumstances but also with a school system that is regularly fully unknown to them. This situation is challenging for children, parents, and teachers, as also teachers are only not well prepared for this situation and thus feel uncertain.

Although the handling of cultural diversity and multilingualism is an important part of teacher training programs at German universities, it commonly falls within the scope of mandatory courses, so that students or teaching staff are often insufficiently prepared for this problem. A sensitization of all parties involved in school for questions of immigration is fundamental in order to be able to adequately cope with this situation, as next to a professional dealing with multilingualism, the cooperation with external partners is necessary, for instance due to traumatic stress or impeding deportation of children.

MENTORING AS AN INTEGRATION AND PROFESSIONALIZATION STRATEGY

It is known as a result of an investigation within the framework of a study of the World Vision Institute (2016) about the living conditions of children with flight history in Germany that often, the situation of such children is doubly precarious. They suffer from the conditions and consequences of the flight and also from the initially uncertain situation in the host country. As children, they have special needs and live through a biographically sensitive phase. In this matter, the exclusion from leisure time activities and from contact to peers due to economic, linguistic, and administrative impediments has particularly severe effects (Berthold, 2014). Their life at the new place of residence changes between being welcome and the threat of deportation (Schröeder, 2016). At the same time and in spite of all obstacles, children are mostly positive and open-minded towards their new home, school, and the possibility to find new friends, as interviews with newly arrived children show (World Vision Germany, 2016). The thought of integration through education draws on these potentials by offering room and opportunities to perceive oneself as accepted and competent as well as to contribute and simultaneously extend one's cultural and linguistic knowledge.

Hence, there is a need for well-trained teachers and pedagogues who are appropriately prepared for this task. Here, "one size, fits all" – solutions cannot be utilized as the variety of the children and their experiences is simply too big. The challenge is rather to newly find out what works in every individual case. This also means to reflect upon one's personal thinking and actions, to overcome stereotyping patterns, and to search actively for potentials and similarities.

Against this background, the mentoring project *"GeKOS – gemeinsam entdecken Kinder ihren Ort mit Studierenden"* (Children discover their place together with students) was developed at the University of Koblenz.

1. The project wants to contribute to the *professionalization* of prospective teachers and pedagogues when dealing with immigration and multilingualism. The challenge to address current social and political developments in university teaching, to make it an accessible experience for students and to classify it scientifically rises from this perspective.
2. The project should also *make a civic contribution*. From this perspective, it is vital to improve living conditions particularly with regard to refugee children in Germany.
3. The university is integrated as a place of *research* that generates *new solutions* for challenging situations – thereto belongs not at last the acquisition of knowledge about pedagogical work with children of refugees.

Therefore, it deals with three issues, the contribution to the *integration of children with a flight history* in the present time, *the qualification of prospective teachers*, who will work with them in the future, and the *obtainment of scientific insights* for all those who face similar challenges.

GeKOS – A Mentoring Project

"Education is the door opener for individual participation and developmental possibilities in our society" (BMBF, 2012). This is the formulation of the National Action Plan for Integration; therefore, the improvement of educational participation of immigrated people is an important education policy as well as pedagogical task. Here, education comprises more than what is learnt at school or in integration courses. They are without a doubt important parts for succeeding integration, but not sufficient when standing alone. Younger studies call attention to the fact that the reasons for unequal education participation of immigrants, as opposed to children and adolescents born in Germany, are not to be found at school or in financial equipment, but in the differences in social and cultural capital. An important example for this is *informal learning* in the context of the leisure time behaviour of children and their peers. Children and adolescents without migration backgrounds in tendency have more options for leisure time activities, they are integrated into greater friendship networks and therefore have more possibilities to try out various activities and to develop interests (Harring, 2011). Simultaneously, leisure time contacts which overcome ethnic borders lead towards a *reduction of inequalities* and a *degradation of stereotypes on both sides*. In principle, these connections count in the same way or perhaps even stronger for children with a flight history. In their families, it does not only lacks means and support opportunities to take part in leisure time activities, for instance through clubs. The parents are also newcomers who often do not know which leisure time possibilities are offered to their kids by their new home. Other important factors are the exertion of the flight and the uncertainty about the family's resident status, which directs the attention towards other and apparently more urgent problems.

With regard to these considerations, GeKOS pursues the objective to offer children opportunities that are in between educational offers on the one hand and family life on the other hand. The project aims at enabling the children to experience leisure time during which they can incidentally learn about their new home as well as about regional habits and particularities. Thereby, they do not only come into contact with new places, acitivities, and persons but above all with the new language. Such learning processes, which are summarized under the term *incidental learning* (Schugurensky, 2000), signify a main resource for integration and learning at school. Therefore, tandems in which each adult mentor is responsible for one child with a flight history as their mentee stand in the center of GeKOS. As experiences in other mentoring projects show, a one-on-one situation offers enormous potentials on both sides (Baquero Torres & de Boer, 2011). Once a week, the tandems create their leisure time together and gain manifold experiences in doing so. They for instance play parlor games, go to the zoo or the movies, paint or do handicrafts and show each other their favorite places. While at the beginning, it is mostly about *building a relationship* and making offers to the child, the tandems increasingly determine what they want to do together and develop *reciprocity*. On the part of the project, there is a budget for activities and material that the tandems can use in their favour.

The shared time enables the children to experience new things and to step out of their everyday life for a while. The adult reference person shows them new possibilities and supports them even when they experience things or actions that are new, irritating, or appear strange. Vice versa, the children get the chance to participate in the shared leisure time organization, to be appreciated for and be able to implement their ideas. In order to communicate, both tandem partners have to learn something about the language of the respective other; the children thus extend their language skills, as well.

The tandem work is supervised intensively and accompanied at university by various flanking events and reflexion instruments during these nine months:

1. At first, the students have to register for the project with a registration questionnaire. It inquires their prior experiences with regard to multilingualism, interculturality, dealing with children and their perception of their own strengths, preferences, and interests.
2. On basis of these information, the matching process is performed. The project coordination and contact teachers of the cooperation schools exchange views and build tandems which take into consideration the preferences, interests, and preconditions of the children and students and pair them in an adequate way.
3. The project starts with a two-day block seminar in which the project goals,

organization, procedure, and evaluation are introduced. Thereto belong the introduction into the legal backgrounds as well as the recognition of concrete indications of and opportunities for consultation in case of traumas, and the development of concrete proposals for activities for first acquaintances through to the handling of one's own resources and limits of responsibility and competence. The students get sufficient space to ask their own questions and simultaneously get used to the task waiting to be dealt with. The students also meet "alumni" there, who share their experiences and are open for questions. Additionally, they get to know their supervisors, who will accompany them during the project round.

4. On starting day, the students and children meet and get to know each other for the first time and arrange their first meeting. The starting day takes place at the cooperating schools and is organized as a festive afternoon with music, games, and a shared meal. The children come attended by their families and the contact teachers, school administration, volunteer refugee helpers and the project team are there, as well.

5. During the course of the project, the mentors are supported in small groups in biweekly coaching sessions and are at the same time offered thematic workshop possibilities.[2] Additionally, there are conversations with the contact teaching staff at the schools, where the students can sit in on classes, as well. (The project is connected to university curriculum structures and is allowed for the corresponding ECTS credits).

6. With a last day, which is celebrated similarly to the first day with all participants, the project round is finished together.

Due to the modular BA/MA structure of the course of study at university, it is difficult to engage students for such projects for a couple of years. Thus, one project round lasts for two semesters. However, the children and students can participate in further project rounds if desired.

GeKOS in the Context of Other Mentoring Projects

The term mentoring refers back to the universally applicable principle of a mentorship between one older or more experienced and a younger or less experienced person with the objective of supporting the latter. The classic form consists of a face-to-face or one-on-one relationship of mentor and mentee (Neumann & Schneider, 2011). Mentoring projects in the context of university teacher training rely on *reciprocity*, because students can learn on different levels during the shared time with their mentee, as well. The existing studies focusing on the effectiveness of mentoring programs are as diverse as the existing mentoring approaches. American studies prove that mentoring programs take full effect especially for children and adolescents in the context of *environmental disadvantage* (Neumann & Schneider, 2011). German studies by Klemm and Klemm (2010) talk about the strengths of mentoring especially in the area of *"soft impact factors"*, such as *improved self-consciousness* and *better learning motivation, emotional stabilization, improvement of educational opportunities* on the side of the children, and *reduction of prejudices* as well as *increase of skills regarding conflict, communication* and *integration* on side of the mentors.

It became visible within the framework of different studies that the success of mentoring projects is linked to various factors (Neumann & Schneider, 2011, p. 226):

- professional organization and coordination (including funding)
- training and support of mentors
- avoidance of situations of excessive demand
- demand-driven application at schools (expression of personal need)
- regularity and intensity (ibid., p. 222)
- quality of emotional relationships between both partners
- the degree of reciprocity (ibid.)

In the context of the EU project "mentor migration", there was a network group in which students of various universities in Europe mentored elementary school children and met weekly with their mentees for nine months between 2007 and 2009. The Freiburg project "SALAM – Spielen, Austauschen, Lernen, Anerkennen und Miteinander sprechen" (*Play, Exchange views, Learn, Acknowledge, and Talk with each other*) is a German project following from this context that still exists today. It aims at pupils with a migration background between 8 and 12 years and at students.

Investigations in the context of this project (Wenzler-Cremer, 2016, p. 255) show that students and children experience "*resonance*" and explore "*their own and the foreign*", by which important opportunities for learning emerge. Examples of statements from guided interviews with the participating students enabled the reconstruction of challenging experiences in the project. In this context, Baquerro-Torres and de Boer (2012) uncovered that one particular problem appears to be that mentors do not always perceive difficulties in the project as learning opportunities and that the danger of reproducing stereotypes occurs especially in situations which the students perceived as challenging.

As "homogenization thinking" of teachers impedes the adequate handling of heterogeneous learning groups in everyday school life, the analysis of questions of migration-dependent heterogeneity is vital for the development of professional attitudes and approaches of prospective teachers. It is necessary to build professional action patterns so that pupils with a migration history are not discriminated or disadvantaged at class due to teachers' poorly reflected culturalizing and ethnicizing interpretation patterns. For the development of a professional dealing with migration, teacher training has to prepare prospective teachers for school in a professional way.

The project "GeKOS" wants to prepare future pedagogues to develop professional action patterns when dealing with the increasing diversity of the life context of children and to contribute to a reflexive examination of *experiences of foreignness*. The students obtain valuable insights into other cultures and the life contexts and biographies of people who had to flee. As the students meet the children and their families on a regular basis for nine months and reflect their experiences in the context of supporting events and tasks in a focused manner, they become aware of and question their own observations, prejudices and judgements, fears, and stereotypes, and identify learning needs and develop competencies to interpret, understand and act in the context of diversity experiences.

It is a special challenge that the group of refugees is not only heterogeneous with regard to its national origin but also with respect to education and class-specific composition. Currently, families and individuals from Syria and Afghanistan but also from Kosovo, Albania, Macedonia and Serbia come to Koblenz and ask for asylum. While families and individuals from Syria are most likely to be accepted as asylum seekers, families from the countries of the Western Balkans and currently also from Afghanistan cannot expect an acceptance of their application for asylum, as their country of origin is not recognized as a crisis region. In this matter, the mentors do not only need background knowledge about the current refugee issue, asylum situation, asylum law and the consequential questions when dealing with children but also need knowledge about the distinct writing and education culture in the countries of origin.

THEORETICAL PERSPECTIVES ON PROFESSIONALIZATION IN PEDAGOGICAL WORK WITH MIGRANT CHILDREN

The project objectives of GeKOS draw on theories about professionalism, which in turn influence the scientific methods employed in the research. Ideas about professionalism permeate all three levels of research regarding university students' experiences during the project:

1. Research on the first level deals with the structure (as in the inner logic) of professional pedagogical action in the mentoring of migrant children
2. Research on the second level focuses on professionalization for the work with migrant children as a process
3. Research on the third level analyzes case-sensitive understanding as a specific professional ability

There seems to be a consensus that professionals need to be able to reflect on their actions and adjust them to the case at hand in the discourse on pedagogical professionalism (Schön, 1983). The mentioned reasons, however, vary between different theoretical approaches and so do the general assumptions about how exactly professional action can be understood (Terhart, 2011). In this chapter, we outline the project's underlying assumptions regarding professional pedagogical work with refugee children.

Structural Approaches and Criticism on Intercultural Competence

When talking about pedagogical work with migrant children, there is a widespread use of theories about intercultural competence. These theories assume that professionals possess certain competences – latent dispositions which allow them to act in a

7

professional way when the contextual need arises. Auernheimer (2013), one of the proponents of intercultural competence as a framework for pedagogical professionalism, has for example proposed that intercultural competence comprises knowledge, attitudes, and practical skills in four specific domains that qualify professionals to adequately deal with intercultural situations. Competence-focused theories thus tend to reduce professional action to a function of competence, which in turn means that professionalism could be equated with having acquired all or most of the necessary competences. This view has been criticized for its dependence on stereotypical forms of knowledge about 'the others' that legitimize universal prescriptions, but fail to take the singular nature of pedagogical cases into account (Mecheril, 2013).

Because of this, GeKOS is grounded in theories which employ the idea that science cannot prescribe solutions but can instead describe the recurring and often dilemmatic demands faced by pedagogical actors. Understood in these terms, professionalism means that the actor balances such demands in a way that is adequate for the case at hand. In order to describe the demands faced in mentoring, we refer to structural views on pedagogical professionalism. Structural approaches draw on the assumption that the defining characteristic of professions is that they deal with practical problems faced by their clients and that they do so through direct interaction with them (Helsper, 2014). A number of challenges arises from this constellation from a structural point of view. These challenges take the logical structure of antinomies in that they require the professional to adhere to two contradicting orientations at once (Helsper, 2002). Because professionals process their client's individual problems, the professional him- or herself cannot solve the client's problem but needs to rely on the client's cooperation as well as on his or her specific resources. Additionally, he or she needs to establish a connection to the client's specific situation (Helsper, 2014). Under these conditions, professionals cannot employ universal rules of dealing with a problem unless they want to risk that the solution fails to address the problem's unique structure and thus the problem itself (Helsper, 2014). As Abbott (1988) puts it, there is no direct way from diagnosis to treatment in professional domains, as a step of inference that cannot be formalized through abstract and universal rules needs to be involved. Abbott instead refers to it as a form of hypothetical reasoning which sets the professional's logic of action apart from that of other occupations. This professional form of reasoning draws on abstract scientific knowledge in order to reconstruct the case at hand in theoretical terms without subordinating its unique features under stereotypical categories (Helsper, 2014). In structural terms, this is called a "reconstructive understanding of the case" (Helsper, 2014; transl. by the authors) and regarded as the backbone of pedagogical professionalism. This form of understanding needs to oscillate between the unique features of the case and the subsumption under scientific knowledge. It therefore takes the form of an antinomy in which *both* references are needed *at the same time*.

Against this background, professionalism can be defined as acting in a way that balances these antinomic demands in a way that is adequate to the case at hand (Helsper, 2014). This demands from professionals the ability to reflect on his or her own actions in order to answer the question whether the specific way of dealing with the challenges of the case at hand is appropriate. *Pedagogical* professionalism is characterized by its special function: Other than a therapist's work, which begins after the client has faced problems he or she cannot solve him- or herself, the professional educators' task is to provide their clients with abilities that help them solve their own problems before they become unsolvable (Helsper, 2014). This is achieved through a mediation between the client on one side and the society's accumulated knowledge and norms on the other side (Helsper, 2014). Because of this special focus, the general challenges to professional action take a particular form reflected in special antinomies and fields of tension (Helsper & Hummrich, 2008, p. 65):

1. heteronomy – autonomy
2. asymmetry – symmetry
3. order – justification
4. subsumation – reconstruction
5. routine – uncertainty
6. universalism – particularism
7. distrust – trust
8. distance – closeness

Compared to competence-centred theories, the structural approach is more sensitive to the dilemmatic nature of pedagogical work. According to the structural approach, professional action is dynamic by nature, demanding constant attention towards and reconfiguration in these dimensions. The structural framework thus draws the researcher's interest to situations in which the 'right' action is not immediately obvious to the protagonist(s). By analysing the recurring logic of these situations, patterns pointing towards characteristic challenges in a specific area of pedagogical work can be identified.

From Structural Demands to Professionalization as a Process

This form of analysis remains on a structural level. As GeKOS is also interested in students' individual processes of professionalization, we also ask how they reflect on these challenges and how their way of dealing with them changes over time. Because of this, the structuralist view on pedagogical professionalism is supplemented by a focus on professionalization as a form of what is called *Bildung* in German.

The above-mentioned biographical perspectives on professionalization focus on how structural demands on professional action are processed and dealt with in individual professionalization processes. Through this lens, professionalism is acquired through reflecting one's own experiences and finding solutions that are adequate for and in accordance with both the challenge at hand and one's own identity. The specific concept we draw on has been proposed by Hericks (2006), who employs Havighurst's (1972) ideas about developmental tasks in order to analyse professionalization. Developmental tasks in professionalization are defined as tasks that arise predictably in one's way to become a professional and need to be solved to further develop one's professional capacity (Hericks, 2006). They are placed at the intersection between structural demands for professional action and biographically acquired resources for dealing with them on behalf of the actor. The main difference between this concept and competence-focused concepts is that the tasks are universal, while the solutions may be highly individual. Moreover, the biographical perspective entails a processual view on professionalization in that it does not only register whether someone has already found a solution or not but also provides a conceptual framework for the description of partial solutions along the way.

Hüpping (2017, pp. 255–259) has recently identified four domains in which professionalization processes are needed with regard to working with migrant children.

1. First, she points out the tendency of teachers to implicitly refer to a different cultural background as a deficit, while at the same time not being aware of the fact that they draw on their own cultural background as a norm.
2. Second, their reasoning about challenges in pedagogical work with migrant children hinges on dichotomous and often stereotypical categories that differentiate between the majority culture and a supposedly homogenous minority culture.
3. This is especially true of parents but also applies to children, which leads to her third finding: Intercultural education often draws on simplistic and folkloristic assumptions about the relationship between culture and individual, resulting in constructions that reduce children to representatives of their presumed culture.
4. Fourth, some topics, especially religious ones, are largely avoided due to insecurities and fears resulting from a lack of knowledge and experience.

In our view, these challenges cannot be dealt with by learning alone but require changes that reach deeper into how professionals conceive the relationship between themselves, migrant children, their families, and society. To differentiate between learning and these deeper changes, we draw on phenomenologically grounded concepts of learning and *Bildung*. Phenomenological concepts assume "that experience is characterized by the occurrence of something appearing to us *as something*, i.e. not in an arbitrary way, but with a particular meaning, a particular form or structure" (Koller, 2017, p. 38). The ascription of meaning draws on our presumptions and expectations about the world, the sum of which Koller (2017, p. 38) calls an "order". Processes of learning and *Bildung* are triggered when an experience seems unfamiliar in the sense that our expectations are not met and our order fails to make this understandable. This failure brings with it a situation of foreignness and irritation. The unfamiliar "intrudes our order by haunting and disturbing us" (Koller, 2017, p. 38) and demands an answer we do not have yet. In the case of learning, this answer is acquired as a form of adding new knowledge, skills, and attitudes, as in learning a new concept that does not challenge the ones we already hold; *Bildung*, however, fundamentally transforms our order and thus the way we relate to others, the world, and ourselves. As this process profoundly changes a person, Koller (2017) refers to it as transformative *Bildung*.

GeKOS tries to initiate and support not only processes of learning but also of transformative *Bildung*, in which the students experience challenges that are new to them and have to find new ways of relating. The concept of transformative *Bildung* has recently been expanded towards the processual aspects of professionalization (Bonnet & Hericks, 2013), is used for the substantiation of GeKOS' goals and as a means of analyzing similar professionalization processes. Due to the open nature of *Bildung*, there is no deterministic relationship between experiences of foreignness and irritation and new ways of relating to oneself and the world. It thus becomes an empirical question in how far processes of *Bildung* take place during mentorship. The accompanying research of GeKOS reflects this question and specifically looks for traces of irritation and changed perspectives in the students' descriptions.

APPROACH AND EMPIRICAL RESULTS OF THE ACCOMPANYING RESEARCH

Methodology and Methodological Design

On the basis of the theoretical-conceptual basics elaborated above, the accompanying research focuses on two concerns:

- Firstly, the evaluation research aims at a review of the goal attainment of the project on behalf of its stakeholders – children and parents with a refugee background, participating students, and sponsors;
- Secondly, the project is to contribute to the current state of research and the level of knowledge about school pedagogy beyond the immediate project context by gaining insights into professionalization demands and living conditions of children with a migration background. Following the approach of transfer-oriented research our findings are discussed with regional school and seminar administrations.

Considering this double addressee and objective structure, aspects of the process and results of the project are investigated on two levels. In addition, we evaluate the organization and support structure for the tandem work (project organization, support program for students, cooperation with all participants). Methodologically, the project refers to instruments of interpretative-reconstructive social research.

- In order to register the project's contribution to the social and cultural integration of children with an immigration background, the social-spatial references of the children, i.e. significant social relationships, locations, and leisure time activities, are investigated following the method of the network analysis of the World Vision Children Studies (Schröder et al., 2013) at the beginning and the end of the study. To this end, the current living environment of the children is built and photographed in a playful manner with building bricks and tokens (Figure 1.2).

11

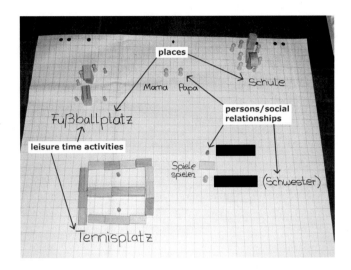

Figure 1.2. Live-world constellation

This building process is accompanied by the children's oral explanations, which are recorded and transcribed. The resulting transcripts and photography protocols are analyzed in a category-conducted, quantitative and qualitative way.

• In order to examine the professionalization of the student mentors, the individual learning and educational experiences are on the one hand documented in a process-accompanying way. The computer-assisted analysis was conducted with the text analysis software MAXQDA and the help of a qualitative content analysis (four elicitation points at an interval of two months). On the other hand, case vignettes help to investigate the improvement of skills to understand and solve cases in a professional way. They are also analysed with content-analytic pre- and post-comparisons in order to be able to assess the impact of project participation on the level of individual professionalization development.

Figure 1.3 displays the levels and examination methods of the accompanying research with regard to the level of child- and student-related objective in chronological sequence.[3]

Meanwhile, there are findings for 90 tandem pairs of two project rounds – 2015/2016 and 2016/2017.

Furthermore, the project-related professional requirements as well as learning and educational experiences are explained both in the light of the elaborated theoretical-conceptual basics and building on the empirical results of the project. Therefore, the results of the qualitative content-analysis of the learning diaries are displayed and interpreted from a profession-theoretical point of view with the help of case examples. The aim is to contribute to the empirical determination and further development of pedagogical professionality and professionalization requirements

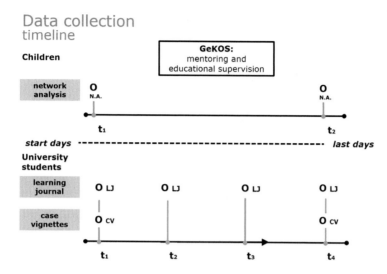

Figure 1.3. Levels of accompanying research and data collection in the passage of time

beyond the pedagogical discourse on professionalization. In doing so, the focus is on three key questions.

1. *Action- and demand structure in the field:* Which tasks and challenges towards pedagogical practice do university students face when mentoring immigrant children?
2. *Types of dealing with such situations:* How do university students handle these challenges? Which overarching action patterns towards these challenges can be identified?
3. *Learning- and educational experiences as well as professionalization processes:* Which learning experiences do university students have when dealing with the respective challenges?

Action and Demand Structures in the Context of Mentoring

The content analysis of the learning diaries takes place in two steps: At first and based on a frequency determination, content areas which the students reflect as crucial are revealed, systematized and theoretically classified. Secondly, selected demand structures are elaborated and particular case structures are exemplarily reconstructed.

Figure 1.4 gives an overview over the project's demand structures, which are arranged according to frequency and reflect the central challenges as mentioned in the learning diaries of the student mentors. It refers to all four points of data collection and calculates frequency in percent of overall learning diaries.[4]

The displayed challenges can be subdivided into three groups:

13

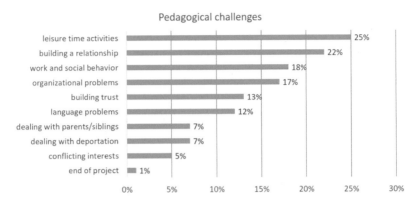

Figure 1.4. Educational challenges in the context of GeKOS

- The four demands that are addressed most often in the learning diaries comprise the finding or design of child-appropriate leisure time activities ('Leisure time activities', 25% of all learning diaries), problems in building a pedagogical relationship ('Building a relationship' 22%), the work attitude and social behaviour of the child ('Work and social behaviour', 18%), and organizational and work agreement issues ('Organizational problems', 17%), which belong to the main demands regarding overall tandem work.
- 'Building trust' (13%) and 'Language problems' (12%) in the fifth and sixth place are challenges which especially shape entries in the first learning diaries and mostly decrease during the course of the project.[5]
- 'Dealing with deportation' (7% of all learning diaries), 'parents/siblings' (also 7%) and 'conflicts of interest' (5%) build the third group of challenges, which only occur in specific tandem constellations and are therefore only described by affected students. Thereto belong difficulties in processing the project's completion (in 1% of all learning diaries).

On the one hand, this overview displays that the challenges in this mentoring project are located at different levels, as beside *pedagogical tasks of daily tandem and relationship work when dealing with the child*, particularly *dealing with parents and siblings* and *organizational problems* (e.g. work agreements), are named. On the other hand, the learning diary entries reflect some of the specific characteristics of the target group, as important challenges for the students were *the level of language, trust building*, or, depending on the respective case constellation, *dealing with deportation*. Thus, the mentoring work indicates a phase structure in which *'long-term tasks'* (leisure time activities, building a relationship, work and social behaviour, organizational problems) can be differentiated from more *phase-specific tasks* such as 'building trust' and 'language problems' at the beginning or 'ending of project' towards the end of the project.

The quantitative count of frequency of the subject areas described in the learning diaries only gives a general overview and abstracts necessarily from concrete demand structures. Thus, particular requirements are differentiated for three central task areas in the project – *child-oriented leisure time design* and *relationship formation, dealing with parents* as central cooperation partners, and *dealing with linguistic and cultural differences.*

Child-Oriented Leisure Time Design and Relationship Formation

The main tasks within the framework of GeKOS concern dealing with the mentee and comprise the development of a trustful relationship with the child, the design of leisure time activities that are appropriate for it, and supporting the children in getting to know their new environment, the German language and cultural norms and values via informal learning.

Trust can be regarded as the foundation of pedagogical relationships and determines how far children talk about themselves or engage actively in leisure time activities.

> At the beginning, he [Kamal] was very distanced and calm. Meanwhile, he is still calm but becomes more open. I recognize more and more that there are topics he likes to talk about and then he also starts to talk on his own. He tries to avoid speaking about other topics. We approach each other in very small steps, but it is getting better. He needs a lot of time to establish a connection. (LTB1, Anna)[6]

A closer look on the basis of the learning diary entries about this task area shows further challenges beyond the aspect of trust with which the students have to cope with, in particular

- Finding leisure time activities that are adequate for the individual interests or wishes of the child, keeping the weekly meetings varied and interesting.
- Overcoming the limited linguistic possibilities of the child in order to articulate own needs as well as situational passivity through to resistance by the child.
- Difficulties in determining and enforcing limits and rule structures with regard to unrealistic wishes of the child, needs of the group, or in dangerous situations.
- Coping with concentration or motivation difficulties of the child.
- Coping with difficult work or social behaviour, coping with social conflicts.
- Organization of the end of the project.

The overall assessment of the diary entries of the students shows that challenges the students are confronted with emerge from typical needs and development tasks appropriate to the children's age.

> Damian would prefer to do five things at a time. Often, he is restless, overexcited and distracted by the activities of other tandem pairs. I try to draw his attention to the things that we do and to react to his desires as well as possible. (LTB 1, Lisbeth)

When dealing with children, the setting of rules is a central challenge for students. Their confidence to do so as well as their ability to judge increase during the course of the project, where they are partly supported by coaching.

> Due to the insights which I gained during coaching, I will make sure to treat Chadi's behaviour more consequently and give him a chewing out after he has a stubborn phase, as in "Well then we'll have to go home now" and then actually walk the talk. (LTB 3, Isabel)

Furthermore, it becomes clear that typical demands in dealing with children are dependent on the individual case characteristics (e.g. the individual language competence, cultural prerequisites or the degree of support from parents or volunteers) with regard to the particular preconditions of children with a migration background.

> When I propose something that we could do, I always get the answer "Everything is okay". So far, I don't know the interests of my mentee because I only hear "doesn't matter", "you decide", or "whatever you like best" as answers. (LTB3, Jessica)

In this context, the students need to learn that it is difficult for some children to formulate their interests, which can have various reasons. Coaching offers some help, which Gundula's learning diary shows. Her mentee "did not want to come to any meeting anymore and completely cloistered herself away. Thanks to the coaching, I was able to get a grip of the situation. It was nice to see that it was not always my fault and that everything cannot always be perfect. This made me stronger" (LTB 3, Gundula).

Interaction with Parents

Working with parents is of central importance within mentoring, because the design of leisure time activities needs the parents' formal acceptance as well as a relationship of trust and continuous agreements with the legal guardians (e.g. for excursions, appointment arrangements for picking up the children at a certain place, obtaining permissions). The reviewed learning diaries display the central importance of visiting the families for many tandems. This contributes to the strengthening of the relationship and enables insights into the living conditions of the families here in Germany as well as into culturally conveyed ways of living. Especially in this context, the mentors experience special cordiality and hospitality for their work:

> Visiting the family was also always meaningful to me, as we strengthened the relation to the parents and also to the children, because we gained insights into their culture and way of living and especially into their lives before they came to Germany, which I see as very helpful information for the work with the children. By welcoming us like this again and again, the parents make it

clear how thankful they are that we take care of their children, but also how hospitable and simply happy they are to get to know people here. (LTB1, Isabel)

Frequently, the students become part of the children's lives throughout the course of the project due to the visits in their homes (e.g. when they play together at the parent's house or attend their birthdays). However, this also confronts the mentors with needs and partly culturally conducted expectations on the side of the parents (e.g. hospitality).

> In the beginning, it was a little bit difficult for me that Luana's family offers me tea, chocolate and so on every single week after the meetings. Of course I am happy about this hospitality and the openness which they show towards me. But I don't always have the time after a long day at Uni and with Luana to stay on the family's couch and drink tea. However, I don't want to appear unfriendly and disappoint the family, who is happy about the distraction from their one-sided everyday life. Especially at the beginning, I did not know exactly how to handle this without dissatisfying anyone – the family or myself [...]. (LTB1, Karolina)

A detailed analysis of the learning diary entries shows the diversity of the emerging relationships, the dependency on the respective condition constellation, and the individuality of the respectively emerging demand structures, especially in the area of parent work: The relationship between mentor and parents of the child often develops – as the following quote shows – in a positive and cooperative way:

> I have a good relationship with Carima's mother. Her German gets better and better and I can talk to her without having Carima translate. I have a feeling that she is very thankful that I spend the time with Carima and I feel very welcome by them. When she is at home, she mostly sits in the living room with us and plays along in board games or practices reading with us. We talk more than initially, because the linguistic barrier becomes smaller as she gets better with the German language. (LTB2, Alina)

In other cases, only little contact emerges. Here, agreements fail or the relationship stays on a superficial or sporadic level, as can be demonstrated with an example[7]: Ella expresses as a central challenge "Parent work!!! Agreements frequently do not work. But there is nothing you can do about that" (LTB3, Ella). To the question "How has the relationship to your tandem child developed?", she answers "Badly. The parents probably do not understand the meaning of the project and do not want any contact" (LTB 3, Ella).

In order to clarify the opposite pole of a succeeding relationship and the large range of the field, Isabel's learning diary entry can be presented as an example expressing the connection between mentor and family: "As already described, the relationship to the parents developed very well. According to Habib, the father, we are already part of the family. They always serve us delicious food and alternatingly bring along self-made cookies. We also exchange recipes with Nabila, the mother" (LTB2, Isabel).

Regarded in higher resolution, the following aspects can be named as challenges that students have to cope with particularly when working with parents:

- Making contact with and establishment of parental trust as a basis for the tandem work
- Establishment of a reliable cooperation relationship and reaching of arrangements
- Positioning and distancing with regard to culturally mediated social expectations and need for closeness of the parents (e.g. when dealing with daily invitations for food or tea in the case of students' limited time resources, dealing with invitations that are perceived as too personal such as participation in family events or gestures of gratitude)
- Support of parents in administrative processes and daily struggles (e.g. fill in forms, help with apartment search, make telephone calls), but also in care tasks (e.g. babysitting).

The last point illustrates that the parents are not only cooperation partners in the pedagogical work of the students with the child but appear as persons in need, as well.

More challenges we came across rather deal with the family, who we get along well with. However, it becomes more and more difficult for us to leave again when we are at their house. I am asked more and more often to help them with problems, for example telephone calls or apartment search. I want to help and I have already made several phone calls for them or have translated documents. But I cannot help with everything, for example I am not well versed regarding the housing market and I know only little about regulations for refugees with respect to apartments. I am also hardly familiar with telephone contracts. I always feel a little over-challenged when I have to help with this. (LTB2, Isabel)

Dealing with Context-Specific Challenges Regarding Linguistic and Cultural Difference

Dealing with *linguistically and culturally determined heterogeneity* poses a central challenge for prospective teachers, which is in centre of current theoretical debates about teacher professionality in the context of immigration (Hüpping, 2017). This assessment empirically proves to be true for the context at hand, whereby findings suggest the necessity of a differentiated consideration of the heterogeneous conditions of the children and their families (existing language skills, cultural backgrounds) as well as of the way of dealing with linguistic and cultural differences.

Thus, the analysis of the learning diaries displays on the one hand that *dealing with language barriers* signifies a central challenge for many tandems both in weekly meetings with the child and in cooperation with the parents until the second part of the project. In this respect, the mentoring context shows that language influences various aspects of teamwork and takes a central part when working together and putting effort into integration. Here, the learning diary entries partly reflect the success of the accompanying educational efforts at school and in adult education, which make a significant contribution, as well.

> The language barrier was a special challenge, mainly in the informal context. It was almost impossible to inform the parents about cancelled meetings or other appointments or to explain it to Abdal himself. I mostly solved this with the help of written information, so that the parents could have them translated. Meanwhile, the children's German has become considerably better and the father visits a German class, which facilitates the communication a lot. (LTB3, Sophie)

At the same time, the great creativity and skills of the tandems to overcome language problems manifests itself especially on the level of language via alternative forms and means of communication – for instance nonverbally via facial expressions, gestures, or images – or joint learning, whereby they create a shared level:

> A small dictionary often helps us, as she can show me words and vice versa. So we both learn from each other. (LTB1, Juna)

Students reflect *culturally based distinctions* – e.g. hospitality, which is perceived as particularly strong, the greater importance of the family, patriarchal structures or religious festivals – in many learning diaries due to the great closeness of the students to the families. The aspects "culture" and "cultural difference" have, however, a smaller role, at least compared to students' other considerations regarding context-specific challenges, especially dealing with language, oppressive flight experiences, or an insecure residency status. The dimension of culture is oftentimes only experienced in closer contact to the families, which can be illustrated with the following diary entry by Sophie:

> I have learnt that cultural differences in "working" with a child only hardly play a role. Of course, the differences become clear in the language, but Abdal is a kid like all the others. It is not before I enter the apartment and see the furniture, food, and family life that I become aware of the differences to the German culture. At our house, everything is more orderly, we eat at the table, with cutlery, not on the ground with our hands. But we are also not as hospitable and ask every stranger to eat with us in our home. We usually clearly have fewer siblings, and headscarfs are only an exception for German women. (LTB3, Sophie)

Against this background, there is need for a differentiated reflection and closer analyses of the significance of culture and cultural differences in the context of elementary school work with children with an immigration history, as exemplified by GeKOS.

Mentoring in the Context of Immigration as an Antinomic Structure

The reflection of the analysis data first shows that students have to deal with partly ambivalent, emotionally charged situations, as the following case example shows:

19

Her birthday was simultaneously nice and sad to me. I was at her place and we had coffee with the whole family. This was very pleasant. Rather depressing, however, was how fast she wanted to leave the house with me. On the one hand, I am glad that she likes to spend time with me, but on the other hand, it saddens me that she prefers staying with me in the quiet room to the company of her friends and all the people who came there just for her. I think this may be caused by the fact that she lacks a quiet room at home as well as time for herself. Everyone sleeps in a single room and there is no space to withdraw and be for yourself. In contrast, our meetings give her an opportunity for peace and 'Leyla-time'. (LTB 1, Claudette)

In the presented situation, the student is happy that her mentee wants to spend time with her alone on her birthday, but simultaneously is concerned that the child wants to escape from her oppressive living conditions.

The described findings additionally display antinomic constellations full of tension from a structure-theoretical point of view. They are in part consistent with constellations that are typical of elementary school work with children in general, for instance tensions between

- the child's desires on the one hand and the necessary rules on the other hand,
- the prior didactic design and the flexible adjustment to situational demands,
- the child's need for closeness and the simultaneous need for role-conform distance,
- and the handling of the principal insecurity and defectiveness of pedagogical action situations in the context of child-oriented organization of leisure time.

Against this background, it appears more adequate to focus on the fact that refugee children are first and foremost children (Maywald & Wiemert, 2016) who act independently from their nationality and cultural affiliation. In this sense, pedagogical work faces challenges which are typical of children and to some extent emerge from developmental tasks.

Furthermore, there are context-specific antinomic constellations (cf. chapter 3.2) and fields of tension which emerge on the one hand from the particular life situations of families with an immigration history (especially of linguistic and cultural difference, insecure residency status, partly precarious living conditions, and the handling of flight experiences and traumas) as well as from mentoring constellations with children on the other hand.

1. *Regulation of closeness and distance in the light of insecure residency conditions:* At first, the pedagogical constitutive regulation of closeness and distance intensifies in the light of partly insecure residence permits and the accordingly uncertain prospects of permanent residence: While the students have to build an emotional relationship with the children and their parents as a prerequisite for a succeeding tandem work, they also need to keep professional distance for their own and the child's sake.

2. *Offering help while keeping the integrity of the families as well as one's own responsibility and competence limits:* When the parents also appear as needy and ask for help when coping with daily struggles, students can offer individual autonomy-supporting help. At the same time, the integrity of the family needs to be protected and too far-reaching assistance has to be avoided. With regard to the complexity of this task and the necessity of interdisciplinary collaboration, the students fathom their own responsibility and competence limits.

3. *Dealing with flight experiences while keeping self-defense and avoiding retraumatization:* In the light of the sometimes intensive domestic contact to the parents, students are often confronted with oppressive stories of flight experiences as well as psychological trauma. Here, they try to understand due to both pedagogical and personal reasons, but also try to avoid too intensive analyses of the biographic background in fear of retraumatization.

4. *Dealing with precarious living conditions while avoiding too much compassion or one-sided dramatization:* On the one hand, the partly precarious living conditions of families with a flight history (e.g. restricted housing conditions, limited material possibilities) necessitate the examination of the living conditions as well as a serious consideration of this situation as a basis for a pedagogical-professional case understanding; on the other hand, it is crucial for adequate behaviour to avoid too much compassion as well as a one-sided dramatization of the circumstances (cf. Budde & Hummrich, 2013, regarding the general field of tension of dramatization and de-dramatization).

5. *Situationally adequate judgement in the field of tension between difference blindness and difference fixation:* With regard to the meshing of challenges that are unspecific and those emerging from the particular difference characteristics of children with a flight history, another antinomy is, according to Mecheril (2009), the development of an adequate case understanding in the tension field between difference blindness and fixation.

6. *Field of tension between expectations of different actors within the project:* Considering the necessity of the cooperation of various groups of persons within the framework of mentoring as well as the integration of the program into university education, the students hold an intermediate position within the cooperation and role structure, from which potential expectations and inter-role conflicts emerge. During the course of the cooperation, they are not only confronted with the expectations of the children but also with those of parents, teachers, and volunteers, which they have to mediate.

7. *Acting in the field of tension of the prospective teacher on the one side and current friendship on the other side:* Tension results from the change in roles and system relations. For example, in the context of homework supervision, the students on the one hand have to try to avoid excessive demands when taking the perspective of the children and their parents and have to critically reflect education demands, while on the other hand representing education norms and learning expectations as prospective teachers.

Moreover, the project comprises demands within the framework of accompanying research (e.g. with regard to life-world constellation) in addition to the immediate pedagogical and organizational tasks. And of course, the students are not only mentors and students but also employees, friends, or mothers due to their student status and the participation in other occupational or family contexts, so that various tasks have to be harmonized.

Types of Dealing with Pedagogical Contingency and Uncertainty

The analysis of the learning diaries clarifies the diversity of the tasks in the context of GeKOS. Moreover, the reflection from the structural point of view reveals that depending on the case constellations the mentors are confronted with complex and partly paradox situational demands, which cannot be solved in a technological manner or without any discrepancies.

The comparative and process-related observation of the learning dictionaries shows that there are differences in the student body concerning how they deal with the tasks and with fields of tension, where the various manners of processing equally refer to *the problem of dealing with insecurities, with the lack of knowledge, and with the lack of calculability.*

In this matter, students who do not have the urge to have a plan or instructions at hand for every situation do best in and are most satisfied with the situation.

- In problem cases, they try to develop solutions together with the children and their parents,
- they communicate with all persons involved,
- they make their needs transparent (when in contact with schools, project coordination, supervisors, and parents),
- and they develop not only situationally flexible solutions but also expand their own limits.
- They neither perceive language nor culture as dividing but focus on similarities and especially the potentials of the children.
- They perceive themselves as learners and are grateful for the possibility for experiences in the project. They want to change and professionalize their own behaviour and see the tandem work as a great opportunity to develop.

In comparison, a significant number of students does not feel prepared for the work with these tensions:

- A characteristic is the search for "recipes" and detailed instructions for every single situation,
- the wish for calculability and controllability during all phases of the tandem work,
- taking only little responsibility for their behaviour,
- and the search for responsibility or experts for supposedly failed situations.

Between those two contrastive, ideal-typically built patterns of working, there are various 'mixed cases' which display, amongst others, the dependency of the way of processing tasks on the respective individual constellations and framework conditions.

Additionally, the experiences in the project underline that in certain cases – e.g. when the child is under particular strain in combination with aggravating external factors – students can become overstrained or even resign in spite of the given support opportunities through coaching and the project management.

> It occurred to me that I cannot change Onur's behaviour. The time was too short and I was too unprofessional. Onur always displayed behavioural problems and I was often unable to reach him. Eventually, the project only meant "passing the time". (LTB 4, Lara)

Education and Professionalization Experience in the Context of the Project

The overview clarified that during the mentoring work, the students have learning experiences with regard to both general pedagogical tasks when working with children (leisure time, relationship building, completion and farewell design) and to overall aspects of vocational orientation and personality development across the project. Additionally, there are gains which refer to the specific pedagogical challenges in working with children with a flight history and their parents. Changes that affect action are due to the sensitization for specific challenges and the development of a personal attitude through context-specific practical knowledge.

> I once again became very aware of how difficult it can be to work with people. You never know what the person in front of you has experienced or gone through. During the tandem meetings, I therefore always try to react as sensitive as possible to my mentee. (LTB 3, Heike)

Additionally, the mentoring work brings latent prejudice structures to mind and enables differentiated views, which is also supported by technical and specialist information and pedagogically accompanying reflections within the framework of coaching.

> Especially the talk by Mrs. Kohlhammer and the coaching give food for thought. You get confronted so often with statements that the refugees here have it too good etc. Through caring for Carima, I get the possibility to develop my own idea on this. I never have the feeling that she is unwell. I also have the feeling that she owns relatively many things, at least more than I would have thought. But you should never forget the other circumstances. They live in a small apartment with five children (I have not seen it from the inside yet, unfortunately) and I cannot assess what they had to go through in their own country or during the flight, or what status they had to give up in their own country. Mrs. Kohlhammer shared many enriching experiences with us in her talk, and the meetings with Carima strengthen my positive and open attitude towards people with a flight history,

because although she is a child and probably cannot really reflect what she owes to Germany, she is very polite and courteous towards me. (LTB1, Alina)

As presented in Chapter 3, transformative educational processes can be triggered when the acting subject goes through emotionally accompanied experiences of crisis in the course of the failure of existing behavior and routine knowledge when being confronted with the strange and unknown. From this point of view, more profound education experiences are thus characterized by negative experiences of *losing existing knowledge* (skills, convictions, interpretations patterns, etc.) before a possible *gain of knowledge* (Meyer-Drawe, 1996). Thereby, familiar knowledge loses its ground. These occasions build new problematic situations, which cannot be processed in an adequate way with the prior means at hand (Koller, 2017).

It has to be put first that transformative educational processes in Koller's sense can hardly be observed directly and empirically on the basis of learning diaries, as interpretations can only be made in retrospective due to the portrayed experiences (Koller, 2012, p. 29). Nevertheless, there are 'traces' of more complex and profound formative processes in the learning diaries, as the case example with a context-specific problem structure illustrates.

The reason and structure of a student mentor's process of change can be clarified with the following example: Here, the mentor experiences how in her presence, her mentee talks to another child in his mother tongue, which, next to the pedagogically motivated requests to talk German, evokes a personally motivated (unpleasant) feeling of exclusion in the mentor:

> One time, Carima began to talk Arabic with another boy. After a while, I told them to talk in German, because I could not understand anything. This was not meant as a prohibition of the other language; in other situations, I have already asked a couple of times what a certain term means in Arabic. But in this moment, I was of the opinion that the children could formulate very well in German, and to have them practice it and also because I can understand them too, a little bit. (LTB t1, Alina)

First of all, it becomes clear that in the past, similar situations signified opportunities to learn the language – to learn particular Arabic terms – for the mentor and thus represented simple learning processes; however, it is central that in this situation, more profound processes of change were triggered due to the following reflections, as well:

> The topic of language prohibition came up during coaching […] and I have gotten a new perspective: When children communicate in their language and I do not understand anything, I basically feel similar to how they must have felt when they came to Germany, with the distinction that we could always switch back to communicating in German in this situation. However, this was a discovery I had to think of at first and that might change my behaviour in the future. (ibid.)

It becomes clear that this situation and the reflections during coaching irritate existing pedagogical perspectives and behaviour concepts and one's own experiences of being excluded become the basis of understanding people with a flight history, for whom experiences of subjectively unpleasant exclusion necessarily belong to their daily lives due to language barriers. Although it also becomes visible that the impact on action cannot be ensured through learning experiences, at least the professional skill to change perspectives has been supported through the irritation of existing concepts and reflective practical experiences.

The central educational as well as potentially also professionalization-effective momentum of this experience is the Other, which – if it is not subordinated to existing experience schemata and therefore rejected – opens space for the development of new points of view as well as for changed attitudes and behaviours through the irritation of prior knowledge. Especially in the context of pedagogical work with children with an immigration background and their families, the emerging moment of a change in perspective is of particular significance for professionality.

CONCLUSION

Education and Professionalization Possibilities within the Framework GeKOS

The learning diaries display that the students took part in various life situations of the children. Thereby, they themselves became a part of the children's live-world. Consequently, they have learned much about the particular living conditions of children with a flight history and their parents. Situations such as home visits or the participation in family life, attending birthdays, and excursions were of particular meaning for this. It becomes clear in the learning diary entries that the gained insights into the life situations of refugees in Koblenz as well as into their experiences during the flight often touch the students in an emotional way: for example the experience of the families' lives in cramped conditions, the lack of silence at home, insights into difficult material situations of families with a flight history, the omnipresent danger of deportation and traumas of the children. Overall, three distinct experience topics can be identified:

- *Child-related experiences*: Hereto belong experiences that deal with the building of trust as well as the dealing with limits in the sense of the necessity to set rules; but also the experience of the importance to step back from one's own expectations in order to adapt to the perspective of the child.
- *Experiences of success and coping with pedagogical challenges*: Hereto belongs the coping with situations that are subjectively perceived as insecure, in spite of initial fears. These experiences are especially about the insecurity to communicate orally with the children and their parents; to learn to deal with a great number of invitations by the parents; learn to handle the children's unpredicted behaviour.
- *Experience with and processing of the complexity of pedagogical situations*: This group comprises the experience of and involvement in complex, challenging

25

situations in the tandem work, such as ambivalences and unpredicted difficulties. This mainly concerns the experience of the deportation of a mentee, or the dealing with traumatized children.

To sum up, the project offers experiences which signify central challenges and concern both the relationship and the task dimension of pedagogical work. Here, an interesting finding is that there are problems and constellations of tension which are typical of the work with children in general, and others which particularly touch the work with refugee children. The project repeatedly asks the mentors to direct an outer perspective towards the pedagogical place 'school'. During the project, the students experience school from the perspective of their mentees and their parents, while they only experience the teacher's role during their internships. From the project perspective, weaknesses and contradictions are revealed. The parents, for instance, get untranslated letters which they cannot understand. It is similar for homework, which the students repeatedly experience as an excessive demand for the children. In one-on-one supervision, it becomes clear that the mentees, although they are in Germany already for a year, for example do not know numbers or letters, which is not found out in their classes. The mentors also find that children only barely have room to play in their new homes, and also only a small space for discovery or too little opportunity to test themselves outside of it. Many children and parents therefore report back their gratitude for the offers that the tandems can try out together. The students experience hospitable parents who invite them for food week after week and are simultaneously just as needy for support as their children. Many parents search for contact to the students, also to train the new German language or to be able to pose informal questions which they cannot ask the teachers. Most of the mentors experience a first impression of the family life of children and parents in the project.

Within GeKOS the students do not only meet the children and families in their usual role as a prospective teacher or the representative of the majority society but also get to know the side of the addressees of the respective requirements. The antinomic structure of the demands from both perspectives reveal that they are equally important and cannot be solved in a one-sided way. The students experience first-hand why the educational or social demands towards children and parents with a flight history cannot always be managed easily and develop an understanding of their perspectives.

Discussion of Mentoring as a Professionalization Strategy

The antinomic behaviour constellations in the project lead towards situations and dilemmas loaded with tension, which do not offer an unmistakable solution without argument. These situations comprise a momentum of crisis, which signifies an opportunity for processes of education and professionalization (Bonnet & Hericks, 2013). However, they only become formative experiences when they lead to new orders and behaviour patterns.

The success of the tandem work depends on the concrete challenges which the child poses, the situational support, and also the respective student. The central category on the part of the students is the adoption of *responsibility for their own behaviour,* the *willingness to question their own expectations, reflect behaviour patterns, and try out unknown paths.* The consciousness of one's own competencies and responsibilities is also important. In this respect, the complexity of the demands as well as the principal limits in the ability to plan and didacticize student learning and educational processes surface in mentoring.

The case of the student who called herself "too unprofessional" points towards the fact that there are students who become aware of the limits of their own behaviour, i.e. who are plunged into a crisis and lack the resources to either develop their own solutions or use support offers and who therefore resign. From this perspective, the support systems of the project play a key role, although they cannot anticipate the solutions. Still, it is important that the support is tailored to the challenges of the respective field of action. The supporting function of coaching is that it demands from the students to reflect upon their own thoughts and actions and that it confronts them with alternative ways of thought and action.

Based on the accompanying research, favourable ways of acting towards the challenges can be identified: Mentors who succeed in taking responsibility act at eye level with their mentees in most of the cases and establish a symmetrical relationship culture that is characterized by reciprocity. They see themselves as profiteers of the project and feel as learners. They use coaching sessions for their own questions, describe their own learning and education process concretely and can identify future learning needs. It became striking through the accompanying research, however, that the work with online learning tasks turns out in various ways: There are students who process a task in a minimalistic way and do not name any areas of development, while others reflect on their experiences in a detailed and concrete way and define learning tasks for themselves. In the sense of the considerations which were unfolded in the article, this group displays 'professionalization as a process of self-*Bildung*'. Further research is needed on what causes these differences.

For the practical project work, it should in any case be a focus to make possible benefits of reflection instruments and formats accessible for students. Thus, the particular challenge to make the significance of reflection in learning diaries more transparent for the students or to look for individually adequate formats arises for the next project round. The benefits of supervision and coaching offers for all participants or the attractiveness of the offers have to be increased, as well.

On the one hand, the general demand arising from these considerations lies in a better curricular accessibility of such projects in order to help students create cross-relations to other content areas. On the other hand, our findings indicate that coaching, reflection, and supervision offers are needed not only within the limits of elective subjects in teacher training, but for everyone going to work with migrant children.

NOTES

1. http://www.hofmanngoettig.de/?p=96177, retrieved on 08/22/2017
2. The workshops comprised the following offering in the project round 2016/2017: "Refugee children in Koblenz", "Working with migrant parents", "Multilingual education", "Escape routes", "Gender, roles and identity in different cultures", "Refugees and traumatization", "Refugee children in schools", "Values and norms in education", "Culture as a topic in social science education", "Developing a gender identity and the influence of culture", "Germany through the eyes of a migrant", "Multilingualism in teaching and learning German".
3. The evaluation of the offer and organization structure (support program, project organization, cooperation of all participants) accompanied the process and was analyzed through discourse with the students as well as project meetings and result-oriented with the help of a standardized satisfaction query of the students, which was analyzed in a descriptive-analytical manner.
4. The learning diaries of the mentors was the data basis, which conveyed the spectrum of the occurring tasks. Content-wise, the illustration refers to question 3: "Have there been challenges for you in the tandem work so far? How did you manage them?"
5. Hence, students reflect upon "communication and understanding problems" in 21.2 % of all cases and about "trust building" in 18.2 % of the first learning diary (t1) which is filled out towards the ending of the second project month.
6. The names of students, children and parents have been substituted by codenames.
7. Correspondingly, it can first be mentioned that more than half of the learning diary entries categorized the relationship to the parents as distanced or as a parallel existence with the help of a six-point Venn diagram. In other cases, it is linked to partly difficult challenges such as boundary definitions for the students, despite or perhaps precisely because of intensive contact.

REFERENCES

Abbott, A. (1988). *The system of professions: An essay on the division of expert labor*. Chicago, IL: University of Chicago Press.

Auernheimer, G. (2013). Interkulturelle Kommunikation, mehrdimensional betrachtet, mit Konsequenzen für das Verständnis von interkultureller Kompetenz. In G. Auernheimer (Ed.), *Pädagogische Professionalität und interkulturelle Kompetenz* (4th ed., pp. 37–70). Wiesbaden: Springer VS.

Baquero Torres, P., & de Boer, H. (2011). Studierende im Übergang. Zwischen der Konstruktion hilfebedürftiger Migrantenkinder und der Reflexion eigener Konstruktionsprozesse. In D. Kucharz, T. Irion, & B. Reinhoffer (Eds.), *Grundlegende Bildung ohne Brüche* (pp. 237–240). Wiesbaden: Springer VS.

Berthold, T. (2014). *In erster Linie Kinder. Flüchtlingskinder in Deutschland*. Köln: UNICEF.

Bonnet, A., & Hericks, U. (2013). Professionalisierung bildend denken. In K. Müller-Roselius & U. Hericks (Eds.), *Bildung – Empirischer Zugang und theoretischer Widerstreit* (pp. 35–54). Opladen: Budrich.

Budde, J., & Hummrich, M. (2013): Reflexive Inklusion. *Zeitschrift für Inklusion 4*. Retrieved August 24, 2017, from http://www.inklusion-online.net/index.php/inklusion-online/issue/view/20

Bundesamt für Migration und Flüchtlinge (BAMF). (2015). *Aktuelle Zahlen zu Asyl. Dezember 2015*. Retrieved July 7, 2016, from http://www.bamf.de/SharedDocs/Anlagen/DE/Downloads/Infothek/Statistik/Asyl/aktuelle-zahlen-zu-asyl-dezember-2015.pdf?__blob=publicationFile

Bundesministerium für Bildung und Forschung (BMBF). (2012). *Nationaler Aktionsplan Integration*. Retrieved September 30, 2016, from http://www.bundesregierung.de/Content/DE/_Anlagen/IB/2012-01-31-nap-gesamt-barrierefrei.pdf?__blob=publicationFile

Harring, M. (2011). *Das Potenzial der Freizeit. Soziales, kulturelles und ökonomisches Kapital im Kontext heterogener Freizeitwelten Jugendlicher*. Wiesbaden: Springer VS.

Havighurst, R. (1972). *Developmental tasks and education*. London: Longman.

Helsper, W. (2002). Lehrerprofessionalität als antinomische Handlungsstruktur. In M. Kraul, W. Marotzki, & C. Schweppe (Eds.), *Biographie und profession* (pp. 64–102). Bad Heilbrunn: Klinkhardt.

Helsper, W. (2014). Lehrerprofessionalität – der strukturtheoretische Professionsansatz zum Lehrberuf. In E. Terhart, H. Bennewitz, & M. Rothland (Eds.), *Handbuch der Forschung zum Lehrerberuf* (2nd ed., pp. 216–240). Münster & New York, NY: Waxmann.

Helsper, W., & Hummrich, M. (2008). Arbeitsbündnis, Schulkultur und Milieu – Reflexionen zu Grundlagen schulischer Bildungsprozesse. In G. Breidenstein & F. Schütze (Eds.), *Paradoxien in der Reform der Schule. Ergebnisse qualitativer Sozialforschung* (pp. 43–72). Wiesbaden: Springer VS.

Hericks, U. (2006). *Professionalisierung als Entwicklungsaufgabe.* Wiesbaden: Springer VS.

Hüpping, B. (2017). *Migrationsbedingte Heterogenität. Pädagogische Professionalität von Grundschullehrkräften im Umgang mit Vielfalt.* Wiesbaden: Springer VS.

Koller, H.-C. (2012). Anders werden. Zur Erforschung transformatorischer Bildungsprozesse. In I. Miethe & H.-R. Müller (Eds.), *Qualitative Bildungsforschung und Bildungstheorie* (pp. 19–33). Opladen: Budrich.

Koller, H.-C. (2017). Bildung as a transformative process. In A. Laros, T. Fuhr, & E. Taylor (Eds.), *Transfomative learning meets bildung: An international exchange* (pp. 33–42). Rotterdam, The Netherlands: Sense Publishers.

Maywald, J., & Wiemert, H. (2016): Ich empfehle, den Begriff Flüchtlingskind einem Kind nicht wie einen Stempel aufzudrücken (Interview). *Jugendhilfe-Report Köln, 10*(1), 7–11.

Mecheril, P. (2009). Weder differenzblind noch differenzfixiert. Für einen reflexiven und kontextspezifischen Gebrauch von Begriffen. In IDA NRW (Ed.), *Reader zum Fachgespräch "Rassismus bildet". Bildungsperspektiven unter Bedingungen rassistischer Normalität* (pp. 103–114). Innsbruck: Universität Innsbruck.

Mecheril, P. (2013). "Kompetenzlosigkeitskompetenz". Pädagogisches Handeln unter Einwanderungsbedingungen. In G. Auernheimer (Ed.), *Pädagogische Professionalität und interkulturelle Kompetenz* (4th ed., pp. 15–35). Wiesbaden: Springer VS.

Meyer-Drawe, K. (1996). Von anderen lernen. Phänomenologische Betrachtungen in der Pädagogik. In M. Borrelli & J. Ruhloff (Eds.), *Deutsche Gegenwartspädagogik* (pp. 85–98). Baltmannsweiler: Schneider.

Ministeriums für Bildung, Wissenschaft, Weiterbildung und Kultur (MBWWK). (2015). *Unterricht von Schülerinnen und Schülern mit Migrationshintergrund.* Retrieved January 1, 2017, from http://migration.bildung-rp.de/fileadmin/user_upload/migration.bildungrp.de/geaenderte_VV_Unterricht_von_Schuelerinnen_und_Schuelern_mit_Migrationshintergrund_September_2015.pdf

Neumann, U., & Schneider, J. (2013). Mentoring-Projekte: Einschätzung und Forschungslage. In U. Neumann & J. Schneider (Eds.), *Schule mit Migrationshintergrund* (pp. 220–323). Münster: Waxmann.

Schön, D. (1983). *The reflective practitioner: How professionals think in action.* New York, NY: Basic Books.

Schröder, D., Fegter, S., Andresen, S., & Gerarts, K. (2013). Die qualitative Studie: Soziale Netzwerke und Gerechtigkeit – 12 Portraits von Kinderpersönlichkeiten. In World Vision Germany (Ed.), *Kinder in Deutschland: Wie gerecht ist unsere Welt?* (Vol. 3, pp. 204–293). Weinheim: Beltz.

Schroeder, J. (2016). Unterricht im Asylverfahren und in der Duldung. In G. Markmann & C. Osburg (Eds.), *Kinder und Jugendliche mit Fluchterfahrungen in der Schule* (pp. 72–79). Baltmannsweiler: Schneider.

Schugurensky, D. (2000). *The forms of informal learning: Towards a conceptualization of the field.* Toronto: Centre for the Study of Education and Work.

United Nations High Commissioner for Refugees (UNHCR). (2015). *Global trends: Forced displacement in 2015.* Retrieved July 25, 2016, from http://www.unhcr.de/service/zahlen-und-statistiken.html

von Dewitz, N., Massumi, M., & Grießbach, J. (2015). *Neu zugewanderte Kinder und Jugendliche im deutschen Schulsystem. Bestandsaufnahme und Empfehlungen.* Köln: Universität zu Köln.

World Vision Deutschland. (2016). *Angekommen in Deutschland. Wenn geflüchtete Kinder erzählen.* Friedrichsdorf: World Vision.

Heike De Boer
Koblenz-Landau University
Koblenz, Germany

Benjamin Brass
Koblenz-Landau University
Koblenz, Germany

Henrik Bruns
Koblenz-Landau University
Koblenz, Germany

FABIO DOVIGO

2. WE'RE IN IT TOGETHER

Inclusive Approaches from Refugee Education in Italy

INTRODUCTION

The tragic events related to the recent wave of migrants arriving in Europe, fleeing from war or difficult living conditions, have revealed the real nature of this phenomenon, which can no longer be considered exceptional or temporary. Both the number of people escaping and the different types of countries involved highlight the permanent character of these migratory movements. They confront us with the need to make choices that go beyond the current emergency and implement systematic policies for resettlement and inclusion as a means of significantly tackling the outbreak of fear and intolerance that we are witnessing in many European countries.

Promoting systematic inclusion policies means recognizing that the arrival of migrants and refugees, many of whom are children, is a challenge and a great educational opportunity for the European school system. Helping rootless people to regain a sense of stability and direction for their lives requires developing an intervention that takes into account not only the socioeconomic, but also educational, psychological and cultural factors that widely contribute to building this path (European Commission, 2015a).

Even though a large body of literature on the social inclusion of refugees is available today, investigations into refugee children and their education remain relatively underdeveloped, especially as regards the implementation of school-based interventions and programmes (Hamilton & Moore, 2004; European Commission, 2015b; Pinson & Arnot, 2010). Research shows that refugee children have multiple complex needs, as they can suffer from psychological trauma and are likely to be emotionally distressed. Moreover, they are required to rapidly adjust to a new language and culture, as well as to build a sense of personal identity and belonging to the new place (McBrien, 2016; Isik-Ercan, 2012; Naidoo, 2015; Pastoor, 2017).

Generally, schooling in the new country proves to be a difficult experience for refugee children, as they face significant challenges in terms of linguistic and cultural adaptation. Children with little or no prior education in their country of origin are frequently unable to cope with the demands posed by the new educational settings. Language barriers have a special impact both on the participation and academic success of refugee students (Bal, 2014; Bigelow et al., 2017; Dryden-Peterson, 2016). As a result, they can experience a sense of disengagement and loneliness.

© KONINKLIJKE BRILL NV, LEIDEN, 2018 | DOI:10.1163/9789004383227_002

A lot of the research emphasises that the process of inclusion is not only related to the educational success of refugee students, but also to the ability of involving the community in which they will settle in the endeavour of overcoming barriers to learning and developing valuable resources for that purpose. Accordingly, adopting a holistic and whole-school approach is vital for promoting the inclusion of young refugees in school (Block et al., 2014; Hek, 2005; Pastoor & Lutine, 2016; Pugh, Every, & Hattam, 2012). This approach focuses on school ethos, welcoming environments, good induction communication, first and second language support, home liaison, community links, pastoral care, and preventing racism and bullying. Participation and learning fostered through a holistic and whole-school approach help refugee children build a sense of belonging and self-confidence that in turn enable them to develop new relationships inside and outside of school (Peterson, Meehan, Durrant, & Ali, 2017; Pinson, Arnot, & Candappa, 2010). They also help all local children and adults to see refugee students not just as aliens or victims, but as valuable partners and resources for promoting learning and intercultural understanding.

However, achieving this level of inclusion through improving refugee education requires that institutions deal with several economic, social, and cultural barriers, as the Italian case highlights. Schools and health and social services usually suffer from a shortage of investment and coordination that, in turn, originate from a narrow perspective on the refugee situation, still frequently perceived and described as an endless emergency (Bradby et al., 2015; IPPM, 2011; Newbigging & Thomas, 2011). Therefore, a lack of resources as well as policy fragmentation significantly limit the ability of the school system and connected services to ensure access and integration for refugee children in Italy. Nevertheless, our research shows that a remarkable set of good practices is emerging from collaboration between local schools and services, paving the way for reconsidering the current paradigm and building a more effective and sustainable approach to refugee children's education.

REFUGEE CHILDREN IN ITALY: AN OVERVIEW

In the last few years, Italy has been one of the main gateways for the vast majority of unaccompanied and separated children arriving to Europe through the Mediterranean Sea (UNHCR, 2017a; UNICEF-IOM, 2017). Once in Italy, children are the responsibility of local administrations, usually supported by voluntary associations as well as national and international NGOs. Even though the growing number of unaccompanied or separated children arriving in Italy has been a matter of concern for public and private bodies involved in providing immediate humanitarian response, until recently, data on children's country of origin, migration trajectory and, more generally, living conditions, have not been collected systematically. Reports based on primary and secondary data show that refugee and migrant children arrive in Italy escaping from poverty and/or conflict areas, where basic rights to security, freedom, and protection are scarcely guaranteed, or not guaranteed at all (REACH, 2017;

Direzione Generale dell'Immigrazione e delle Politiche di Integrazione, 2016). Children come from a variety of countries, especially from West Africa, Eritrea, and Somalia. Most of them are unaccompanied (91%), aged 16 to 17 (93%), and boys (92%). Moreover, some children want to settle in Italy to pursue an educational and future working career, while others express the intention of joining their relatives in other countries. However, children's plans soon come up against the time required by the public administration to track down documentation and grant the required asylum permits. Faced with the intricacies of a bureaucratic system they can barely comprehend, children often decide to flee or depart from the reception system, seeking to reach their target destination in illicit and dangerous ways that expose them to the risk of exploitation and violence.

The decision to migrate is almost always made by the individual child, who usually takes the migration route in order to flee from ethnic or political persecution in their home country, as well as from a situation of family violence or economic troubles at home. Getting to Europe is the goal of nearly half of all migrant children, who are looking for a country that will offer better human rights conditions and access to education. Other children are initially led to a neighbouring or North African country, essentially seeking work. Many interviewed children disclose they didn't know about the risks involved in the journey (Rigon & Mengoli, 2013). Conversely, others admit they were aware that their life might be in danger during the long journey, but were still resolved to leave at any cost. On average, the length of the journey is one year and two months, but for some children – for example those from The Gambia and Guinea Conakry – it takes even longer as they have to work (usually illegally and exploitative conditions) to pay for the journey.

Most children leave their country without thinking of Europe as a final destination, as they are simply looking for a place where there will be more job opportunities or better education. However, after they move to North Africa they frequently change their minds, as they face widespread violence or abuse. Children also report the sea crossing towards Italy as the worst event they have to deal with during their journey. Nevertheless, the decision to embark on this dangerous crossing is usually driven by the terrible conditions they are living in in Libya: during their stay, many of them are indiscriminately arrested and taken into custody without charges, while others report that their families had to pay a ransom after they were kidnapped (Attanasio, 2016).

The few children traveling with siblings also underline that being separated by accident from other family members was a constant risk throughout the journey. Separation usually takes place during the transfer, but sometimes it also happens after arrival in Italy.

Once in Italy, children have to deal with new issues in terms of access to international protection and/or achieving legal permissions for onward travel (ASGI, 2016). Indeed, obtaining legal status in Italy as a refugee can take several months (or years, in some cases). Likewise, the process of assigning a legal guardian to unaccompanied children can take almost one year in some cases. The appointment of a legal guardian was only recently removed as a requisite for applying for international protection or a residence permit, enabling children to benefit from enrolment in education. As a consequence, children often live in a kind of prolonged limbo that hinders their ability to plan their future and settle in the country. As most of the children are 16 to 17 years old, they are particularly exposed to the risk of discouragement and disempowerment. On the one hand, they are not allowed to work and acquire economic independence; on the other hand, this long wait puts them at risk of losing the special protection ensured by the norms as long as they are minors.

Similarly, children who rule out settling in Italy – as they aim to travel onward to join relatives who are living in other European countries – find it very difficult to reach this goal while complying with the legal requirements. As procedures addressed at examining the claims for family reunification or relocation are still unclear, each process usually takes more than one year to be managed. As a matter of fact, over the years only a minor proportion of migrant children have actually been transferred from Italy to another country for reunification or relocation purposes.

This issue is worsened by the complexity and lack of clarity that affects bureaucratic practices connected to the application process (Gruppo di studio sul sistema di accoglienza, 2015). Scarce information, intricate procedures, and uncertain timelines contribute to increasing children's anxiety and sense of vulnerability. By law, newly arrived unaccompanied children should stay in short-term accommodation structures for no longer than thirty days. After this period of time, they should be relocated to specific long-term accommodation structures managed by the Protection System for Asylum Seekers and Refugees (SPRAR). However, the shortage of available places in long-term accommodation structures actually forces children to remain in short-term reception centres longer than expected, hampering their access to the educational system (Save the Children Italia, 2017; SPRAR, 2017).

Living in centres with a lack of perspectives and few activities, children already marked by distressing experiences easily feel abandoned once more. Accordingly, some of them escape from reception facilities and try to reach services located elsewhere in Italy, assuming that they will be able to speed up the procedure. Many others decide to break with the Italian reception system to continue their travel in hiding, once again putting themselves at risk of exploitation and violence.

Access to education would be a primary resource for reducing that risk and promoting personal health and wellbeing, especially considering that many children undertook the journey precisely in order to access better education (Catarci, 2012, 2016). However, by law in Italy, it is mandatory only for unaccompanied and separated children living in secondary reception centres to be enrolled in school. As children spend, on average, six months in primary reception centres, most of them cannot attend school at all or, at most, are able to spend only a few hours a week in school.

In March 2017, a new law established a number of measures to improve the protection level of refugee children on the basis of the "best interest of the child" principle. These measures include, among other things, the prohibition on executing border rejection of unaccompanied and separated foreign children, reducing the maximum amount of time spent in first-line reception centres to 30 days, extending opportunities to assign guardians to children, improving procedures for age assessment, and guaranteeing children's right to access health and educational services. As for the latter, the analysis that follows will introduce the main features of the organisation of the refugee children's education system in Italy.

THE FRAMEWORK OF REFUGEE CHILDREN'S EDUCATION IN ITALY

As we noted, education is seen as a protective factor for refugee children. Nevertheless, even though in the last few years the number of asylum-seeker and refugee children in Italy has increased significantly, we still lack official figures indicating how many of them enrol in schools and where. Moreover, although the Italian government has promoted some actions to sensitise schools about this situation, so far no long-term educational policies have been put in place with the aim of providing systematic inclusion in education for refugee youths. As the current system puts local municipalities in charge of the management of newly arrived adults seeking asylum, the government similarly assumes that refugee children will be managed by local schools within the wider framework of immigrant education (Giovannetti, 2014). Consequently, while the Ministry of Education recently launched a campaign to spread information about students with refugee experience, schools have not been provided with clear-cut plans or stable resources to specifically meet their needs.

Evidence from countries with extensive experience with refugee education shows that the ability of schools to provide immediate and appropriate support is pivotal for favouring a smooth accommodation process that will ensure settlement, safety and security for children (Education Unit Division of International Protection, UNHCR, 2016; Taylor & Sidhu, 2012). Conversely, inadequate school support often translates into students' absenteeism, disengagement, feelings of disempowerment, poor relationships with peers, and early school leaving. This, in turn, can affect not only school achievements of refugee children, but also their coping strategies and resilience, undermining future prospects in terms of employment and socio-economic status, and heightening social exclusion (Korac, 2003). According to Italian law, all minors, both native and foreign, have the right to education within the national school system until age 16, regardless of their legal status. Even if their legal status is irregular, foreign children have equal rights to education as Italian children. They are subject to compulsory education and entitled to receive assistance and arrangements in case they have special needs. When a refugee child applies to attend a school, the required documents should be the same as for Italian children. In addition, child enrolment should be ensured even if documents related to identity, health, or school certificates cannot be provided. Even if the child is not able to produce an identity document, s/he should be registered on a reserve list that enables him/her to attend classes and get the final certification related to school attendance.

However, until recently, formal education for asylum-seeking children has not received special attention in Italy, as it has been assimilated into the ordinary activities already aimed at first or second-generation migrant children. Not being considered a population with a specific profile, the insertion of unaccompanied children in education has not been monitored over time, so we lack comprehensive information about their age, gender, and the overall path they follow when they enrol in the Italian education system (MIUR, 2017). To reverse this trend, in 2015 and 2016 the Ministry of Education launched two calls to submit programmes asking schools to design programmes to ease the integration of unaccompanied children by providing psychological support and providing courses in Italian as a second language, specifically targeting refugee pupils. Moreover, a share of European Funds on Asylum, Migration and Integration (FAMI) has been used to develop administrative staff and teachers' skills with regard to refugee education and training courses on linguistic-cultural mediation. It also supported projects that addressed the promotion of school activities focused on deepening the understanding of human rights in relation to migration issues. Furthermore, based on a Memorandum of Understanding signed with the UNHCR, a website has been developed to inform teachers and students about unaccompanied minors' personal and educational trajectories, as well as to help develop projects aimed at increasing awareness of refugee children' rights and opportunities.

The regulation differentiates between children under and over 16 years of age. The former should be enrolled in a grade corresponding to their age in compulsory education. However, after assessing the curriculum provided in the country of origin and the competences already acquired by the child, school teachers can opt to assign the pupil to the class immediately below or above the one corresponding to his/her age in order to adjust school integration to the actual level of skills. Enrolment can take place at any time throughout the school year. According to the Ministry of Education, the number of foreign students in school classes should be limited to 30%. Preparatory classes are not planned at the national level, as Italian laws do not allow schools to organise special classes for foreign students. Moreover, schools are not obliged to provide specific language support for newly arrived students. However, taking advantage of the relative degree of autonomy granted by the Italian education system, some educational institutions expand what is ordinarily offered by organising additional courses for refugee youths. According to the level of competence of foreign students, the school can implement some adaptations to curricula and adopt individual or group interventions to promote inclusion. By law, educational institutions should also ease the learning of Italian as a second language through the organisation of specific workshops in schools, delivering about 8–10 hours per week (about 2 hours per day) over 3–4 months.

Students over 16 are no longer subject to compulsory education in Italy. Nevertheless, they are eligible to study to obtain an upper secondary school diploma (5 years) or a professional qualification (3 to 5 years). As a consequence, to be enrolled in school immigrant children have to provide evidence of all skills required to apply for the class they would like to attend. This usually implies that children must receive extra help from voluntary teachers or associations in order to obtain the competences they need. Those who do not have a lower secondary school certificate or are not able to show an equivalent level of competence can be enrolled in a CPIA (Provincial Centres for Adult Learning) in order to acquire this certification. Children enrolled in such courses are entitled to obtain the final certification even if they turn 18 years while attending the course.

However, effective school enrolment and attendance of refugee children in Italy is often hindered by some important factors: first of all, reception centres are sometimes located in areas far from schools or even not reachable by public transportation. Moreover, even where schools are close to the reception centres, they cannot ensure that places are available to accommodate refugee students. Additionally, although all children between 6 and 16 are entitled by law to go to school whenever they arrive in Italy, some schools exert direct or indirect pressure to discourage their enrolment. On the one hand, there is a lack of knowledge of the norms and national decrees related to the rights to instruction of refugee children. On the other, school personnel often feel overwhelmed and unable to cope with the breadth of the educational tasks the attendance of refugee children would imply having to deal with. Additionally, although the law establishes the principle that refugee children should be enrolled in classes corresponding to their age, it is very common to find children who are allocated to school grades merely on the basis of language and educational skill assessment, even though they are two or even three years older than their peers. Some schools also have to face the reactions of Italian parents, as the attendance of a large group of immigrant children is perceived as having a negative effect on a school's reputation. Finally, it is not uncommon for refugee children to refuse to go to school or be dissuaded by family members, as they do not see education as an investment or, more often, consider Italy just a temporary stop of their journey to another European country (Grigt, 2017).

These factors notwithstanding, many schools are doing their best to use the limited degree of autonomy currently allowed by the centralised Italian educational system to identify and leverage the residual resources available for promoting refugee education. Good practices addressed at bettering the educational experience of refugee students are constantly being developed, especially with regard to children whose curriculum has to be accommodated according to their specific linguistic or personal needs (Santagata & Ongini, 2016). As we will examine in the next paragraph, in this respect the most important challenge Italian schools are facing nowadays is the lack of coordination and networking between those initiatives. Good practices tend to be fostered on the basis of individual, voluntary efforts made by teachers. Even when actions that have been proven to work are adopted by the entire school, they are rarely systematised, documented and, above all, disseminated to other schools. As a consequence, the knowledge one school develops about how to solve administrative or educational issues related to refugee children's attendance is generally confined to that same institution, or even limited to the know-how of individual teachers. This explains the wide gap between the rights to integration and education that the law, in the abstract, guarantees for refugee youths and the good, but isolated, practices many schools are trying to put in place to manage the arrival of this new population of students (UNHCR, 2017b).

With regard to school levels, barriers to accessing education in early childhood are a critical issue for refugee families. Education in kindergarten is not compulsory in Italy. Nevertheless, more than 90% of children are enrolled in pre-primary schools, which are divided into public (managed by national government or municipalities) and private (fee-paying) institutes. A large number of studies highlight that pre-school access plays a pivotal role in ensuring children from a migratory background develop learning and participation that will help them to succeed in further school levels. However, refugee families often find it difficult to enrol their children in pre-primary school. Institutes managed by the national government are free, but frequently crowded. Consequently, places are limited, especially for children arriving in the middle of the school year. In turn, municipalities usually link access to pre-primary schools (and connected services such as transportation and meals) to legal proof of residence in the area, which refugee families cannot provide. Finally, private institutes are generally not available to refugee families to enrol their children in for financial reasons.

Another weak point of the Italian educational system in terms of granting access to refugee youths is the upper secondary school level. By law, from the age of 14 all children can enrol in secondary education, provided that they can demonstrate the required associated competences. For those who do not have a lower secondary school certificate, the teachers' board can make an assessment based on oral and/ or written tests in order to admit them to the secondary school. Even though the educational path of refugee children has been not systematically documented in Italy, empirical evidence shows that most of them, generally aged between 16 and 18, are usually enrolled in CPIAs or, alternatively, in the vocational education and training school system managed by regional authorities, so as to attend training courses aimed at providing professional qualifications for the labour market.

A major problem for refugee children succeeding in enrolling in upper-secondary school is that once they turn 18 they lose the rights connected with being underage. Consequently, they have to prove they have a passport, as well as available accommodation and a suitable livelihood for the time left until the end of their schooling. These requests are rarely compatible with the completion of a course lasting 3 to 5 years. Moreover, some vocational education and training centres adopt discriminatory policies by declining to register unaccompanied children who do not have a residency permit. Actually, most refugee children aged over 16 are not able to demonstrate that they possess the required qualifications or competences to attend upper secondary education. As a consequence, they often enrol in CPIAs, where they can find basic literacy and Italian language courses (including a test for the residency permit for long-term residents), first-level education courses leading to obtaining the lower secondary school certificate, and second-level education courses created to guarantee a technical, professional, or artistic preparation diploma. Even though CPIAs offer valuable support to refugee students' education, both in terms of effective assessment of competences developed in non-formal settings and instruction provided to foreign language speakers and illiterate children, they also have some relevant shortcomings. Firstly, CPIAs were originally conceived to support adult workers' education through the provision of lifelong learning courses. Their mission only recently expanded to include remedial courses for early school leavers aged over 16. As a consequence, the organisational ability of CPIAs to accommodate refugee youths' educational requirements is quite limited. With the exception of a few centres, children are not usually enrolled in specific courses aimed at minors. Because of the lack of resources, they attend classes devised for adult students, which do not take into consideration the different learning and psychological needs of refugee children. In addition, classes mostly take place in the evening, as they were created for adult workers. Consequently, refugee children can attend only a limited number of class hours per week. As a result, opportunities for education are reduced with regard both to class content and rates and, more generally, the impact education can have on the daily life of children. More adequate organisation would imply an investment of specific resources in terms of time and teachers involved in refugee children's education, as well as comprehensive inter-professional and multi-agency cooperation with other practitioners (Edwards et al., 2017). Finally, the number of young Italian students enrolled in CPIAs has steadily decreased over the years. While they attend adult classes in the evening, refugee children naturally tend to group together. As the chances to meet other Italian peers are very limited compared with mainstream schools, opportunities to develop social interaction through school attendance are scarce in this context. As a result, CPIAs risk becoming an umpteenth segregated environment that hinders children's integration.

As we noted, the availability of a number of skilled practitioners, as well as inter-professional and multi-agency cooperation are pivotal for ensuring that schools can foster a smooth integration process for all asylum-seeker and refugee students. Head teachers play a key role in this sense, as they are not only legally responsible for the management and coordination of all interventions planned in school, but should also take the lead on sensitising all school personnel to this topic and to the importance of developing adequate organisational and pedagogical strategies to help refugee children to settle in school. Furthermore, as public funding is conceived as ensuring only the basic functioning of mainstreaming schools, head teachers are also compelled by the lack of resources to find alternative ways to provide viable educational opportunities for all children with specific needs, including the implementation of integration activities aimed at refugee students.

Administrative support staff, too, play a central role, as they are usually the first point of contact with school for refugee families or children's guardians. Moreover, they are responsible for managing the highly complex procedures related to the children's enrolment, as norms on this subject are frequently subject to further revision and specification. Administrative support staff are also involved in preparing school applications for getting external funding from the Ministry of Education. These applications are aimed at acquiring additional resources to promote "special" linguistic and/or educational projects addressed at refugee children. However, many schools suffer from endemic administrative understaffing, so they are often unable to deal with the large bureaucratic load involved in the application and report process.

As for teachers, it is important to consider that since the 1970s, the Italian approach to inclusion has traditionally been based on the accommodation of all children – regardless of disability or specific needs – in mainstream schools. This means that organising separate classes (for example with the aim of offering preparatory linguistic courses to refugee children) cannot be devised within the normal framework of schools. However, by law, educational institutions can deliver specific support to disadvantaged students in terms of additional small-group activities aimed at learning Italian as a second language. Such activities have been defined by the Ministry of Education as a weekly intervention providing 8 to 10 teaching hours that should be developed over a period of 3 to 4 months. However, only a few schools actually have educational staff teachers who are specialised in teaching Italian as a second language and/or can afford to devote extra time to this activity. As a consequence, linguistic support is offered only for a very limited number of hours per week, usually by unspecialised teachers who are essentially working on a voluntary basis.

In addition to Italian as a second language, refugee children also need the help of other subject teachers, as many of them are illiterate or, more generally, have received very little education in their country of origin. Italian law affirms that students with specific socioeconomic, linguistic and cultural needs – as is the case with refugee children – are entitled to follow personalised school paths, which can be adapted to meet the skill levels and learning pace of each student. Indeed, in pedagogical terms, refugee students constitute a considerable challenge for teachers, whose teaching skills should be expanded to acquire the basic level of intercultural competences needed to work with refugee children. More precisely, it is important that intercultural competences are not confined to the interventions of specialised teachers or other consultants, but become a common ground for all teachers, especially in schools where refugee children are attending classes (Fiorucci, 2015). Through this, it would be possible to improve both the accuracy of the evaluation process used to assess refugee children's skills as they enrol in school, and the ability of teachers to adapt the curriculum according to the needs and potential of this specific population of students.

Such arrangements are mandatory to favour the enrolment and success of refugee youths in school. Therefore, investing in the provision of dedicated training courses for teachers on these topics is pivotal. However, so far teacher training in Italy has been underdeveloped, especially at the secondary school level. While a master's degree in early childhood education – commonly including classes about intercultural education – is currently delivered by many Italian universities to prospective teachers, training that addresses future secondary teachers is still limited and fragmented. This lack of preparation and guidance is especially detrimental, as most refugee students are usually enrolled in secondary schools. As a result, educational projects focused on refugee children are frequently supported by individual, well-intentioned teachers, instead of being part of a systematic and shared effort towards inclusion supported by the whole school. In upper secondary institutions (including most vocational schools), the situation is further complicated by the fact that schools are regularly crowded, often including up to 30 children per classroom. This large number of students significantly hinders the ability to successfully integrate refugee children by providing the level of care and attention they need. As a consequence, some schools are indirectly discouraging children from enrolling in or persevering with attending classes, while others categorize them according to the places available on the spot, rather than on the basis of their actual age or skills.

Furthermore, to pursue refugee students' inclusion, teachers' interventions must be associated with other contributions from specialised practitioners, especially in terms of linguistic and cultural mediation, as well as psychological support (Catarci, 2011). The role of mediators is critical, especially in the initial phase immediately following the enrolment of refugee students in school: on the one hand, the mediator can provide vital information to teachers and other practitioners about the child's migration story and current situation; on the other, s/he facilitates the child in gradually getting to know and integrating into the new educational setting. Moreover, where the child is accompanied by parents or other relatives, the mediator ensures that smooth communication about the child's education and effective integration can take place. Mediation services are usually offered by external partners, such as asylum-seeking reception centres or local municipalities. However, these activities are provided on a limited and irregular basis, covering only a small portion of the actual schools' requirements for mediation.

As regards psychological support, a large number of studies show that refugee children are at a high risk of developing psychological disorders related to their forced migration experience, especially in terms of post-traumatic stress disorder, distress, anxiety, and depression. Research emphasizes that improvements in children's mental health are strongly associated with the development of safe conditions characterized by stable settlement and social support. In particular, school participation, acquiring language proficiency, and building a network of local friends are all factors positively associated with children's levels of wellbeing and resilience. Even though appropriate health care access should be provided to all refugee children in Europe – as a right guaranteed by the first host country – the organisation of public health services in Italy, coupled with the poor competences of health staff in this particular area of intervention, tend to reduce the actual opportunities for children to receive proper help in psychological terms. As a result, specific support for refugee children's mental health is not as widespread as it should be, as it is mostly delivered by private organisations on a voluntary basis.

Another final point that needs to be highlighted is the chronic underfunding that affects Italian schools, which undermines their ability to ensure refugee students school access, permanence, and success. In 2015, the Ministry of Education launched an annual call for applications for funding for school projects related to the inclusion of refugee youths. The call for applications to the fund, which allocates one million euros per year, aims to implement activities promoting refugee students' integration through the provision of linguistic, cultural, and community support. However beneficial this initiative could be, it has a number of shortcomings. First of all, the allotted funding is not sufficient to guarantee that the minimum range of actions required to ensure school enrolment and attendance of all refugee students over one year will be covered. Secondly, being a competitive call for applications, it implies that institutions will invest extra time and resources in applying for the funds. As a consequence, disadvantaged and/or understaffed schools, which would be the primary target of the funding, are often unable to sustain the workflow required by the application process. Moreover, the irregular flow of refugee children arriving in Italy throughout the year does not match the rigid procedures and deadlines of the application system. Therefore, schools that welcome refugee children in the middle of the year are excluded from the opportunity to obtain additional resources in a timely manner. Finally, as funding is provided on a yearly basis, school projects are at risk of being discontinued, even if children's attendance lasts for longer than one year – as is usually is the case.

Italian delays in envisioning and implementing clear-cut policies on this issue reflect the prolonged invisibility of asylum-seeker and refugee children within the official educational paths. This void has, to a certain extent, been filled by NGOs and voluntary associations. However, when responding to the needs of refugee children, such organisations risk framing them as a homogenous group, even though we know that being a refugee is more an outcome of bureaucratic process, than an homogeneous reality (Rutter, 2006). This way, they tend to adopt a one-dimensional view of refugees' backgrounds, typically focused on a "victim's history", which often fails to take into account how refugee biographies differ widely according to individual experiences and feelings. Moreover, NGOs and associations are usually concentrated in large towns in Italy, whereas current administrative policies tend to scatter asylum-seekers and refugees to small towns for reasons essentially related to public order. Therefore schools, along with social services, are the only public agencies left that could offer widespread and extensive educational support to refugee children. In addition, while social services may be unfamiliar or be regarded with suspicion as they are frequently connected with legal requirements, schools are generally respected and appreciated by refugee families, which consider them as an opportunity for socio-economic mobility (Dutton et al., 2000). However, this implies that schools would have to increase their ability to organise outreach, assiduously working to involve individual students and families in educational activities instead of restricting themselves to applying bureaucratic procedures for enrolment.

All in all, the current approach to the integration of refugee students in Italian schools is shaped by manifold positive interventions. Nevertheless, such interventions are fragile, as they are mostly based on short-term funding (provided by the central administration or private bodies) or on voluntary contributions. This poses a question about the actual perspective from which refugee children education is seen and managed in Italy. On the one hand, we find a legal framework that ensures a high degree of protection and promotion of the educational rights of refugee children. On the other, actions taken to fulfil those rights are not adequately supported as they are based on short-term funding. Planned interventions still seem to refer to a conception of refugee children's arrival and integration in schools as a temporary (or even exceptional) event, even though international reports highlight that it is an enduring, probably permanent phenomenon. Without proper allocation of funding, refugee children not only end up being excluded from educational experiences they would be entitled to participate in, but are also increasingly exposed to the risk of going underground and, consequently, being exploited or even abused. However, the introduction of regular long-term funding schemes is a necessary but not sufficient condition for ensuring sustainability of actions related to refugee children's education in Italy. Faced with the extended development of valuable, but scattered and often isolated practices emerging from institutions that work on fostering refugee youths' school experiences, it is also pivotal to promote greater coordination and cross-dissemination of interventions, so as to ensure that positive actions can be spread and reinforced in all schools in an effective way.

CHALLENGES AND OPPORTUNITIES OF REFUGEE CHILDREN EDUCATION IN ITALY

As in many other countries, school culture in Italy is increasingly permeated by neoliberal tendencies that restrict educational experiences to the ability to pass tests and get good grades. The INVALSI survey, conducted yearly in the framework of the OECD-PISA program, is a good example of how a supposedly neutral instrument for measuring performance leads to reinforcing a vocabulary made of "attainment", "ranking", and "excellence", diverting attention from actual key points such as participation, equity, and collaboration. However, the assessment of schools' abilities to handle increasing diversity cannot be based only on individual performances in languages or mathematics. We also need indicators for the way schools successfully contribute to increasing awareness of the value of extended citizenship and cultural differences by building alliances with parents and community members (Bergset, 2017; Kia-Keating & Ellis, 2007). The limited independence from the central administration gained recently by Italian schools can be greatly improved by involving parents, guardians, and other figures in decision-making processes related to school life. Adopting a participatory approach that engages parents and other partners in choices concerning the education of children is essential to ensuring refugee pupils' settlement as well as to transforming it into an opportunity to foster wider community empowerment.

To this end, teachers play a key role in coordinating all efforts aimed at guaranteeing the effective enrolment and transition of refugee youths. However, this poses a professional challenge, as refugee education cannot be considered as just a variation of the usual intercultural education programmes. Consequently, Italian teachers need to receive both pre-service and continual professional development in refugee education as a stable part of their training. It is important to note that, with regard to pre-service teachers, training programmes have been implemented successfully in countries that have a long history of tackling refugee emergencies. For example, since 2007 a large number of future teachers from Greater Western Sydney have attended Refugee Action Support (RAS) programmes, which include participation in community-based service-learning as a parallel practicum experience for student teachers (Ferfolja, 2007, 2009; Ferfolja & Naidoo, 2010; Ferfolja & Vickers, 2010; Naidoo, 2013). This programme requires pre-service teachers to spend their service learning time working as tutors for a period of twelve weeks in tutoring centres located in high schools with a large population of refugee students. Schools participating in the programme host a team of three or four pre-service teachers, and every tutor works with a group of three to four students. Even though the programme has been put in place to support refugee students, it is open to all students seeking assistance. As a result, RAS groups favour the socializing and acculturation process of students from different backgrounds (mainstream, ESL, and refugee). The programme embraces a holistic and whole-school approach, based on reciprocal learning, where tutors and students offer cultural scaffolding to each other, thereby acquiring deeper knowledge and understanding from the educational interaction. This way, future teachers can expand their professional competences while developing a reflective (and sometimes critical) stance towards traditional forms of teaching and learning, by comparing them to the actual practices promoted in schools participating in the programme. Moreover, by mixing refugee, Italian-as-a-second-language and mainstream students, this kind of programme has proved to be effective at ensuring not only academic achievement and social integration of refugee children, but also additional support for all students attending classes.

Experiences based on the RAS, as well as other educational approaches, emphasise that Italian schools have to develop deeper knowledge of the multiple, complex needs of asylum-seeker and refugee pupils. This entails school practitioners acquiring a broader awareness of how children experience high mobility, displacement, replacement, dealing with a new language and culture, enduring poor housing and health problems, facing changes in family relationships, and sometimes anxiety or feelings of guilt about leaving behind or surviving other family members. The sense of emergency usually leads teachers to focus on primary educational needs, by concentrating essentially on helping refugee pupils to acquire basic language and literacy skills and to adapt to the culture and expectations connected to formal education. As we saw, many schools support the learning of Italian as a second language, both by fostering specific linguistic programmes implemented by teachers and favouring interaction with native peers. However, it is not uncommon to see refugee children reported to health and social services as their struggle to conform to the expectations of teachers is interpreted as an unwillingness to comply with the school's rules. Consequently, refugee and asylum-seeker children are usually overrepresented within the growing population of pupils with elusive diagnoses such as SLD, ADHD, ODD and so on, which transform the cultural gap into an individual deficit.

Moreover, not all schools are putting clear anti-bullying policies in place to tackle racism and discrimination which, to varying extents, many refugee students often face. Schools need to be aware that refugee children are natural catalysts for all kinds of negative projections about diversity. Therefore, they are frequently envisioned as deviant subjects that can put local health, safety, and the welfare system at risk. More subtly, they are often blamed for "slowing down" classes because of their poor performance, undermining other pupils' ability to receive adequate instruction. Yet, it is worth noting that refugee children also mobilise strong positive projections, especially connected to their condition as victims of war or abuse. A large body of literature emphasises how violence and loss have a deep psychological impact on asylum-seekers' lives, hindering their ability to accommodate and actively become a part of their schooling (Bronstein & Montgomery, 2011; Campbell III, 2017; Chopra & Adelman, 2016; Hayward, 2017; Rutter, 2006). Nevertheless, forcing refugee students into the narrow category of "victims" does not do justice to the complexity of their identity, especially because the Western conception of "trauma" overlooks the multiform ways through which other cultures enable individuals to cope with distress, drawing on their own personal and social resources. A balanced view of refugee students cannot be reduced to a psychological assessment aiming to measure risk or protective factors as internal characteristics of children. It also requires careful consideration of external conditions that affect post-migration experiences in terms of being in a poor economic situation, unstable housing, and social marginalisation, not to mention uncertainty related to current procedures for the recognition of international protection (Cabot, 2013; De Gioia, 2017). In short, compelling refugee students alternatively into the role of aggressor or victim diminishes schools' capacities to perceive them as human beings with all their complex needs and facets. Therefore, it is important to avoid not only demonising refugee pupils for crimes they have not committed, but also to avoid forcibly medicalizing them for diseases they do not actually have.

Medicalisation is especially visible in the deficit model implicit in the way refugee youths are prevalently seen as victims requiring medical and psychological treatment (Braun, 2016; Keddie, 2012). This approach risks diverting attention from the impact that economic conditions and social barriers have on their lives. Moreover, it leads to underestimating refugee students' potential, as well as their ability to develop resilience and build on their strengths (Hek, 2005; Ziaian et al., 2017). This model is also reflected in categories that schools usually use to assess refugee children's educational needs. On the one hand, categorising children is seen as a mandatory step in order for them to access special provision for refugee students from the central administration; on the other, the same process frequently leads to the creation of labelling policies focused on negative descriptions, which hinder the inclusive path expected from school education and increase the risk of segregation of refugee children (Madziva & Thondhlana, 2017; Masocha, 2015; Matthews, 2008). Therefore, a double shift is required to enable schools to work effectively with those students. Firstly, refugee needs are not special, but specific. That implies that refugee pupils cannot be segregated into special categories, as the trite rhetoric of SEN managed to do with other groups in the past. Specific just means precise, so there is no reason to put them outside the supposed realm of normalcy. Secondly, refugee students are more than their needs. They also have aspirations, projects, dreams. Consequently, inclusive schools should commit to sustaining students through a process of empowerment, so as to help them become able to exercise agency in their lives by pursuing and achieving personal and community goals (Daley, 2009; Dryden-Peterson, 2011).

Research shows that educational policy and support provided to asylum-seeker and refugee children can take different forms according to the conceptual framework adopted by schools (Arnot & Pinson, 2005; Madziva & Thondhlana, 2017). In Italy, we can identify five models that describe the way refugee pupils are managed, focusing, respectively, on protection of children seen as especially helpless and at risk (vulnerable children model), school admission and induction (new arrivals model), safeguarding of cultural minorities against discrimination and underachieving (ethnic minority model), and Italian as an additional language acquisition (IAL model). Several authors have suggested that these programmes are less effective than approaches based on a holistic model that is able to recognize refugee youths' experiences as a complex tangle of educational, emotional, and social dimensions. Such dimensions should be addressed by seeing provisions "not as an aim in itself but as a means to promote the pupils' ability to fulfil themselves as learners, to access the curriculum and to be socially included" (Arnot & Pinson, 2005, p. 40). Consequently, the holistic approach is as much interested in supporting children's participation and well-being throughout the school and community, as it is in the development of literacy and curriculum. Implementing a holistic model of supporting refugee pupils in schools requires a shared commitment to social justice and inclusion; sensitivity to and celebration of cultural diversity; developing cooperation between schools involved in refugee programmes; sustaining parents' engagement in school activities and mutual support; and promoting a distributive leadership approach to strengthen partnerships with local agencies.

Accordingly, helping refugee students to settle in a new environment involves more than just adding further provisions beyond those already in place. It entails setting in motion an organisational change in schools that helps to identify and remove the barriers to learning and participation that affect cultures, policies, and practices which are deeply embedded in educational structures. In turn, this implies that schools need not only external aid, in the form of linguistic mediators and psychological advice, but also additional teaching resources to offer specific support for pupil enrolment and transition, as well as work on the adaptation of teaching and curriculum. In this regard, recent school reforms in Italy added quantity (in terms of the number of teachers), but also removed quality and undermined inclusion by dismantling team teaching and reducing the time teachers could previously devote to developing good practices for all pupils. As we noted, the literature emphasises that in refugee students, school access and academic achievement correlate positively with an increased sense of safety and self-efficacy (Ahmadzadeh et al., 2014; Education Unit Division of International Protection, UNHCR, 2016; Kislev, 2016; Schnell & Azzolini, 2015). However, schools are also prone to replicating inequality and marginalisation by implicitly rewarding pupils who correspond to a specific profile (in terms of culture, language, gender, economic conditions, social capital, and so on), and excluding others (Sidhu & Christie, 2007; Taylor & Sidhu, 2012). For this reason, facilitating refugee students' ability to fulfil their needs and make the best use of their potential cannot be achieved just by focusing on them and their families. It requires working on transforming the whole school, drawing from principled interventions based on inclusive values, and extended cooperation with other agencies.

MULTI-AGENCY WORK AND REFUGEE CHILDREN EDUCATION: A CASE ANALYSIS

Due to the dramatic increase in the influx of refugee children in the last few years, Italian schools and child psychology services are currently facing a number of new professional challenges. In fact, children and families from a refugee background seem to escape the technical view usually adopted by educational and health practitioners, which is based on a mixture of diagnostic tests and special needs policies, as we previously remarked. This approach struggles to cope with the multiple requirements – in terms of health, culture, language, and learning – involved in taking care of refugee children (Dwivedi, 2002). As a consequence, even though services have multiplied their efforts to ensure consultation and support, experiences of frustration and inadequacy about reciprocal relationships are quite common among practitioners and refugee families. Misunderstandings during meetings frequently arise due to insufficient mastery of the Italian language or a lack of linguistic mediators, as well as from the mismatch between different cultures and communication frameworks. Despite a high investment of human and time resources from schools, health, and social services, activities are characterised by a significant degree of entropy, while rates of success in case management tend to be low.

Research on inclusive school development suggests that promoting change in educational settings involves working on three main institutional dimensions: culture, policies, and practices (Booth & Ainscow, 2011). This complex goal can be better achieved by leveraging not only internal resources, but also external partnerships with parents, caregivers and, more generally, school stakeholders. The literature shows that supporting refugee children's education requires fostering an even broader inclusive approach, as alliances are pivotal to ensuring the effectiveness of intervention. Accordingly, we assume that this would imply a shift from a school-centred view to a network-based perspective focused on active cooperation between services and communities.

To test this hypothesis, at the suggestion of educational and health and social services in Italy we carried out an action research study that aimed to understand how schools and services can increase the effectiveness and quality of programmes aimed at refugee children and families/caregivers. The study was carried out in two lower secondary schools and two health and social services, all located in a large urban area in northern Italy. The two schools were attended by a population of around 450 students, many of whom are from a first- or second-generation migrant background, and 52 mainstream and support teachers. The health and social services take care of the evaluation, diagnosis and treatment of children affected by psychological and learning disorders. The services' teams, comprising child psychiatrists, psychologists, speech therapists, psychomotor therapists, and social workers, see around 1200 children per year. Overall, one third of these children are from a migrant background. At the time the investigation was held, a total of 37 cases related to unaccompanied minors or children whose families had been or were applying for international protection. Of these, 19 children were enrolled in the two lower secondary schools investigated.

The inquiry was developed using an action research approach, as the primary goal was to help practitioners and refugee families to collaborate in order to address and solve key problems in their organizations and communities (McIntyre, 2008; Reason & Bradbury, 2008). The data collection process was conducted through extensive fieldwork over ten months, based on the collection of services' and schools' documentation, participant observation, conversations and semi-structured interviews held with refugee families, as well as practitioners working in the health and social services, schools, and other community services. The investigation focused on three research questions:

- What are the structural reasons behind the persistent difficulties of services and schools in managing refugee children's and families' cases?
- Are examples of good practices emerging from the activities of practitioners in services and schools and, if so, what are their specific features?
- How could the knowledge embedded in emerging good practices be promoted and disseminated throughout services and schools?

Data collected from gathering services' and schools' documentation, doing participant observation, and recording conversations and semi-structured interviews have been reported fully (using verbatim transcription of conversations and interviews). All content was then analysed through the qualitative content analysis approach, which makes it possible to generate concepts that describe the research phenomenon by identifying specific codes and categories. These codes and categories are created using both an inductive (originated from the data) and deductive (derived from close reading) method. The analysis process was carried out with the help of Atlas-ti© software in order to manage the coding activity and the subsequent identification of categories and generation of concepts. To check coding reliability (Miles et al., 2014), we adopted a verification procedure aimed at systematically comparing codes elicited by researchers to ensure inter-coder agreement (k1/41.22). Subsequently, emergent themes (or second level codes) were developed by establishing connections and relationships between codes that proved to be reliable, thereby providing a higher level of abstraction that still reflected the source material. As a final step, we selected and then grouped together emergent themes according to similarities, so as to produce the global interpretation of data through the generation of general concepts (Friese, 2014).

As a result, data analysis highlights that repeated difficulties of services and schools with managing refugee children and families can be attributed to five main causes:

1. Linguistic mediation was available in schools and health and social services only upon formal request and for a limited time. Consequently, the institutions we investigated usually prefer not to hire linguistic mediators, with very few exceptions, assuming that communication with children and families would be managed anyway. This option produces a double negative effect on conversations with refugee families. On the one hand, children and parents are perceived as uncooperative by practitioners, as they tend to be silent during the meeting. However, silence is produced not only by a respectful attitude towards authority, but also by the immigrants' inability to follow conversations held in the Italian language and riddled with technical terms. On the other hand, faced with what they assume is resistance from families to comply with the suggestions they are offering, practitioners tend to patronise refugee children and even adults as if they were stubborn or had cognitive impairments.

2. Practitioners often adopt an implicit "vulnerability" view in dealing with refugee youths and families. This view is rooted in the widespread belief that refugee children have been exposed to shocking events before or during migration. Accordingly, teachers tend to primarily relate to refugee students as suffering and traumatised children, while health and social services develop interventions specifically based on the framework of post-traumatic stress disorder. Certainly, the refugee children and families we met during interviews had experienced a high level of fear and stress that cannot be underestimated. Most of them were still visibly disoriented and distressed. However, a prevalent focus on trauma risks reinforcing institutional control by producing a view of the refugee children population as being more uniform than it is. This view overlooks the complexity of pre-exile experiences, as well as the manifold issues refugees have to deal with as they try to settle in the new country. Problems connected to social and economic conditions, housing, marginalisation and racism cannot be reduced to an individual mental disorder subject to medicalisation from health services.

3. The diagnostic model usually adopted by schools and health and social services to complete the screening of newly arrived minors tends to focus on separated parts of the individual. The child is seen as an aggregate of specific functions

defined in terms of level of intelligence, attention, language, stress, and so on. This separation is furtherly exacerbated by the division of labour currently in place in services that take responsibility for refugee children. According to the specific need involved, a single child can be assisted by teachers, support teachers, child psychiatrists, psychologists, speech and psychomotor therapists, and social workers, each focused on his/her professional area of intervention. If not harmonised, the piling up of different languages and approaches, which separate specialists use while they are dealing with the same child, tends to produce a sense of fragmentation and increased alienation, instead of integration and connectedness.

4. It is common in the schools and services we visited to make reference to an idea of a standard to which refugee children and their families are constantly referred. Children are repeatedly assessed according to the typical level of educational, health, and social skills they are expected to conform to within a short period of time. This practice is usually carried out using psychological or educational tests that have been developed with "normal" children in mind, with no migration background. Therefore, they reflect a narrow view of standards that systematically produces a negative description of the refugee children and their families. Accordingly, the refugee child is depicted through a detailed list of abilities s/he lacks: s/he does not speak Italian, does not pay sufficient attention, does not control emotions, and does not develop adequate relationships with peers. In fact, this kind of repeated negative description not only underestimates refugee children's potential, but also contributes to worsening their disadvantaged condition by undermining motivation, thereby hindering the process of empowerment on which integration is primarily based.

5. Finally, interviews with refugee children and families highlight that their needs are not limited to economic or psychological conditions, but also refer to the possibility of establishing stable relationships with the new environment they are trying to settle into. The social capital of refugees is usually low compared to other migrants, as they often had to flee from their home country without having the time to connect with or develop social networks in the new country. This situation, which is especially difficult for unaccompanied minors, is further worsened by national policies that frequently disperse refugees by accommodating them in different regions in Italy. As a consequence, very isolated children are commonly sent to school at very short notice in the middle of the school year. This widespread practice contributes to producing cultural clashes within school, as well as poor group and classroom relationships between the refugee child and peers. Even though efforts are made by teachers to combat possible expressions of racial denigration and harassment, the risk of the child being marginalised is high, as s/he often undergoes a "second exile" experience at school.

Faced with the difficulties encountered by the schools and health and social services, several examples of good practices are also emerging from the activities of the practitioners involved in managing refugee children's cases. Even though they are still at an early stage and not implemented systematically, such good practices can play an important role in developing strategies that would help schools and services to overcome some of the issues we previously described:

1. Instead of assuming that a lack of mastery of the Italian language will not affect communication with children and their families, a group of practitioners formed by one psychomotor therapist, one social worker, two teachers, and one support teacher insisted on having a linguistic mediator available during the meetings with families, although this implied managing draining paperwork and having harsh discussions about budget issues. As a result, children and parents previously labelled as "dull" or "stubborn" immediately became able to show a relevant level of problem-solving capacities and cooperation with schools and services in finding viable solutions to what were previously considered seemingly unresolvable issues. Moreover, communication eased by linguistic mediators helped to promote less unidirectional communication from practitioners to refugees and more interaction based on reciprocal learning and appreciation.

2. After attending an external seminar on ethnopsychiatry, another mixed group composed by health consultants and teachers called into question the view, taken for granted, that equated children to their condition of vulnerability, especially with regard to the automatic association between refugee experiences and post-traumatic stress disorder. Although the group did not negate the impact that stress and other negative factors related to painful events have on refugees' identities, they proposed widening the focus of attention beyond the mere psychological profile of children. According to the group, this can be done by including other experiences related to the economic, social, cultural and educational dimension of refugee youths and their families. Moreover, such dimensions should be regarded not only through the negative lens of a child's trauma and vulnerability, but also through the positive perspective of the abilities children were able to preserve in terms of resilience and empowerment, despite the terrible events they were exposed to.

3. The same group of practitioners also questioned the condition of professional separation that the traditional division of labour produces among practitioners. This condition was especially evident between teachers and health and social consultants, as they were reporting to different structures and organisational cultures. However, it was also affecting each institution internally, as practitioners were frequently working in silos, focusing on separate areas of intervention related to different features of children's and families' integration issues. This fragmentation produced a sense of frustration both in practitioners and refugee families, which in turn resulted in increasing disaffection with services and schools. To counteract this trend, the group proposed strengthening coordination within and between educational and health and social services by fostering multi-agency work to address improving inter-professional collaboration. To this

end, an experimental practice called "whole child/whole family" was initiated by designing adhocratic, temporary teams based on a more holistic and cross-sectional model of evaluation and intervention.

4. During one evaluation meeting, professionals working in refugee reception centres raised explicit concerns about the negative descriptions produced by the assessment instruments usually employed by schools and health and social services. In their opinion, those instruments ended up discouraging children and families from attending school and trusting services. After quite a confrontational debate, the schools and health and social practitioners committed to revising their protocols in order to offer a more balanced view, in which the classification of children's shortcomings with regards to expected levels of education or behaviour would be complemented by the identification of existing competences and potential. This implied modifying the medical and educational case files usually employed by practitioners so they would comprise not only scores pinpointing a child's deficits related to tested abilities, but also a depiction of his/her actual and potential areas of proficiency. The assessment finally incorporated a qualitative part that allowed the children and their families (as well as other stakeholders involved in supporting the refugee settlement process) to have their voices heard and documented.

5. As for the lack of connections that usually affects refugee children and families, both schools played a pivotal role in helping them to expand their social network within the school area. As a teacher recalled, this question had traditionally been considered a private matter for migrant families or, at most, individual teachers who committed to helping on a voluntary basis. However, the recent influx of refugee children dramatically emphasised the need to design a more systematic and integrated approach. This has been achieved by developing a community-based approach that enabled teachers to enlarge the picture to the opportunities available both inside and outside schools. Consequently, a resource bank has been created by the schools, in collaboration with NGOs and other charities, to spread information through notice boards and Facebook about existing social networks related to sport, cultural, educational, or recreational events in the area. Unaccompanied children were supported in finding in- and out-of-school activities that would help them to strengthen their personal network. During the interview, a group of teachers commented that, as the bank was proving effective in providing information and connections to refugees, they were working on building a special "task force" project leveraging such databases in order to ease the management of recurring emergencies related to refugee children's enrolment in the middle of the school year.

CONCLUSIONS

It is a commonplace that a crisis situation, such as that which we are now experiencing with refugee children, can become an opportunity for education. In ancient Greece, opportunity was portrayed as a running youth, Kairos, bald except for a long lock of hair hanging down from his forehead. He represented the propitious moment or the moment of something coming into being (Stern, 2004). The only way to grab him was from the front, before he moved on. It is easy to link this image to the dramatic pictures of newborns rescued from rubber boats in the Mediterranean Sea nowadays. Thus, it is possible see an opportunity in the crisis of refugee children only if we are able to identify what it is important to grasp in this situation – that is, a chance to improve access to equitable and quality education for all. This implies some specific actions that must be taken in Italy to ensure that educational experience is fully accessible and fruitful for all refugee children. Firstly, children's rights to accessing education, currently guaranteed only on paper, should really be implemented and monitored, especially for minors lacking identification documents or residence permits and/or living in short-term accommodation facilities. Secondly, the enrolment of refugee children should be facilitated and supported, especially with regard to access to pre-primary schools, regional vocational schools, and provincial centres for adult learning. Appropriate procedures for standard assessment of students' certificates and/or skills should be put in place at the national level. Thirdly, financing for educational institutions enrolling refugee students should be guaranteed with a long-term and more flexible perspective, so as to enable schools to develop appropriate actions to support children's educational, linguistic, social, cultural, and psychological needs. This is also pivotal for enabling timely welcoming and integration procedures even when a refugee child arrives in the middle of the school year. Fourthly, intercultural training, as well as specific training on refugee education, should be provided to all pre-service and in-service teachers and professionals working in health and social services in order to ensure that practitioners develop a basic and shared level of skills in this area of intervention. Such training should include preparation and refreshment courses on teaching Italian as a second language to refugee children. Finally, as shown in our case analysis, both schools and health and social services should favour the development and spread of good practices emerging from fieldwork, especially those based on a holistic perspective and aimed at fostering multi-agency work through the dissemination of inter-professional collaboration, as a means for promoting the effective inclusion of refugee children in schools and communities.

REFERENCES

Ahmadzadeh, H., Hashem, L., Al Husseini, J., Wahby, S., Alasil, M., Bali, Z., & Waziri, H. (2014). *Ensuring quality education for young refugees from Syria (12–25 years)*. Oxford: Refugee Studies Centre, Oxford Department of International Development University of Oxford. Retrieved November 30, 2017, from http://s3.amazonaws.com/inee-assets/resources/rr-syria-youth-education-2014.pdf

Arnot, M., & Pinson, H. (2005). *The education of Asylum-Seeker and refugee children: A study of LEA and school values, policies and practices.* Cambridge: The University of Cambridge.

ASGI. (2016). *Asylum information database* (National Country Report). Retrieved November 30, 2017, from http://www.asylumineurope.org/sites/default/files/report-download/aida_it_2016update.pdf

Attanasio, L. (2016). *Il bagaglio. Migranti minori non accompagnati: il fenomeno in Italia, i numeri, le storie*. Rome: Albeggi.

Bal, A. (2014). Becoming in/competent learners in the United States: Refugee students' academic identities in the figured world of difference. *International Multilingual Research Journal, 8*(4), 271–290. Retrieved from http://doi.org/10.1080/19313152.2014.952056

Bergset, K. (2017). School involvement: Refugee parents' narrated contribution to their children's education while resettled in Norway. *Outlines-Critical Practice Studies, 18*(1), 61–80.

Bigelow, M., Vanek, J., King, K., & Abdi, N. (2017). Literacy as social (media) practice: Refugee youth and native language literacy at school. *International Journal of Intercultural Relations, 60*, 183–197. Retrieved from http://doi.org/10.1016/j.ijintrel.2017.04.002

Block, K., Cross, S., Riggs, E., & Gibbs, L. (2014). Supporting schools to create an inclusive environment for refugee students. *International Journal of Inclusive Education, 18*(12), 1337–1355. Retrieved from http://doi.org/10.1080/13603116.2014.899636

Booth, T., & Ainscow, M. (2011). *Index for inclusion: Developing learning and participation in schools* (3rd ed.). Bristol: CSIE.

Bradby, H., Humphris, R., Newall, D., & Phillimore, J. (2015). *Public health aspects of migrant health: A review of the evidence on health status for refugees and aslum seekers in the European Region* (pp. 1–29). Copenhagen: WHO Europe. Retrieved November 30, 2017, from http://www.euro.who.int/__data/assets/pdf_file/0004/289246/WHO-HEN-Report-A5-2-Refugees_FINAL.pdf?ua=1

Braun, V. (2016). Standpoint theory in professional development: Examining former refugee education in Canada. *In Education, 22*(2), 72–86.

Bronstein, I., & Montgomery, P. (2011). Psychological distress in refugee children: A systematic review. *Clinical Child and Family Psychology Review, 14*(1), 44–56. Retrieved from http://doi.org/10.1007/s10567-010-0081-0

Cabot, H. (2013). The social aesthetics of eligibility: NGO aid and indeterminacy in the Greek asylum process. *American Ethnologist, 40*(3), 452–466. Retrieved form http://doi.org/10.1111/amet.12032

Campbell III, J. A. (2017). Attitudes towards refugee education and its link to xenophobia in the United States. *Intercultural Education, 28*(5), 474–479. Retrieved from http://doi.org/10.1080/14675986.2017.1336374

Catarci, M. (2011). *L'integrazione dei rifugiati. Formazione e inclusione nelle rappresentazioni degli operatori sociali*. Milano: FrancoAngeli.

Catarci, M. (2012). Conceptions and strategies for user integration across refugee services in Italy. *ECPS Journal, 5*, 75–107.

Catarci, M. (2016). Intercultural mediation as a strategy to facilitate relations between the school and immigrant families. *Revista Electrónica Interuniversitaria de Formación del Profesorado, 19*(1), 127–140. Retrieved November 30, 2017, from 10.6018/reifop.19.1.244161%5Cn http://search.ebscohost.com/login.aspx?direct=true%7Band%7Ddb=fua%7Band%7DAN=112740048%7Band%7Dlang=es%7Band%7Dsite=ehost-live

Chopra, V., & Adelman, E. (2016). The pursuit, practicality, and potential of refugee education. *1'17 ZEP, 18*, 4–9.

Daley, C. (2009). Exploring community connections: Community cohesion and refugee integration at a local level. *Community Development Journal, 44*(2), 158–171. Retrieved from http://doi.org/10.1093/cdj/bsm026

De Gioia, K. (2017). *Giving voice to families from immigrant and refugee backgrounds during transition to school*. In S. Dockett, W. Griebel, & B. Perry (Eds.), *Families and transition to school*. London: Springer.

Direzione Generale dell'Immigrazione e delle Politiche di Integrazione. (2016). *Report di monitoraggio sui minori stranieri non accompagnati (MSNA) in Italia*. Rome: Ministero del Lavoro e delle Politiche Sociali.

Dryden-Peterson, S. (2011). Refugee education. *Policy Development and Evaluation Service, 45*, 95. Retrieved from http://doi.org/10.3102/0013189X16683398

Dryden-Peterson, S. (2016). Refugee education in countries of first asylum: Breaking open the Black box of pre-resettlement experiences. *Theory and Research in Education, 14*(2), 131–148. Retrieved from http://doi.org/10.1177/1477878515622703

Dutton, J., Hek, R., Hoggart, L., Kohli, R., & Sales, R. (2000). *Supporting refugees in the inner city: An examination of the work of social services in meeting the settlement needs of refugees.* London: Middlesex University and London Borough of Haringey.

Dwivedi, K. N. (2002). *Meeting the needs of ethnic minority children: Including refugee, Black, and mixed parentage children: A handbook for professionals.* London: Jessica Kingsley Publishers.

Education Unit Division of International Protection, UNHCR. (2016). *Mainstreaming refugees in national education systems.* Retrieved November 30, 2017, from http://www.unhcr.org/560be1493.html

Edwards, A., Montecinos, C., Cádiz, J., Jorratt, P., Manriquez, L., & Rojas, C. (2017). *Working relationally on complex problems: Building capacity for joint agency in new forms of work. In agency at work.* London: Springer.

European Commission. (2015a). *Selected publications on refugees' and migrants' integration in schools.* Retrieved November 30, 2017, from http://ec.europa.eu/libraries/doc/refugees_and_migrants_integration_in_shcool.pdf

European Commission. (2015b). *VET and Adult education helping newly-arrived refugees in Europe: Challenges, ideas and inspiring practices.* Retrieved November 30, 2017, from http://ec.europa.eu/dgs/education_culture/repository/education/documents/school-vet-adult-survey-refugee_en.pdf

Ferfolja, T. (2007). *Refugee Action Support (RAS) program: A collaborative initiative between the University of Western Sydney, the Australian Numeracy and Literacy Foundation and the NSW Department of Education and Training* (Interim Report). Sydney: University of Western Sydney.

Ferfolja, T. (2009). The refugee action support program: Developing understandings of diversity. *Teaching Education, 20*(4), 395–407. Retrieved from http://doi.org/10.1080/10476210902741239

Ferfolja, T., & Naidoo, L. (2010). *Supporting refugee students through the Refugee Action Support (RAS) program: What works in schools.* Penrith: University of Western Sydney.

Ferfolja, T., & Vickers, M. (2010). Supporting refugee students in school education in greater Western Sydney. *Critical Studies in Education, 51*(2), 149–162. Retrieved from http://doi.org/10.1080/17508481003731034

Fiorucci, M. (2015). La scuola e la prospettiva interculturale/The school and the Intercultural perspective. *Pedagogia Oggi, 77–90.* Retrieved November 30, 2017, from http://www.siped.it/wp-content/uploads/2015/12/Pedagogia-Oggi-2-2015-ONLINE_fiorucci.pdf

Friese, S. (2014). *Qualitative data analysis with ATLAS.ti.* London: Sage Publications.

Giovannetti, M. (Ed.). (2014). *V Rapporto ANCI-Cittalia. I minori stranieri non accompagnati in Italia.* Retrieved November 30, 2017, from http://www.cittalia.it/images/file/Rapporto%20Cittalia_Anci_MSNA.pdf

Grigt, S. (2017). *The journey of hope: Education for refugee and unaccompanied children in Italy.* Retrieved November 30, 2017, from https://download.ei-ie.org/Docs/WebDepot/Journey_Hope_EN.pdf]

Gruppo di studio sul sistema di accoglienza. (2015). *Rapporto sull'accoglienza di migranti e rifugiati in Italia. Aspetti, procedure, problemi.* Retrieved November 30, 2017, from http://www.libertaciviliimmigrazione.interno.it/dipim/export/sites/default/it/assets/pubblicazioni/Rapporto_accoglienza_ps.pdf

Hamilton, R. J., & Moore, D. (Eds.). (2004). *Educational interventions for refugee children: Theoretical perspectives and implementing best practice.* New York, NY: RoutledgeFalmer.

Hayward, M. (2017). Teaching as a primary therapeutic intervention for learners from refugee backgrounds. *Intercultural Education, 28*(2), 165–181. Retrieved from http://doi.org/10.1080/14675986.2017.1294391

Hek, R. (2005). The role of education in the settlement of young refugees in the UK: The experiences of young refugees. *Practice, 17*(3), 157–171. Retrieved from http://doi.org/10.1080/09503150500285115

IPPM. (2011). *Study on educational support for Newly Arrived Migrant Children (NAMS).* Retrieved November 30, 2017, from http://www.sirius-migrationeducation.org/wp-content/uploads/2013/09/Educational-Support-for-NAMS.pdf

Isik-Ercan, Z. (2012). In pursuit of a new perspective in the education of children of the refugees: Advocacy for the "family". *Kuram ve Uygulamada Egitim Bilimleri, 12*(Suppl 4), 3025–3038. Retrieved from http://doi.org/10.1080/13603110802504523

Keddie, A. (2012). Pursuing justice for refugee students: Addressing issues of cultural (mis)recognition. *International Journal of Inclusive Education, 16*(12), 1295–1310. Retrieved from http://doi.org/10.1080/13603116.2011.560687

Kia-Keating, M., & Ellis, B. H. (2007). Belonging and connection to school in resettlement: Young refugees, school belonging, and psychosocial adjustment. *Clinical Child Psychology and Psychiatry, 12*(1), 29–43. Retrieved from http://doi.org/10.1177/1359104507071052

Kislev, E. (2016). The effect of education policies on higher-education attainment of immigrants in Western Europe: A cross-classified multilevel analysis. *Journal of European Social Policy, 26*(2), 183–199. Retrieved from http://doi.org/10.1177/0958928716637142

Korac, M. (2003). The lack of integration policy and experiences of settlement: A case study of refugees in Rome. *Journal of Refugee Studies, 16*(4), 398–421. Retrieved from http://doi.org/10.1093/jrs/16.4.398

Madziva, R., & Thondhlana, J. (2017). Provision of quality education in the context of Syrian refugee children in the UK: Opportunities and challenges. *Compare: A Journal of Comparative and International Education, 7925*, 1–20. Retrieved from http://doi.org/10.1080/03057925.2017.1375848

Masocha, S. (2015). Construction of the " other " in social workers' discourses of asylum seekers. *Journal of Social Work, 15*(6), 569–585. Retrieved from http://doi.org/10.1177/1468017314549502

Matthews, J. (2008). Schooling and settlement: Refugee education in Australia. *International Studies in Sociology of Education, 18*(1), 31–45. Retrieved from http://doi.org/10.1080/09620210802195947

McBrien, J. (2016). *Refugees and asylum seekers.* In R. Hattam, M. Zembylas, & J. Arthur (Eds.), *The Palgrave international handbook of education for citizenship and social justice.* London: Palgrave Macmillan. Retrieved from http://doi.org/10.1057/978-1-137-51507-0

McIntyre, A. (2008). *Participatory action research.* Thousand Oaks, CA: Sage Publications. Retrieved from http://doi.org/10.1017/CBO9781107415324.004

Miles, M. B., Huberman, M. A., & Saldaña, J. (2014). *Qualitative data analysis: A methods sourcebook.* London: Sage Publications.

MIUR. (2017). *Gli alunni stranieri nel sistema scolastico italiano. A.S. 2015/16.* Retrieved November 30, 2017, from http://www.istruzione.it/allegati/2017/Notiziario_alunni_Stranieri_nel%20sistema_scolastico_italiano_15_16.pdf

Naidoo, L. (2013). Refugee action support: An interventionist pedagogy for supporting refugee students learning in Greater Western Sydney secondary schools. *International Journal of Inclusive Education, 17*(5), 449–461. Retrieved from http://doi.org/10.1080/13603116.2012.683048

Naidoo, L. (2015). Educating refugee-background students in Australian schools and universities. *Intercultural Education, 26*(3), 210–217. Retrieved from http://doi.org/10.1080/14675986.2015.1048079

Newbigging, K., & Thomas, N. (2011). Good practice in social care for refugee and asylum-seeking children. *Child Abuse Review, 20*(5), 374–390. Retrieved from http://doi.org/10.1002/car.1178

Pastoor, L. de W. (2016). Rethinking refugee education: Principles, policies and practice from a European perspective. *Annual Review of Comparative and International Education, 30*, 107–116.

Pastoor, L. de W. (2017). Reconceptualising refugee education: Exploring the diverse learning contexts of unaccompanied young refugees upon resettlement. *Intercultural Education, 28*(2), 143–164. Retrieved from http://doi.org/10.1080/14675986.2017.1295572

Peterson, A., Meehan, C., Durrant, I., & Ali, Z. (2017). *Inclusive educational provision for newly-arrived unaccompanied asylum-seeking and refugee children: A study in a single school in Kent* (Research Report). Canterbury: Canterbury Christ Church University.

Pinson, H., & Arnot, M. (2010). Local conceptualisations of the education of asylum-seeking and refugee students: From hostile to holistic models. *International Journal of Inclusive Education, 14*(2), 247–267. Retrieved from http://doi.org/10.1080/13603110802504523

Pinson, H., Arnot, M., & Candappa, M. (2010). *Education, asylum and the 'non-citizen' child: The politics of compassion and belonging.* Basingstoke: Palgrave.

Pugh, K., Every, D., & Hattam, R. (2012). Inclusive education for students with refugee experience: Whole school reform in a South Australian primary school. *Australian Educational Researcher, 39*(2), 125–141. Retrieved from http://doi.org/10.1007/s13384-011-0048-2

REACH. (2017). *Children on the move in Italy and Greece*. Retrieved November 30, 2017, from http://www.reachresourcecentre.info/system/files/resource-documents/reach_ita_grc_report_children_ on_the_move_in_italy_and_greece_june_2017.pdf

Reason, P., & Bradbury, H. (Eds.). (2008). *The Sage handbook of action research participative inquiry and practice: Themes in education*. Thousand Oaks, CA: Sage Publications. Retrieved from http://doi.org/ 10.1177/1476750311414740

Rigon, G., & Mengoli, G. (2013). *Cercare un futuro lontano da casa. Storie di minori stranieri non accompagnati*. Bologna: EDB.

Rutter, J. (2006). *Refugee children in the UK*. Maidenhead: Open University Press.

Santagata, M., & Ongini, V. (2016). *Alunni con cittadinanza non italiana. La scuola multiculturale nei contesti locali. Rapporto nazionale A.S. 2014/2015*. Retrieved November 30, 2017, from http://www.istruzione.it/allegati/2016/Rapporto-Miur-Ismu-2014_15.pdf

Save the Children Italia. (2017). *Atlante dei Minori Stranieri non Accompagnati in Italia*. Retrieved November 30, 2017, from https://www.savethechildren.it/sites/default/files/AtlanteMinoriMigranti2017.pdf

Schnell, P., & Azzolini, D. (2015). The academic achievements of immigrant youths in new destination countries: Evidence from Southern Europe. *Migration Studies, 3*(2), 217–240. Retrieved November 30, 2017, from http://doi.org/10.1093/migration/mnu040

Sidhu, R. K., & Christie, P. (2007). Spatialising the scholarly imagination: Globalisation , refugees and education. *Transnational Curriculum Inquiry, 4*(1), 7–16.

SPRAR. (2017). *Rapporto annuale SPRAR: Atlante SPRAR 2016*. Retrieved November 30, 2017, from http://www.sprar.it/wp-content/uploads/2017/06/Atlante-Sprar-2016-2017-RAPPORTO-leggero.pdf

Stern, D. N. (2004). *The present moment: In psychotherapy and everyday life*. New York, NY: W. W. Norton & Co.

Taylor, S., & Sidhu, R. K. (2012). Supporting refugee students in schools: What constitutes inclusive education? *International Journal of Inclusive Education, 16*(1), 39–56. Retrieved from http://doi.org/ 10.1080/13603110903560085

UNHCR. (2017a). *Desperate journeys; Refugees and migrants entering and crossing Europe via the Mediterranean and Western Balkans routes*. Retrieved November 10, 2017, from http://www.refworld.org/ docid/59ad23046.html

UNHCR. (2017b). *Focus group on integration* (Final Report). Retrieved November 30, 2017, from https://www.unhcr.it/wp-content/uploads/2016/01/UNHCR_Report_ENG_web.pdf

UNICEF – IOM. (2017). *Harrowing journeys: Children and youth on the move across the Mediterranean Sea, at risk of trafficking and exploitation*. Retrieved November 30, 2017, from https://www.unicef.org/ publications/files/Harrowing_Journeys_Children_and_youth_on_the_move_across_the_ Mediterranean.pdf

Ziaian, T., de Anstiss, H., Puvimanasinghe, T., & Miller, E. (2017). Refugee students' psychological wellbeing and experiences in the Australian education system: A mixed-methods investigation. *Australian Psychologist* (Online), 1–10. Retrieved from http://doi.org/10.1111/ap.12301

Fabio Dovigo
Department of Human and Social Sciences
University of Bergamo
Italy

HERMINA GUNNÞÓRSDÓTTIR

3. "DO YOU TEACH ABOUT REAL KNOWLEDGE?"

Different Ideas between Parents and Teachers from Unlike
Cultures about the Role of Schools and Education

This qualitative research aims at understanding how parents of immigrant and refugee children and their teachers construct their ideas on the roles of schools and education. It presents data from an ongoing project on immigrant and refugee education in Iceland. Data was gathered by group interviews with 38 teachers, ten in-depth interviews were conducted with parents of immigrant students who have a European background and two Syrian parents (a couple) were also interviewed. The research draws on theories and literature on home-school collaboration, structuralism and post-structuralism and Hofstede's cultural dimensions' theory. The findings indicate that parents and teachers hold different ideas about teaching and education and how their cultural background shapes their beliefs.

INTRODUCTION

The world is on the move as never before and for various reasons. In the last few years we have witnessed how a flow of people has had to leave their home countries because of war, unstable political environment or simply in the search for a better life. Some countries are more attractive destinations than others, often depending on closeness to the home country, access (both geographically and bureaucratically) or how welcoming the host country presents itself. In many cases, people do not have a choice; they simply go where they have the chance to find shelter and the opportunity to live a better life than before. Families with school age children who settle in a new country have to learn a new language and engage with a new culture. The schools in the host country may or may not be experienced in recognising and responding to the multiple needs and challenges faced by the students and their families.

Iceland is one of the countries that have seen an increase in immigration in the past decade. According to Statistics Iceland (2016) 1.9% of the total population of Iceland were foreign citizens in 1996 but by 1st January 2017 immigrants in Iceland were 10.6% of the population. Students who do not have Icelandic as their mother tongue in compulsory schools (age 6–15) follow this number as they were registered to be 9.3% in 2016. Although the percentage of immigrants in Iceland is not high, or around 10–11% the changes have been fast and for a small nation of 330,000 inhabitants this can have a major impact on small towns and villages and their schools.

Akureyri is an industrial and service town in the North of Iceland with 18,000 inhabitants, but at the same time it is the second largest town in Iceland. Immigration to Akureyri has been less than in Iceland as a whole and for 2016 the ratio is 5%. Children under 18 years of age with a foreign background have been rare so far in schools in Akureyri. In 2000, only 30 children with foreign backgrounds were registered living in Akureyri but in 2016 this number had tripled to 120 children (Statistics Iceland, 2016). By children of foreign backgrounds, we designate those born in Iceland of immigrant parents, or children who moved to Iceland with their foreign parents at an early age. It can thus be safe to say that in Akureyri the population has so far been rather homogeneous in terms of native born versus foreign born individuals. Also, it goes without saying that with such a small number of immigrants' schools may not have been addressing issues related to immigrants as a high priority in their operation.

In January 2016 Akureyri welcomed four families from Syria who had been living in refugee camps in Lebanon for some time. The four families consist of 23 individuals, 13 children were of school or kindergarten age. After an adaptation period of two weeks they went to their neighbourhood school or kindergarten.

Icelandic education policy is based on principles of inclusive education and equal opportunities for all learners (Ministry of Education, Science and Culture, 2012). However, in Icelandic schools issues on multiculturalism in education have not received much attention or focus, although some regions and schools are exceptions from this. The most recent research on multicultural issues and education reveals certain inadequacies of the school system when it comes to responding effectively to the educational needs of immigrant students (Magnúsdóttir, 2010; Tran, 2007). This is also confirmed by the findings from The Programme for International Student Assessment – PISA[1] which shows that immigrant children are worse off than their Icelandic counterparts regarding educational attainments and social adaptation (Garðarsdóttir & Hauksson, 2011; Halldórsson, Ólafsson, & Björnsson, 2013).

This chapter presents findings on different ideas that emerge among parents and teachers about the role of schools and education. The aim of the chapter is to explore and understand these different perspectives, their nature and how they can be used to improve the education of the students concerned.

THEORIES AND LITERATURE

This research draws on three main strands from theories and literature; home-school collaboration, structuralism and post-structuralism and Hofstede's cultural dimensions theory.

Home-School Collaboration

The literature on home-school collaboration emphasizes the importance of building a culturally responsive relationship (Ameta, 2013) where the school plays a leading role in communicating with the parents. Both parties, parents and teachers, need to have an active role with a focus on the student and his education and well-being. Too often the communication is characterised by one-way communication on behalf of the school which can cause parents to become passive listeners (Abadeh, 2014). Parents' cultural diversity which causes an additional difference from their new country of residence can create complexities for teachers in their communication with the parents. Joshi, Eberly, and Konzal (2005) have emphasized that in order to create a learning environment for students of different cultures, teachers need insight into the values, beliefs, and practices of those cultures.

Research findings show that culture can have an impact on students' learning, both negatively and positively (Ameta, 2013; Chumak-Horbatsch, 2012). To become an effective and a positive tool in education, culture needs to be explored deeper than only as ethnicity, race and faith. Schools and teachers need to recognise the broad notion of similarities and differences and how these are reflected in students' multiple social identities (Ontario Ministry of Education, 2009). According to Trumbull, Rothstein-Fisch, Greenfield, and Quiroz (2001) the major barrier to parent-school communication is the failure in trying to understand different beliefs of parents and educators relating to the purposes, goals, and outcomes of schooling. One barrier or failure in this context takes the form of fixed ideas or beliefs about parents' aspirations regarding their children's education. In a new OECD (2015) report containing a Review on Migrant Education this is discussed and concluded that: "Most immigrant students – and their parents – hold an ambition to succeed that in most cases matches, and in some cases surpasses, the aspiration of families in their host country" (p. 5). In the report the well-being of immigrant students is highlighted and it is mentioned that their well-being is affected, not only by cultural differences between the country of origin and the host country, but also by the way schools and communities help this group of students to deal with problems on a daily basis relating to living, learning and communicating (p. 6). In its guidance to policy makers and school systems the report argues that schools need to reach out to immigrant parents as "students do better when their parents understand the importance of schooling, how the school system works, and how best to support their child's progress through school" (p. 10).

Structuralism – Post-Structuralism

Elements within structuralism and post-structuralism are useful to understand social structures and how these affect our way of thinking and being. Post-structuralism is sometimes described as a 'movement' of ideas or a set of theoretical positions which developed as responses to structuralism. Structuralism assumes that there is an inner, universal structure which manifests itself in how society develops, the structure of language, how children learn a language, etc. Structuralism does not, however, account for historical or cultural circumstances; in contrast, post-structuralism considers for instance that our human nature develops through our relationships with others. People are social beings because we have relations with other people. Those relations are historical and social in nature, but not based on universal structures (Jóhannesson, 2010; Peters & Wain, 2003). Post structuralism assumes that the reality is fragmented and diverse.

A constructed practice of education and learning, for example, is how education has most of the time been organised in a traditional way with a group of students, each sitting quietly at a table in a classroom and listening to the teacher who without any doubt controls the lesson; learning and communication. In this situation education means pure academic knowledge obtained from schoolbooks and the teacher. From the mid twentieth century this view of education has been challenged by educational scholars and today we have multiple definitions of education and learning (Slee, 2011; Tomlinson, 2005).

Hofstede's Cultural Dimensions Theory

The cultural dimensions theory developed by Geert Hofstede (de Mooij & Hofstede, 2010). describes how cultures affect societies regarding values held by their members and how these values reflect behaviour and people's entire being. Although the theory was developed in the context of business-orientated organisations it is useful to understand cultural differences between nations in educational settings and study how culture affects people's views on values and rules in societies.

In Hofstede's theory (2011) culture is analysed according to six dimensions:

1. *Power Distance*, relating to the different solutions to the basic problem of human inequality;
2. *Uncertainty Avoidance*, relating to the level of stress in a society in the face of an unknown future;
3. *Individualism* versus *Collectivism*, relating to the integration of individuals into primary groups;
4. *Masculinity* versus *Femininity*, relating to the division of emotional roles between women and men;
5. *Long Term* versus *Short Term Orientation*, relating to the choice of focus for people's efforts: the future or the present and past.
6. *Indulgence* versus *Restraint*, relating to the gratification versus control of basic human desires related to enjoying life.

Hofstede (2011) selected elements within the six dimensions listing which, in the authors opinion, relate to education, home and school (see Table 3.1).

Hofstede's model is a useful tool to shed light on the differences between people in various countries and make us more aware of other countries' cultures in order to avoid misunderstanding and misinterpretations between people from different parts of the world (Hofstede, 2011). His model can thus help us understand other cultures and have respectful cross-cultural relations.

Table 3.1. Selected elements of the six dimensions

Small power distance societies	Large power distance societies
Use of power should be legitimate and is subject to criteria of good and evil	Power is a basic fact of society antedating good or evil: its legitimacy is irrelevant
Parents treat children as equals	Parents teach children obedience
Older people are neither respected nor feared	Older people are both respected and feared
Student-centred education	Teacher-centred education
Hierarchy means inequality of roles, established for convenience	Hierarchy means existential inequality

Weak uncertainty avoidance societies	Strong uncertainty avoidance societies
The uncertainty inherent in life is accepted and each day is taken as it comes	The uncertainty inherent in life is felt as a continuous threat that must be fought
Ease, lower stress, self-control, low anxiety	Higher stress, emotionality, anxiety, neuroticism
Higher scores on subjective health and well-being	Lower scores on subjective health and well-being
Tolerance of deviant persons and ideas: what is different is curious	Intolerance of deviant persons and ideas: what is different is dangerous
Comfortable with ambiguity and chaos	Need for clarity and structure
Teachers may say 'I don't know'	Teachers supposed to have all the answers
Dislike of rules – written or unwritten	Emotional need for rules – even if not obeyed

Individualist societies	Collectivist societies
Everyone is supposed to take care of him- or herself and his or her immediate family only	People are born into extended families or clans which protect them in exchange for loyalty
"I" – consciousness	"We" –consciousness
Right of privacy	Stress on belonging
Speaking one's mind is healthy	Harmony should always be maintained
Others classified as individuals	Others classified as in-group or out-group
Personal opinion expected: one person one vote	Opinions and votes predetermined by in-group
Purpose of education is learning how to learn	Purpose of education is learning how to do

Short-term-oriented societies	Long-term-oriented societies
Most important events in life occurred in the past or take place now	Most important events in life will occur in the future
Personal steadiness and stability: a good person is always the same	A good person adapts to the circumstances
There are universal guidelines about what is good and evil	What is good and evil depends upon the circumstances
Traditions are sacrosanct	Traditions are adaptable to changed circumstances
Family life guided by imperatives	Family life guided by shared tasks
Students attribute success and failure to luck	Students attribute success to effort and failure to lack of effort

(Continued)

Table 3.1. Selected elements of the six dimensions (Cont.)

Indulgent Societies	Restrained Societies
Higher percentage of people declaring themselves very happy	Fewer very happy people
A perception of personal life control	A perception of helplessness: what happens to me is not my own doing
Freedom of speech seen as important	Freedom of speech is not a primary concern
Higher importance of leisure	Lower importance of leisure
More likely to remember positive emotions	Less likely to remember positive emotions
More people actively involved in sports	Fewer people actively involved in sports
In wealthy countries, lenient sexual norms	In wealthy countries, stricter sexual norms
Maintaining order in the nation is not given a high priority	Higher number of police officers per 100,000 population

Perhaps the most relevant dimension for this research is the power distance dimension which is defined as: the extent to which less powerful members of a society accept and expect that power is distributed unequally (de Mooij & Hofstede, 2010). In countries with high power distance parents tend to teach obedience and expect respect, teachers possess wisdom and are automatically esteemed. Inequalities are expected, and may even be desired, thus quality of learning depends on excellence of teachers. Conversely, in low power distance countries parents and children, and teachers and students, may view themselves more as equals (but not necessarily as identical). Equality is expected and generally desired. Thus, quality of learning depends on two-way communication and excellence of students (Marcus & Gould, 2000). For the work in schools this means that teachers and students consider themselves as equals, learning is geared towards the student who is involved in the whole learning process and students are encouraged to take an active role in their education, communication and discussions. The dimension of *uncertainty avoidance* is also relevant here since in cultures of strong uncertainty avoidance, there is a need for rules and formality to structure life. This translates into the search for truth and a belief in experts (Hofstede, 2011). In terms of education and schooling, the educational systems tend to be more centralized and parents and students expect structured learning situations and seek the right answers. Teachers are therefore considered to have all the right answers. By contrast, in a weak uncertainty avoidance school system rules are very general and agreed by the school community and can easily be changed. Parents and students expect open-ended learning situations and discussions. Teachers do not have all the knowledge and may say "I do not know". Learning is geared towards students' own abilities and potential.

Country Comparison According to Hofstede's Model

According to the model national culture is measured on a scale from 0–10 for each dimension. Each country then obtains an index which is comparable to other countries. The index indicates how the culture in general is characterised according to the given dimensions. We can take Iceland and Syria as an example and let the model available on Hofstede's website (https://geert-hofstede.com/iceland.html) compare these two countries (Figure 3.1).

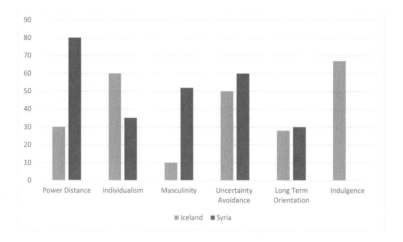

Figure 3.1. Iceland and Syria according to Hofstede's model on culture

The model then explains the scores for each dimension. In this chapter there is, however, not enough space for much detail on the model but selected examples can be explored. The most striking difference here is on the dimension *Power Distance* which deals with power and equality and is defined as follows: "the extent to which the less powerful members of institutions and organisations within a country expect and accept that power is distributed unequally" (Hofstede, 2011). Iceland scores very low on this dimension which, according to the model, means that hierarchy is established for convenience and communication is informal, direct and participative. The high score for Syria, on the other hand, describes a hierarchical society where people accept a designated order in which everybody has a place and needs no further justification. Another large difference relates to *Masculinity*. With a very low score of 10, Iceland is definitely a feminine society which means, according to the model, that people value equality, solidarity and quality in their working lives, conflicts are resolved by compromise and negotiation, free time and flexibility are favoured. The focus is on well-being and status is not shown or emphasized. A high score on masculinity indicates that the society is driven by competition, achievement and success – a value system that starts in school and continues throughout organizational life.

Syria is considered to have a high score (60) on the dimension *Uncertainty Avoidance* which means that rigid codes of belief and behaviour are maintained and there is intolerant of unorthodox behaviour. People have an inner urge to be busy and work hard, precision and punctuality are the norm, innovation may be resisted and security is an important element in individual motivation. There are no results on *Indulgence* for Syria but the score of 67 describes Iceland as an indulgent country where people are willing to fulfil their impulses and desires, especially with regard to enjoying life and having fun. They possess a positive attitude and have a tendency towards optimism, placing a higher degree of importance on leisure time and acting as they please.

METHOD AND DATA

The research is framed within an interpretive paradigm (Berger & Luckmann, 1966; Bogdan & Biklen, 1992) where the aim is to analyse and understand how parents of immigrant and refugee children and their teachers construct their ideas on the roles of schools and education. A qualitative methodology (Creswell, 2007) is applied with the objective of exploring and understanding the living experiences of people within the education sector; that is, the perspectives of teachers and parents of immigrant and refugee students to their education. The study presents data from an ongoing project on the education of immigrants and refugees in Iceland. The data was gathered from various stakeholders in order to gain a broad perspective on the issue. Seven semi-structured (Esterberg, 2002) group interviews (Bender, 2013) were conducted with a total of 38 teachers who have the experience of teaching students with immigrant background (grades 1–10). The majority were women and they were all Icelandic. Each interview lasted approximately 30–60 minutes. One interview was taken with a school counsellor who provides professional support for students and teachers, concerning students with immigrant backgrounds. Ten in-depth interviews were conducted with parents of immigrant students who have a European background – six women and four men. The technique of snowball sampling (Þórlindsson & Karlsson, 2003) was used to access parents who live in the municipality and consider themselves immigrants. The parents are aged from 26 to 60, they are all married or in a relationship and four of the women and all of the men have university degrees. The interviews were conducted in Icelandic or in English, depending on the preference of the participant, and lasted on average one hour. Finally, Two Syrian parents (a couple) were interviewed about their experience of their children's education in Icelandic schools. The interview took place at their home and lasted about an hour and a half. Data was analysed according to thematic analysis (Braun & Clarke, 2006; Matthewes & Ross, 2010).

FINDINGS

The findings are introduced by one main theme that appeared in the interviews with the teachers, the European parents and corresponds to the data from the Syrian parents; *The role of the school as an educational institution* which is divided into five sub-themes; Lack of discipline and respect, academic demands, the relationship between teachers and students, approach to learning, keeping up with their home country curriculum.

Lack of Discipline and Respect

The European parents felt that the Icelandic school system lacked discipline and that there was insufficient academic pressure on their children. Besides, students did not show enough respect for their teachers. By discipline they refer to, for example, the relaxed and loosely structured classroom organisation where students are allowed to "go out of the classroom, come back, eat, drink" when they wish. The parents refer to an opposite structure from their home countries where children are supposed to sit down and be quiet and listen to the teacher who is in charge of the classroom. A mother from Western Europe who also is an educated teacher said when discussing the Icelandic schools:

> For example, there is lack of respect, I'm not talking about "I'm your teacher, I'm better than you and you have to respect me". This is not what I'm talking about. I'm talking about the lack of respect towards the person trying to teach you, and respect for the person who is trying their best to offer you the possibility to learn.

In her opinion, Icelandic students are undisciplined and get away with being lazy and not focusing on their study. She refers to her own teaching experience in Icelandic upper secondary school where students showed behaviour which would not be accepted in her country:

> I'm not used to telling the pupils: "now you shut down your laptops", 80% had laptops at that time, probably 100% now. "Shut down your laptops and listen to what I'm saying, I'm trying to explain something and you have to listen and have to look at what I'm drawing". They closed their laptops and then I turned around and the first ones were already with their laptops up again… and this is something I'm not used to. Put up their feet in the classroom or something like that… it should be more strict… but there's also need for clear rules and they have to respect the teachers, or other people

Another mother reflects on a similar issue that differs from her home country:

> We, I guess… come from a very traditional academic setup, a kind of pedagogy where everything was by rules, you would have to learn your multiplication tables… you don't even have to learn your multiplication tables here anymore. They have hardly any homework, so there's a little bit of conflict here, I sense that the teachers want them to do well, but at the same time they don't want to push them too much

The teachers are well aware of the differences between countries in terms of discipline, respect and demands. In of the teacher groups they referred to an Icelandic student

> who went to Spain, came back and told us that, just in the case of how to address the teacher, over there they show much more respect for their teachers, he said that all the demands were also higher than at home in Iceland… you

can do what you like in Icelandic schools, there are no rules… they experience it a bit like that.

This teacher concluded by saying: "You can do whatever you like in Icelandic schools, there are no rules, they experience it a bit like that".

Academic Demands

The parents feel the Icelandic school does not place enough academic demands on students and other activities than academic learning are given too much space in their schooling. They refer to an attitude in their country towards education where school means a hard work. A mother from Eastern Europe said:

If you went to school in [her native country] you went there to learn, you didn't go there to play or… you had to learn, had to get 10. Here it's like "huh whatever… make friends or something, it's more like that.

A father from Eastern Europe talked in a similar vein and referred to when his daughter joined him in Iceland:

When my wife came from [the home country] with her daughter, she was 8 years old and started going to third year. She sometimes said: "we are doing something in mathematics we learned that in first year in the village". They were two years behind in those areas

The Syrian parents share similar concerns as the other parents regarding the quality and the level of education in Icelandic school, and when asked about their experience of the school so far, they said:

Father:	Nothing… we are used to teaching them, I take the responsibility to teach them and follow their level and their grade exactly. I follow some… I can work in the curriculum, we try at least to follow their grades in mathematics, science and English.
Researcher:	so that is what you try to do at home?
Father:	yes
Mother:	cause we feel they start to lose what they have.
Researcher:	so the school is not enough…?
Father:	yes, correct, absolutely so low, I am surprised, actually.

The parents mentioned that they had had other expectations, "We thought it would be different", and say they had heard that "it's a European country and we thought it would be different, but they used to have more than this in Lebanon and Syria". They feel their children are not learning according their level of ability as they say: "when they were in school they used to have something stronger, we can say". When comparing the two countries, the father said: "there is more organised and more stronger [in Syria and Lebanon]… there is real knowledge, okey in mathematics and science and social science... he knows for example what is the meaning of Maya or what the population of... you know neighbours and something... this is the basic thing for the community" and the mother continued: "do you know the biggest difference between here and Lebanon and Syria is that in Syria and Lebanon we DO follow our children... like they have exams, they have books at home... homework, but here they don't have anything to do at home".

In their conversation, one could feel how they appeared worried about the future; they were concerned as to whether the Icelandic school system would be able to prepare their children properly for further and higher education. Regarding the upper secondary school the father asked if: "the normal school [compulsory school] is enough to prepare the students to go the grammar school?... and if you want to apply to any university outside [Iceland] do they respect the high school here?

The Relationship between Teachers and Students

Some parents struggle with the fact that teachers and students normally have a relationship that is based on equal/peer communication. The Syrian parents are surprised by the relationship between teachers and students and said:

> Yes, this is something we don't have... just strict teachers and there is full respect. But here it is totally different, children can say and can argue and do something impolite... I remember the first time we went to school... it was eighth or seventh grade... they were just sitting and putting their feet on the table... they didn't show any respect. This was the first shock and the teachers were happy; that was also a shock, because they [the teachers] didn't say anything.

But there are parents who see the situation in a positive way. A mother from Germany touches upon one of the characteristics and key elements of the Icelandic curriculum – democracy – when asked about her opinion of the Icelandic school system:

> In general I am very happy with the school system here... especially because the school system in Germany is a scandal in my eyes... they are trying to build up a small democracy inside the class, so they decide how they want to have their rules and this is wonderful... the pupils can decide where they want to be some time of the day, they can say: "I am very angry right now and I need to calm down" and they can lie down with a blanket and relax. They are much more respectful towards the needs of every pupil at every time and I think it is very good. Sometimes I think it's a little bit too much but maybe that's because I am German.

In her comment, she also describes how children are offered to be responsible for their behaviour and actions. A father from Western Europe who is also a teacher with twenty years of teaching experience in Icelandic schools adheres to the Icelandic school policy when he says:

But now it's a lot more, not just thinking about study results, children, most importantly, have to feel good. If they feel good about themselves it is much easier to learn and everyone has the right to feel good in school and that is a wonderful change.

The Syrian mother compares the Icelandic and the Syrian school and said: "I don't like the way we used to have it in Syria it's not very good; sometimes children they don't find time to play, no" and she describes how too much homework affected their play time, "I don't think that was a good way but maybe for the other subjects, like math or science or languages.

Teachers in all the schools tell stories of how they extend their role as teachers and try to support and give advice to families beyond the school, such as searching for a reading books in the students' mother tongue, helping with finding a suitable sport or after school activities in order to stimulate their adaptation. This supportive attitude of the teachers correlates with the experience of the Syrian parents. They said:

The good thing here is they respect our culture and they respect our religion… when they have like Christmas activities they just contact me and ask are your children allowed to do this and this… Before they do anything they just ask.

Approach to Learning

One mother from Poland said she really liked the Icelandic system and referred to her own experience in her home country:

When I was little I hated school because there was a lot of work and we never had time to play and you had to be good in everything. Here you have more options to choose and also my partner's son is 16 and he is not doing his homework at home, he has time at school to do it. First I wasn't sure if this was a good thing and I was like" sit down and learn" but it didn't work and I couldn't help him except for math because I don't know Icelandic. There is less stress at school and they are going to University in Denmark or elsewhere and its ok, it doesn't have to be like education in Poland.

The Syrian parents had not fully understood how the Icelandic school was organised and because their children do not have homework they had difficulty in understanding its function. The mother said: "because they don't have anything to do at home so we just don't know… but we don't know because they have a different way of teaching… they just focus maybe more on activity or something like this to learn at school and in Syria and Lebanon they focus more on books". The parents had also recognised one of the main characteristics of the Icelandic school when asked if they had received information on the Icelandic school system:

Father: we have no idea

Mother: it's just this meeting every autumn… and if we need something extra I can go to the school and I go and ask… but I feel that they deal with every student here as…

Father: individual

Mother: yes, individual, like they focus maybe on something for my son and they focus on another thing for someone else… they just work with them as individuals and I like this way; its good, but sometimes its just, you know, the students who are higher than others they don't get the time because they focus on other children who just need more help.

Keeping up with Their Home Country Curriculum

The teachers' conversations show that they recognise how some parents try to keep up with the curriculum in their home country by extra homework after school; one of them said about one of his students: "she is getting a lot of study material from abroad… she is under a lot of pressure" and they discussed how different the perspectives are with regard to demands and discipline, because the parents' background is rooted in another culture and "the study expectations are sometimes much higher than here". Teachers talk about parents who want their children to be prepared for the school in their home country if and when they go back, as well as their perspective that the Icelandic school is not academically demanding enough for their children. One teacher said:

> She (the mother) has her in private tuition at home and she took a progress exam this spring [exams in her home country], so that she is getting material from abroad which of course is awful as it makes it a very long school day for the child… she dreads going home.

Referring to the mother of this child, teachers mentioned that they feel the mother is pleased with the school "but she always wants more" and one teacher added: "she thinks that just because [the school] is so different, she wants to prepare her for home system… she is very worried that she will not be ready for that… thinks that not enough demands are made here…".

The Syrian parents believe they need to provide their children with learning according to the Syrian curriculum, "cause we feel they start to lose what they have… we do many things extra… we have the Syrian curriculum and… for the mother language we follow the Syrian…".

DISCUSSION

The findings were introduced by one main theme; The role of the school as an educational institution divided into five sub-themes that cast a clearer light on the theme; Lack of discipline and respect, academic demands, the relationship between teachers and students, approach to learning, keeping up with their home country curriculum. The findings will now be discussed and connections made with the theoretical and literature background of the research.

Expectations towards the School and Culture

The findings show that the parents' expectations and perspectives towards the school as a learning organisation related to their home country culture and how the society values and delivers education. Most of the parents value a system that has a rigid and a universal structure which corresponds to ideas of structuralism (Peters & Wain, 2003) where examples of education would be a teacher who controls the lesson and the students are supposed to obey, be quiet and sit still. This perspective also considers the aim of education as being to obtain pure academic knowledge which also features strongly in the way Hofstede (2011) describes societies with a high power distance and strong avoidance of uncertainty. The Syrian parents talk about their shock when they realised that students do not behave in schools as they are used to, and they are uncomfortable with the informal and relaxed relationship between students and teachers. This is indeed a shock to them as their values and norms relating to these elements differ strongly. In Hofstede's model (2011) this is visualised in the bars comparing power distance and masculinity between Iceland and Syria. Parents from European countries – who can be considered to have experienced less difference in culture than the Syrian parents – nevertheless talk along similar lines; inadequate discipline and less focus on real knowledge. At least two European parents seem to adhere more to the Icelandic culture and values in education when they refer to how teachers are working with students in a democratic manner where the students have a voice, and are made responsible for their own behaviour and actions. They also talk about the importance of well-being in education. These parents can be seen as representative of a perspective that has moved away from structuralism towards a post-structural view of education (Slee, 2011) which highlights our human development through relationships with others. From the post-structural perspective, it is also considered normal that reality is fragmented and diverse and teachers' reactions to students are thus based on individuals and their needs (Tomlinson, 2005) rather than universal rules.

Doubtfulness about the System – Lack of Collaboration

Parents' attempts to supplement their children with extra learning according to their home country curriculum relates both to their personal attitudes and perhaps intentions to go back home but also to their lack of trust in Icelandic schools in terms of delivering "a real knowledge". Teachers have noticed how some parents keep a private school at home for their children, where they try to keep on track in their home country curriculum. The teachers are worried about these students as they see how the extra workload causes the students to feel stressed and anxious. The doubtfulness is something that happens when the parents feel uncertain and do not see a place for their beliefs and values. Hofstede's model (de Mooij & Hofstede, 2010) on uncertainty is relevant in this context. According to the model, Icelandic culture is considered to be weak on uncertainty avoidance which means that people are tolerant of divergent persons and ideas and there is curiosity about what is different (Marcus & Gould, 2000); people are even comfortable with ambiguity and chaos, there is a dislike of rules and what is perhaps most opposite to strong uncertainty avoidance is that teachers may say to students "I don't know" (Hofstede, 2011). Parents who come from a culture characterised by strong uncertainty avoidance are used to the opposite; teachers are supposed to have all the answers and there is an emotional need for rules and an inherent need for clarity and structure. When parents recognise that the framework around their basic ideas and values is not there, they become uncertain and suspicious. This is clearly recognised by the example of the Syrian parents who wondered whether the Icelandic school system would be "enough" to allow their children to access higher education and even universities abroad.

Home-School Collaboration

One of the most important roles of home-school collaboration is to involve parents in active participation of their children education. When parents are actively involved in the school life they will be in better position to understand the function of the school and, expectations towards teachers, parents and students. The school has to play a leading role and take the initiative for collaboration (Ameta, 2013). Our findings indicate that the parents are passive listeners rather than active participants. In the case of the Syrian parents, teachers showed some initiative when they asked about the participation of the Syrian kids in Christmas habits in schools and the parents mentioned that teachers are interested and respectful (Eberly & Konzaæ, 2005). What seems to be lacking is a culturally responsive relationship (Ameta, 2013) where parents and teachers engage in mutual discussion on national culture in their home-country and Iceland (differences and similarities) and educational culture in relation to the overall school system in Iceland. As mentioned in the document from the Ontario Ministry of Education (2009) schools and teachers need to recognise the broad notion of similarities and differences and how this is reflected in student and parent identities. Earlier research has identified how failure in trying to understand different beliefs of parents and teachers can act as a barrier to home-school communication (Trumbull, Rothstein-Fisch, Greenfield, & Quiroz, 2011). Our findings indicate that parents have problems understanding the Icelandic school and its function and have doubts about the quality of the education provided as it is very different from what they are used to in their home-country.

CONCLUSION

This chapter presents findings on different ideas that emerge among parents and teachers about the role of schools and education. The aim of the chapter was to explore and understand these different perspectives, their nature and how they can be used to improve the education of the students concerned. One main theme was identified and titled: *The role of the school as an educational institution*. The participants in this research – parents and teachers – appeared to have different ideas about the role of the school which were presented in the findings under following sub-themes: Lack of discipline and respect, academic demands, the relationship between teachers and students, approach to learning, keeping up with their home country curriculum. An underlying element in all the themes are a lack of discussion between parents and schools on *culture* – differences and similarities, aims and expectations of both parties and how both can reach their expectations.

NOTE

[1] The Programme for International Student Assessment (PISA) is a triennial international survey which aims to evaluate education systems worldwide by testing the skills and knowledge of 15-year-old students, see: https://www.oecd.org/pisa/

REFERENCES

Ameta, E. S. (2013). *Building culturally responsive family-school relationships* (2nd ed.). Boston, MA: Pearson.

Bender, S. (2013). Samræður í rýnihópum [Focus group discussions]. In Sigríður Halldórsdóttir (Ed.), *Handbók í Aðferðafræði Rannsókna* [Manual on research methodology] (pp. 299–312). Akureyri: Ásprent.

Berger, P., & Luckmann, T. (1966). *The social constructionism of reality: A treatise in the sociology of knowledge*. Harmondsworth: Penguin.

Bogdan, R. C., & Biklen, S. K. (1992). *Qualitative research for education: An introduction to theory and methods*. Boston, MA: Allyn and Bacon.

Braun, V., & Clarke, V. (2006). Using thematic analysis in psychology. *Qualitative Research in Psychology, 3*(2), 77–101. Retrieved from http://dx.doi.org/10.1191/1478088706qp063oa

Chumak-Horbatsch, R. (2012). *Linguistically appropriate practice: A guide for working with young immigrant children*. Toronto: University of Toronto Press.

Creswell, J. W. (2007). *Qualitative inquiry and research design, choosing among five approaches* (2nd ed.). Thousand Oaks, CA: Sage Publications.

de Mooij, M., & Hofstede, G. (2010). The Hofstede model: Applications to global branding and advertising strategy and research. *International Journal of Advertising, 29*(1), 85–110. doi:10.2501/S026504870920104X

Garðarsdóttir, Ó., & Hauksson, G. (2011). *Ungir innflytjendur og aðrir einstaklingar með erlendan bakgrunn í íslensku samfélagi og íslenskum skólum 1996–2011* [Young immigrants and other youth with foreign background in Icelandic society and in Icelandic schools 1996–2011]. Netla-Veftímarit um uppeldi og menntun. Retrieved from http://netla.hi.is/menntakvika2011/020.pdf

Halldórsson, A. M., Ólafsson, R. F., & Björnsson, J. K. (2013). *Helstu niðurstöður PISA 2012: læsi nemenda á stærðfræði og náttúrufræði og lesskilningur* [The main PISA findings 2012: students' literacy in math and natural sciences and reading comprehension]. Reykjavík: OECD.

Hofstede, G. (2011). Dimensionalizing cultures: The hofstede model in context. *Online Readings in Psychology and Culture, 2*(1), 1–26. Retrieved from https://doi.org/10.9707/2307-0919.1014

Hofstede-insights. (2017, October 1). Retrieved from https://www.hofstede-insights.com/

Jóhannesson, I. Á. (2010). Historical discourse analysis as professional and political reflexivity. In J. Kauko, R. Rinne, & H. Kynkäänniemi (Eds.), *Restructuring the truth of schooling—essays on discursive practices in the sociology and politics of education: A festschrift for Hannu Simola* (pp. 133–149). Helsinki: Finnish Educational Research Association (FERA).

Magnúsdóttir, N. (2010). *"Allir vilja eignast íslenskar vinir": hverjar eru helstu hindranir á vegi erlendra grunn- og framhaldsskólanemenda í íslensku skólakerfi?* [Everyone wants Icelandic Friends: What are the hindrances faced by immigrant students in compulsory and upper secondary schools in Iceland?] (Unpublished master's thesis). University of Iceland, Reyjavík.

Marcus, A., & Gould, E. W. (2000). Crosscurrents: Cultural dimensions and global web user interface design. *Interactions, 7*(4), 32–46. Retrieved from https://laofutze.files.wordpress.com/2010/03/ama_cultdim.pdf

Matthewes, B., & Ross, L. (Eds.). (2010). *Research methods. A practical guide for the social sciences.* Harlow: Longman.

Ministry of Education, Science and Culture. (2012). *The Icelandic national curriculum guide for compulsory schools: General section.* Retrieved from https://eng.menntamalaraduneyti.is/publications/curriculum/

OECD. (2015). *Immigrant students at school: Easing the journey towards integration.* Paris: OECD Publishing. Retrieved from http://dx.doi.org/10.1787/9789264249509-en

Ontario Ministry of Education. (2009). *Realizing the promise of diversity: Ontario's equity and inclusive education strategy.* Retrieved from http://edu.gov.on.ca/eng/policyfunding/equity.pdf

Peters, M. A., & Wain, K. (2003). Postmodernism/poststructuralism. In N. Blake, P. Smeyers, R. Smith, & P. Standish (Eds.), *The Blackwell guide to the philosophy of education* (pp. 57–72). Malden, MA: Blackwell Publishing.

Statistics Iceland. (2016). *Population by sex, municipality and citizenship, 1 January 1998–2016.* Retrieved from http://www.statice.is/statistics/population/inhabitants/background/

Slee, R. (2011). *The irregular school: Exclusion, schooling and inclusive education.* London & New York, NY: Routledge.

Tomlinson, S. (2005). *Education in a post-welfare society.* Berkshire: Open University Press.

Tran, A. D. (2007). Factors affecting Asian students' academic achievement in Iceland. In K. Bjarnadóttir & S. K. Hannesdóttir (Eds.), *Þekking þjálfun þroski: Greinar um uppeldis og fræðslumál* (pp. 191–213). Reykjavík: Delta Kappa Gamma – Félag kvenna í fræðslustörfum.

Trumbull, E., Rothstein-Fisch, C, Greenfield, P. M., & Quiroz, B. (2001). *Bridging cultures between home and school: A guide for teachers.* Mahwah, NJ: Lawrence Erlbaum Associates.

Þórlindsson, Þ., & Karlsson, Þ. (2003). Um úrtök og úrtaksaðferðir [On samples and sampling methods]. In S. Halldórsdóttir & K. Kristjánsson (Eds.), *Handbók í Aðferðafræði og Rannsóknum í Heilbrigðisvísindum* [Manual on methodology and research in the health sciences] (pp. 219–235). Akureyri: Háskólinn á Akureyri.

Hermina Gunnþórsdóttir
The University of Akureyri
Akureyri
Iceland

TÜNDE KOVACS CEROVIĆ, SANJA GRBIĆ
AND DRAGAN VESIĆ

4. HOW DO SCHOOLS INTEGRATE REFUGEE STUDENTS?[1]

First Experiences from Serbia

BACKGROUND

International Experience

Presently Europe is confronted with the need to cater for hundreds of thousands of refugees from the Middle East, mostly from Syria, Iraq and Afghanistan and to ensure their education The importance of education for migrant communities and refugees is based not only on the Universal Declaration of Human Rights and the European Convention on Human Rights, but also on the fact that schooling is an essential means for ensuring life continuity, job prospects, social integration and peer relationships (Kia-Keating & Ellis, 2007; INEE, 2010) through which refugee students are "trying to reconstruct their lives and their self-esteem and develop hope for the future" (Matthews, 2008).

However, literature addressing education of immigrant or refugee children lists a variety of barriers that can hinder education integration and negatively affect education attainment of these children and youth (Kovacs-Cerovic & Vulic, 2016). Being a newcomer, fleeing from hardships to a foreign country, even if it is a desired destination of arrival, is not easy. Neither do education systems grant success to everybody – newcomers seem to be among those at risk of failure. The PISA research on disparities between immigrant/refugee and domicile children directed educational policy analysts' spotlight on immigrant/refugee children already in the early 2000s by showing that students whose parents are immigrants/refugees have weaker performance than native students in some countries on PISA, even after controlling for socio-economic background and language (OECD, 2016). These warnings seem to be corroborated by new research.

The dropout rate of refugee/migrant children in most countries is much higher than that of the domicile group (NESSE, 2008; OECD, 2015b); refugee parents are hampered by stress, trauma, and/or lack of social capital in the new situation (Vlajković, Srna, Kondić, & Popović, 2000).

Migrant students are more likely to be placed in groups with lower curricular standards (Bartlett, 2015), or in special education schools (NESSE, 2008); quality of the teaching–learning process can be endangered by oversized classes and lack of equipment (OECD, 2016); teachers' pedagogical competencies for working in multicultural environments might be low; their expectations for the educational outcomes of refugees/refugee children might also be low (OECD, 2016); differences between home and host country curricula can create difficulties for refugee/migrant children in a variety of ways (NESSE, 2008; UNHCR, 2015); acquiring the language of instruction is a key challenge for refugee/migrant children (UNHCR, 2015); lack of finances, non-conducive ethos, and poor school organization can create loopholes that have the potential of reversing previous integration efforts (OECD, 2016).

The barriers for education integration of refugee children are often unsurmountable already at the level of access. The right to education is not universally granted everywhere or to all categories of refugees/migrants; in some countries only those with permanent papers can access public education, or only primary education (but not secondary or pre-primary) is granted free of charge (Bartlett, 2015). Access can be substantially hindered by logistical problems such as lack of placement capacity in the closest school, distance to school, lack of transportation, and/or lack of safety on the road (Bartlett, 2015; UNHCR, 2015). Newcomers are also facing system divides between education, social support healthcare, registration and many other further public services, which create gaps the vulnerable families cannot manage to overcome (Kovač Cerović, Lakićević, Cenerić, Vainalanen, & Mladenović, 2013). Acceptance of newcomers into a school is mediated by the school's organizational culture and the level of interest to embrace new students at all (NESSE, 2008). Creating additional placement possibilities with enlarged classes can result in negative reactions from the domicile population and requires lots of negotiation and dispute resolution (Bartlett, 2015). The realities and painful backlashes of the aforementioned logistical problems have emerged in situations of refugee crises where language or ethnic differences were not even present, such as with minority students taking refuge during the wars in ex-Yugoslavia in areas where their national group was majority, or more recently in the Ukraine (Kovacs-Cerovic & Vulic, 2016).

Furthermore, the attainment level and quality of education for refugee or migrant students is often limited by residential and school segregation and low expectations by teachers, recreating self-fulfilling prophesies (Rosentahl & Jacobson, 1968; Bartlett, 2015) along the same pattern as for discriminated against vulnerable groups such as Roma in Europe (Daiute & Kovač Cerović, 2017; Roma Education Fund, 2015). As for Roma and other marginalized groups the risk of segregation in education is elevated, especially in the context of segregated neighbourhoods where the newcomer child can become streamlined to schools that are already segregated, aggravating the problem further on. And segregation is very hard to abolish (Rostas, 2012; Rostas & Kostka, 2014), calling for a multitude of well-orchestrated actors, and a series of meticulous organizational innovations (e.g. Kovač Cerović & Lukšić Orlandić, 2016; Kočić-Rakočević & Nagy, 2015; Panayotova & Evgeniev, 2002).

Aside of the aforementioned educational and social barriers to education integration that are common to most vulnerable groups, refugee children and youth can face emotional risks originating from war and exile trauma that can seriously hamper their educational prospects or even their educational demand. Vlajković, Srna, Kondić, and Popović (2000) describe these as "normal reactions to abnormal situations". Arnot and Pinson (2005) provide a comprehensive overview of scholarly research indicating mental health and social psychological problems afflicting refugee children. The list of findings includes suffering from trauma, behavioural problems, feelings of guilt, difficulties developing familiarity with new places, adjusting to a new culture, constructing a new sense of identity/belonging, coping with changes in familial relationships, parents becoming more vulnerable and increasingly dependent on their children, or more protective and authoritarian, feelings of anxiety and uncertainty concerning the future, poverty and poor housing, high mobility, health problems, racial harassment and bullying. There are different views about how prominent role does the history of traumatization play in the efforts of refugee children to engage in education – some authors (such as Rutter, 2006; Neftçi & Çetrez, 2017) argue that dealing with trauma constitutes a significant aspect of being a refugee student that should not be ignored, while others (such as Matthews, 2008; Pinson & Arnot, 2007) view the emphasis on trauma as shifting the attention away from more defining sociological factors such as poverty, marginalization and discrimination. Recent studies conducted in Serbia find that around two third of asylum seekers from the Middle East and Asia suffer from post-traumatic stress disorder, anxiety and depression (Vukčević, Dobrić, & Purić, 2014; Vukčević Marković, Gašić, & Bjekić, 2017). Especially alarming are the findings regarding refugee children and youth – they experienced more traumatic events compared to adult refugees (Vukčević Marković, Gašić, Ilić, & Bjekić, 2017). These findings issue warning to address mental health of refugee children and youth, given that symptoms can become hindrance for academic prospects and overall wellbeing.

Due to all the aforementioned factors progression to higher levels of education is rather an exception than a rule for students from vulnerable groups, including migrant and refugee students. These students are most often swiped towards or opt for non-attractive short vocational courses (NESSE, 2008), but their chances for further education are also hampered by the lack of support and administrative barriers (UNHCR, 2015).

Recommendations for overcoming the barriers and pitfalls in the education trajectory of refugee and immigrant children include measures such as language integration, early childhood education and care, parental engagement, limiting concentration in disadvantaged schools, building the capacity of schools and teachers, and limiting tracking and grade repetition (OECD, 2015a; Nusche, 2009). Also, recommendations on how to address and heal war trauma and the trauma and hopelessness of exile are present both in international scholarly accounts but also in policy documents or hands-on guidebooks used by professionals or civil society activists (e.g. Ignjatović-Savić, 1995; Mikuš Kos & Huzejrovic, 2003; Vlajković, Srna, Kondić, & Popović, 2000). An emphasis on resilience despite disruptive symptoms, exhibiting intercultural values and supporting religion practices are also seen as effective ways of decreasing distress symptoms and countering some of the negative, trauma-connected psychosocial conditions (Neftçi & Çetrez, 2017).

While target countries of migration have been following many of these recommendations in order to ensure effective education of migrant and refugee children and youth (e.g. Kornhall, 2016; OECD, 2015b, 2015c), Serbia was until recently only a transit country for refugees aspiring to move on to more developed countries and its education system was caught unprepared for their integration. Families and children from Syria, Iraq or Afghanistan were placed in refugee centres or supported by humanitarian aid through dispersed service centres. Civil society volunteers worked with children providing non-formal education, playgroups, language workshops, etc., while psychosocial assistance was provided to families and youth by civil society activists during their time spent in Serbia. This changed during Autumn 2016. Since then more refugees stay for a longer period in the country and a number of schools started to prepare and accept students from collective refugee centres. Since the education system in Serbia never before faced a challenge of similar complexity, the process these schools are piloting is a unique opportunity to observe and register the educational changes entailed in enrolling refugee students.

The Case of Serbia

At the end of 2017 about 50 schools in 17 municipalities in Serbia are educating around 400 refugee students, while just 18 months before virtually no refugees were staying long enough in Serbia to consider enrolling their children in school. Serbia was a transit country on the "Balkan route", thousands of refugees passed by on a weekly, sometimes even daily level, staying for a couple of days or weeks in the country before heading on to their destinations of choice in the European Union and the more developed countries. In the summer of 2016 entry to the EU became progressively more restricted for refugees. More and more families realized they might end up staying longer than originally planned in this last non-EU country on their route, and began considering the education of their children in Serbia. At the same time the international debate on the handling of migrants and the resultant changes in admission policies toward migrants, asylum seekers and refugees are reflected in Serbia as well, and the integration of refugees in the Serbian education system proceeds short of a clear governmental policy.

Schools in Serbia were caught unprepared for such a task. However, there were scattered but relevant experiences of schools admitting and educating temporarily displaced children, for example during intense flooding in 2014 or, earlier still, during the Yugoslav wars of the 1990s. Owing to those periods of crises, most schools in Serbia, especially the school psychologist, had some limited knowledge about how to provide support to traumatized children arriving to their schools (Vlajković, Srna, Kondić, & Popović, 2000).

Moreover, in the early 2000s Serbia adopted an inclusive education policy, that was implemented nationwide and contributed to the use of a variety of relevant educational tools including individual education plans (IEPs) making inclusion for children with disabilities in regular schools and classes a reality (Kovač Cerović, Jovanović, & Pavlović Babić, 2016; Kovač Cerović, Pavlović Babić, Jokić, Jovanović, & Jovanović, 2016). Serbia also participated in the Decade of Roma Inclusion, and developed methodologies both at school and community level for integrating Roma students, involving parents, mediating with the community and providing support for Roma students, such as the Roma pedagogical assistants program (Daiute & Kovač Cerovic, 2017) and many others (Kovács Cerović, 2018) that contributed to a significantly higher enrolment and progression rate of Roma students compared to the early 2000s, prior to the Decade. Through these programs as well as some others such as Schools without Violence (Popadic, 2009; Popadic & Plut, 2007), school development planning with school self-evaluation, schools in Serbia also developed thematic school Teams and started to learn and utilize teamwork as part of their daily activity.

All these emerging school processes should be considered as supporting a conducive context for the integration of newly arriving refugee students from the Middle East. But the novel challenge was considerably more complex than what schools managed to overcome previously. To what extend and how the new integration process utilized the existing mechanisms is an empirical question, and as such one of the focal points of our study.

Refugee Integration Project

In response to changing aspirations and needs, in September 2016 the Ministry of Education, Science and Technological Development (MOESTD), in cooperation with the Centre for educational policies (CEP) and UNICEF, launched a one-year pilot project "Supporting the education of refugee/migrant students in the Republic of Serbia" with five elementary schools being selected (out of 12 applicants) to participate based on criteria of (a) proximity to the asylum/refugee centre and (b) estimated capacities for providing quality education in diversified classrooms. The Project design was informed by best international experience, and in accordance with these, refugee children were to be enrolled in regular school classes as well as provided with additional classes targeting language acquisition (Serbian and English), cultural and civic competence building and social adjustment.

The students' enrolment was preceded by a preparatory phase during which schools attended professional training, established Teams for supporting the inclusion of refugee students within each school, and developed their Plan for inclusion specific to each school with the help of external experts ("school mentors"). The main strategic points of these Plans were establishing cooperation between the refugee and domicile students' parents, peer-to-peer support, adjusting extracurricular activities to the needs of refugee students and creating positive school climate regarding their integration.

The Integration Process

During the second semester of academic 2016/2017 about 70 refugees aged 7–17 years entered formal education. The first group consisted of children under care of the Centre for social work, and the second, enrolled later during the semester, comprised of students under parental care. Throughout this period the participating schools were provided with continuous support of the aforementioned external "mentors". Also, a translator was assigned to each school, many of them aided by volunteers and non-governmental organizations. Each participating school prepared a proposal on how to organize a welcome period of several weeks for the refugee students and got a symbolic small grant for accomplishing the designated activities.

The daily organization of the refugee's stay in school was partially determined by the schedule of meals at the collective centres and of their transportation, limiting the time spent in the school to three-four school hours. During that stay, the students had two-school hour language lessons organized separately from regular classes and two regular classes together with domicile pupils. In general, aside from language acquisition the school enrolment focus was on establishing communication with domicile teachers and students, creating a sense of security and acceptance, overcoming stress and overall social adjustment.

The Project aimed to assist the development of a comprehensive strategy of education integration of refugee students throughout the education system in the Republic of Serbia. From transit station Serbia turned into a semi-destination country for refugee pupils, hence obtaining a unique status among the countries responding to the refugee crisis. This, in turn, required a serious shift from the usual way of functioning for schools, and a new capacity for responding to the new situation had to be developed.

Study Aims

The study we are reporting about builds on the pilot project, and its aims are fully pragmatic: we were witnessing the unfolding of a new phenomenon in Serbia that is unique in several ways, and we wanted to take a snapshot of this developing phenomenon in *status nascendi* and learn from what we see, hear and understand. Particularly compelling seemed the following aspects to register: (a) Serbia is a country of emigration and not immigration, and it is not prepared to face sizable cultural and linguistic differences – did children and teachers embrace the differences brought about with the newly arriving refugee students at all and if yeas, how? (b) Schools in Serbia are working under fairly strict curriculum constraints, meagre financing, and have almost no autonomy in their functioning – could they adjust and successfully respond to such an outstanding challenge at all and, if yes, how did they bring this about? We were interested to collect both positive and negative experiences of the schools in order to develop recommendations for the forthcoming nation-wide action. Nevertheless, we observed a process that was exceptional for Serbia, maybe also for other countries working on the integration of refugees; a situation where both schools and students were volunteers in an experiment of integration – which means that it was mainly outspoken, resilient, proactive and motivated refugee students who enrolled in willing schools that had already acquired at least some experience in handling diversity and promoting intercultural understanding in the classroom. These characteristics of the context will be taken into account during the interpretation of the results.

METHODOLOGY

Three interconnected case studies of schools were conducted using a mix-method research design, with quantitative and qualitative research procedures being implemented within two consecutive research phases. Research phase one entailed administration of two different questionnaires for quantitative data acquisition targeting domicile students and teachers in selected schools, giving us coarse, general insights regarding the initial psychosocial climate on the classroom level regarding refugee students' inclusion. The second research phase comprised of focus groups with what we called "inclusion experts": teachers and school associates being the internal, and school mentors as the external professionals. Implementation of the aforementioned procedure (as well as several non-standardised interviews and classroom observations) meant moving the data gathering from classroom- to the school-level functioning, providing us with more in-depth understanding of the refugee students' inclusion process from the vantage point of different school experts. This allowed us to expand the findings obtained by quantitative measures, using phase one data as a direction pointer towards relevant topics for phase two exploration. Let us now present each of the inquiry stages in more detail.

Research Phase One: Quantitative Overview of the General School Climate Regarding Integration

Student sample: Social distance towards refugee students. Mapping the psychosocial environment within which the inclusion process takes place, was the first research step, while noting that in classrooms such an environment is created by both students and teachers. The first variable we measured is social distance that domicile students expressed toward refugee students.

Instrument and data gathering. For that purpose, we administered a version of the Bogardus scale adapted to the Serbian school context and fitting to situations typical for classroom interaction among students in elementary school (Arsenović-Pavlović, Jolić, & Buha-Đurković, 2008). Seven levels of distance, from the most distant to the closest peer-to-peer interactions were, respectively: (7) socializing in school, (6) helping in difficult situation, (5) attending birthday party, (4) sitting next to each other in class, (3) living in the same building, (2) socializing in out of school contexts and (1) falling in love. In order to have a reference point for the magnitude of distance interpretation, each domicile student assessed his/her readiness to participate in certain activities in school context with (a) Serbian, (b) Roma or (c) refugee students.

Data were gathered during April 2017, within one school visit, during regular school classes, with senior-year psychology students taking part as field researchers, as part of their university course activities. Special attention was paid to administer the scale in those classes where refugee students were included together with the domicile students, so the students in the sample had at least some in-school interactions with the refugee students, but at a time when the refugee students were not in school. The questionnaires were in paper-and-pencil format, individually completed, with the process taking approximately 15 minutes.

Sample. 148 students in total participated from three schools, from classes that had refugee students. Out of these 40% were girls and 30% declared themselves as Roma, which reflects student profile in the three selected schools, later discussed at greater length. Figure 4.1 depicts the student sample.

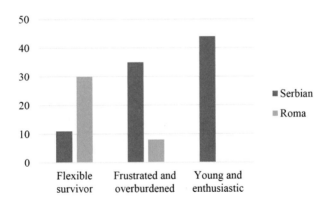

Figure 4.1. Number of Serbian and Roma students in the sample by the school

Data coding and analysis. For each participant total distance was calculated as a score ranging from 0 (accepting zero relations – greatest distance) to 1 (accepting all relations – lowest distance). Social distance of the entire student group was calculated as the arithmetic mean of the individual scores for the two targeted groups separately. Multiple ANOVA and t-tests were performed, details of which are given in the Results section. In general, differences in the dependent variable, namely, social distance, are examined taking into consideration two factors, domicile student group (Serbian or Roma) being the unrepeated one, and student group toward which the distance is assessed (Serbian, Roma or refugee) being the repeated factor.

Teacher sample: teachers' intercultural competence. The most prominent feature of the new classroom environment created by the inclusion of refugee students is the immensely increased level of student diversity, especially the cultural and language versatility within classes. This posed new challenges for teachers regarding their intercultural attitudes and skills that influence the teaching and learning process and the overall wellbeing of students. The second type of characteristics we thus measured as an indicator of psychosocial classroom climate is intercultural competence of teachers.

Instrument and data gathering. Data were collected by using Teacher Intercultural Competence Scale, a recently developed multidimensional instrument that is intended to measure self-reported levels of competence for teaching in culturally heterogeneous classrooms standardized on the Serbian sample (Petrović, Jokić, & Leutwyler, 2016; Zlatković, Petrović, Erić, Leutwyler, & Jokić, 2017; Leutwyler, Petrović, & Jokić, 2017). The scale was developed by nesting the concepts of intercultural competence of Deardorff (2009) and Perry and Southwell (2011) into the theoretical model of teachers' professional competencies developed by Baumert and Kunter (2013), measuring three dimensions of intercultural competence: (a) "Values, Beliefs and Goals" (VBG, 23 items), referring to subjective theories about a specific topic, and the subjective relevance of specific educational aims; (b) "Motivational orientations" (26 items), entailing control beliefs and intrinsic motivational orientations; and (c) "Self-regulation" (19 items) that encompasses appropriate engagement, dealing with frustrations, or maintaining a healthy distance in inter-culturally challenging situations. Each of the dimensions are self-assessed through a number of Likert type items with a 1–4 rating scale. The Scale has 68 items in total and requires approximately 20 minutes to complete.

The Scale was distributed to teachers in paper-and-pencil format by senior-year psychology students during the same visit to schools in April 2017 when social distance data were obtained. Teachers were provided with written request for participation and instructions for scale completion, and were given one week time for the task. Upon its expiration students went back to the school to collect the completed questionnaires.

Sample. 44 teachers in total from the three targeted schools responded to the ICC questionnaire, 91% of which were females, within age range 27–60 (M=43.93, SD=8.13). Their teaching experience expressed in years ranged from 2 to 30 (M=15.48, SD=7.61). 55% reported growing up in a multinational environment and all were of Serbian nationality (with 16% data missing).

Scores calculation and data analysis. For every participating teacher three scores were derived, each being expressed as an arithmetic mean of the items on the three aforementioned dimensions, with higher scores reflecting higher intercultural competence aspects. Two-factor mixed analysis of variance was performed on the teachers' data. The first of the two factors was Intercultural competence dimension and was repeated (by respondents), having 3 levels, one for each dimension of the ICC scale: (1) beliefs, values and goals, (2) motivation and (3) self-regulation. The last of the two factors is unrepeated and represents the three schools wherefrom teachers were asked to participate, each of the selected schools being in more detail described in the last part of the Methodology section.

Research Phase Two: School-Level Qualitative Overview of the Inclusion Process

Refugee students spent the majority of their time in school in the classrooms together with their domicile classmates, participating in teaching and learning activities. In order to ensure a smooth entry and successful learning, the entire school as microsystem underwent a process of preparation and adjustment. The qualitative part of our research aimed to tap into the details of this adjustment process, i.e. the transformation of schools to master the complex task of integrating the refugee students and coping with the unexpected circumstances.

General method. We relied on focus groups as our main research technique, being in our opinion the optimal way to observe and explore the complicated and not always overt processes through which collective norms and practices are construed and exerted (Bloor, Frankland, Thomas, & Robson, 2001). Semi-structured focus groups with local-level experts from the three selected schools were conducted, exploiting the flexibility of this approach compared to techniques which consist of pre-defined questions imposed on the natural flow of the discussion (Gibson & Brown, 2009). Focus-group guidelines were formulated around inclusion-relevant themes, covering several thematic blocks, depending on the participants: school preparation process; domicile students and parents preparation for refugee students' entering schools; day-to-day organization of refugee students' school attendance; cooperation with other relevant institutions; initial expectations and fears; student-refugee and teacher-refugee interactions; cultural differences, barriers and coping mechanisms; typical organizational and instructional problems; available and scarce in-school and system-level resources; examples of good practices and experiences; goal or purpose of the school inclusion process from the vantage point of participating experts and their expectations for the future outcomes.

Informants and data collection. Data were collected from those participants who had direct experience with every-day school inclusion of refugee students: class and subject teachers, members of the Team for the support of inclusion of refugee students, school associates (psychologists, pedagogues), and other relevant staff (Roma assistants), as well as external experts – school mentors. Four semi-structured focus groups were carried out, three of them held in each of the participating schools with internal experts, while the fourth one was organised for the school mentors at the Faculty of Philosophy in Belgrade. Each focus group discussion lasted up to 120 minutes and was conducted with 10 to 20 participants per session, making it around 50 informants in total.

Other important information resources were two targeted meetings with mentors, translators and teachers from the Team for support of inclusion from all three selected schools, with this picture enriched by insights gained through informal class observations (both regular classes with domicile students, and separately organized for refugee students' language learning), informal communication with refugee students, school principals and researchers from the Centre for educational policy who carried out the project.

Data analysis.   Audio tapes from the focus groups (as well as field notes from the meetings, observations and other communication) were summarized in written form for further analysis. Thematic analysis was applied going from particular statements to more abstract themes, with no *a priori* defined coding system, so that the themes would more naturally emerge from data (Patton, 1990). Identified core themes were then interpreted in light of similar international experiences, as well as taking into consideration distinctive features of the national context and of the selected schools. Triangulation and reporting of participants' original statements were used as means for reliability insurance (Willig, 2008).

Three Schools Case Study: Three Similar, Yet Very Different Educational Contexts

The research was conducted in three schools volunteering to engage in the education integration of refugee students. These schools also accepted to be part of our study and wholeheartedly accepted us as researchers allowing us to enter their premises and explore the complexities of the integration process "from the inside". Aside of their willingness and motivation to cooperate with the researchers each of these schools is characterized by several unique features that render its participation in the study exceptionally valuable.

The first school, called the *Flexible survivor*, has several such features. To begin with, this school is both an adult education school using an "accelerated curriculum" where one semester counts as one school year, and a regular basic school. Its students, mostly between 10 and 16, are often from families with a history of hardships in their lives – children who for a variety reasons started education several years later than required, children of families returning from countries where they were denied asylum, etc. More than 80% of pupils are Roma students from low socio-economic status families living on the edge of poverty. The school represents the only provider of educational opportunities for its students. To adequately respond to the needs of their students, representing a very heterogeneous population with a significant share from vulnerable groups, teachers individualize and adjust teaching as much as possible. In this regard, the school represents an important point in the education system that prevents dropping out of at risk students from the system, and providing support for re-enrolment to regular education. Due to these specificities, the school is exempt from regular external evaluation.

This school had enrolled significantly more refugee pupils than the other schools in the project, and was the first school to volunteer for participation. In total,

Over 50 refugee students, mostly boys aged 7 to 17, attended classes here during the project year. They enrolled at different times during the school year. 22 of them, enrolled in the first cycle, were without parental care. However, there were also significant fluctuations in the number of attending refugees. Some would leave the school in order to migrate further, and some, in the case of failure, would come back.

The second school which we named *Frustrated and Overburdened* is a regular 8 grade elementary school, located on the outskirts of Belgrade at a neighbourhood close to the "Deponija" [Landfill] slum mainly inhabited by a deprived Roma population, living in extremely bad conditions. Due to the proximity of this settlement a large number of Roma students are enrolled in the school (over 30% of the student body). In the local community, this school is already sometimes labelled as a "Roma School". Consequently, the school often faces typical "white flight", when parents of the majority population move their children to other schools, leaving our school in fear of closedown or of becoming a truly Roma-only school.

The staff of this school is small, numbering less than 30 teachers, working in one shift only. At the time the researchers entered the school six refugee students had been enrolled, from two families. Five students were enrolled in second grade (one of them was younger than 7 years old, which is less than expected for that grade), and one student attended classes with 6th and 8th grade students.

The third school, *Young and enthusiastic*, is a relatively new regular 8 grade elementary school, located in a suburban area of Belgrade close to the Refugee Centre. The school has more than 1000 students and teaching is organized in two shifts. The teaching staff is young and numerous, many of whom are in their induction period or working only part time in the school. Participation in projects and professional development activities are highly valued. Students enjoy a wide offer of extracurricular activities, with almost all students participating in at least on. Students can also choose between four foreign languages (English, German, Russian and Chinese) and two types of religious education (Orthodox Christian and Muslim). That the school fosters the quality of education is also reflected in students' outcomes – they are ranked 5th out of 18 schools in their municipality in terms of the national test at the end of the compulsory education.

The school has enrolled twenty refugee students, mostly from Afghanistan, in two rounds. First seven boys aged 13 to 15 years without parental care were enrolled and later on an additional group of eight boys and five girls entered the school. The second group was aged 7 to 17, they were all under parental care, but with very diverse prior education experiences.

FINDINGS

Quantitative Assessment of the Overall Attitude Towards Refugees

Social distance towards refugee students. Students' answers obtained by completing Bogardus social distance scale, are presented in Figure 4.2.

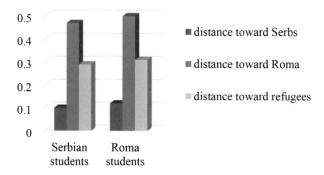

Figure 4.2. Social distance of Serbian and Roma domicile students toward Serbian, Roma and refugee students. Distance towards a particular group shown in proportions on the Y axis (higher value indicates greater distance)

As shown in Figure 4.2, the distance of both domicile students' groups towards refugee pupils is almost identical. In other words, the findings suggest that there is no difference between Serbian and Roma pupils regarding their distance towards the refugee pupils (t (55.05) = .25, p = .804). Findings also show that that the distance of the domicile students' population towards refugee pupils is of a medium level.

The results considered separately for the two groups of domicile students demonstrate that Serbian students exhibit a relatively high distance towards Roma students, which is significantly higher than the distance to their own group (t (89) = 13.75, p <.001), and this distance is also significantly higher than the distance to the refugee students (t (89) = -5.61, p <.001).On the other hand, within the Roma student group there is no statistically significant difference in the distance towards their own Roma group compared to their distance towards Serbian students (t (37) = −1.82, p = .077). There is a significantly higher distance towards refugee pupils than towards Serbs (t (37) = 3.33, p = .002). Hence, the distance of all domicile students towards the refugee population, although larger compared to the distance to their own group, is shown to be lower than expected. This conclusion is further supported by the finding that there is a greater social distance among Serbian students towards a domicile minority (i.e. Roma students) than to refugee pupils.

Teachers' intercultural competence. Let's look at the self-reported intercultural competence of teachers. Figure 4.3 presents the results of ANOVA performed to compare scores on three ICC scale dimensions for teachers from the three participating schools.

What can be said about the findings of this analysis? First, given the fact that the theoretical range of scores goes from 1 to 4 (higher scores point to higher self-assessment of competence), and thus the theoretical expectation is 2.5, Figure 4.3 reveals that teachers report higher intercultural competences than what is theoretically expected. Secondly, the results of ANOVA indicate main effects of

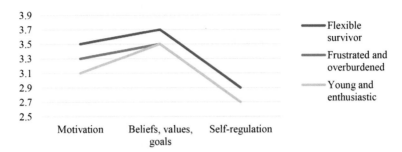

Figure 4.3. Intercultural competences of teachers from three participating schools. Average scores on the three dimensions of ICC on Y axis

both included factors, whereas, as the nearly parallel slopes of the lines shown on the Figure 4.3 imply, the effect of factor interaction was not statistically significant. The main effect of the Intercultural competence factor is significant (F (2, 80) = 97.91, p <.001) and suggests that the scores of all teachers, regardless of which school they belong to, differ for the three dimensions of an instrument for assessing teachers' intercultural competence. The teachers reported highest scores on the scale reflecting their beliefs, values and goals concerning intercultural education. They assessed somewhat lower their own motivation to work in an intercultural environment. Finally, teachers evaluated their self-regulation skills in the situation of teaching in an intercultural environment as being the lowest compared to the other two dimensions.

The second factor, the School, according to the ANOVA results has marginal significance (F (2, 40) = 3.09, p = .056), indicating that teachers from different schools marginally differ in the assessment of their intercultural competence. Teachers from the school labelled as "Survivor" report a higher level of intercultural competences in relation to the other two schools, but a statistically significant difference was registered only compared to the teachers from "Young and Motivated" school. Also, differences were shown only for two of the intercultural competence scale dimensions, motivation for working in an intercultural environment (F (2, 41) = 3.60, p = .036) and self-regulation in the intercultural teaching situation (F (2, 40) = 3.99, p = .026), while the self-evaluation of intercultural values, beliefs and goals was high and equal for teachers from all three schools. We expect that in a larger teacher sample teachers from the "Survivor" school would significantly differ from the teachers from both of the other two schools on all three dimensions of intercultural competence scale.

Let's shift the focus to the implications of the lack of interaction between school and intercultural sensitivity factors for the moment. No matter how different these three school contexts are as it is hinted in the Methodology section, teachers from all of them are similar in their expressed beliefs, values and goals concerning intercultural education, rating them relatively high. This comes as no surprise if we consider the voluntary nature of the schools' participation in the pilot phase of this project aimed at supporting the integration of refugee students in education, and the previous experiences of the selected schools with inclusive education, that gave these schools an edge in dealing with student diversity. On the other hand, estimates of the motivation to work in an interculturally diversified environment were not as high in all the schools, while the self-assessed self-regulation skills for managing the teaching and learning process in diversified classroom conditions proved to be the weakest point of teachers' intercultural competence, showing that favourable attitudes and previous experience are, even for these most prepared and willing schools, perceived as insufficient when it comes to the new challenge of integrating refugee students. It is interesting, however, that on all three subscales the school named *Survivor* had the highest scores – a point deserving further exploration.

These quantitative measures helped us map the overall classroom climate regarding acceptance of refugee children in the targeted schools from both sides of the teaching process, that of teachers and that of students. We used the acquired findings as pointers to the directions we could take during the in-depth exploration through qualitative approach, which is the focus of our next section.

Qualitative Overview of the School-Level Inclusion Process

In the following sections, we present the results of a thematic analysis of the focus groups and other data sources, first linking them to the respective school of the informants and subsequently presenting and elaborating the themes across the schools by category of responses. Finally, we will turn to recommendations in the concluding chapter.

Case Studies of Three Schools

Flexible survivor.   Teachers from this school perceive themselves as highly motivated and dedicated. They point out that they feel identified with the mission of the school, and therefore often invest much more than expected of them. For them it is quite usual to work with the traumatized population in ad hoc circumstances. These are the teachers who have never been "just teachers" – they go to the Roma settlements to visit students' families trying to maintain connections with the parents and to include them as much as possible in the education of their children; they know how to motivate students, create a learning culture, monitor student progress and use all available feedback to improve their practice and the well-being of students. The students refer to their teachers as "mom" and "aunt", which speaks of the relationship that exists between students and teachers, and about the school climate itself. Simultaneously, the proactive and committed school leadership ensures that the school stays mission-oriented. The school principal is a figure that is very visible in the school, and is actively involved in school activities and the very process of inclusion of refugee pupils. Due to the principal's engagement, the school has successful cooperation with numerous (non-)governmental organizations and institutions, where one with health institutions is especially emphasized. These resources are also used for the newly emerging situation regarding the inclusion of refugee students.

As already mentioned, there is no external data on the school's educational efficiency. The facts that it resides on the margin of the Serbian education system and that it is one of a kind, create both advantages and disadvantages for the school. On the one hand, the school can seize the opportunity to be flexible to quickly and freely adapt to new conditions (which other schools do not perceive to have), without fear that this would negatively affect external evaluations. On the other hand, the school lacks a relevant frame of reference regarding its teaching process, the teaching methods and the quality of instruction at the school, and has no clear feedback that could help to guide its further development.

Thanks to the enthusiasm of its staff and the previous positive experiences in working with a heterogeneous student population, the school welcomed refugee students with excitement. Furthermore, the flexible and adaptable modus operandi of the school, its continuous coping with unexpected situations, as well as many years of experience with students at risk, facilitated the integration process. Teachers report on feeling that they could navigate this unstructured process well. However, the teachers' low expectations, as well as the low criteria for student achievement, could be an obstacle for the academic advancement of refugee students. Additionally, a high proportion of Roma students in the school and a lack of interaction with students from the majority (i.e. Serbian) population could lead to a sense of segregation among refugee students, creating a new kind of obstacle to their integration process.

Frustrated and overburdened school. In the context of integrating refugee students, the teachers describe themselves as open, tolerant, and colourful because they work in a school that all students can attend, regardless of their diversity. They are also *engaged, devoted, happy, sociable* and *loud* because they feel they can be in harmony with children and their age-relevant needs. The school staff entered the project in a naive and open manner, they anticipated it would be an easy task for them due to their substantial prior experience with inclusive education and their expertise in teaching children from different cultural, social and economic backgrounds. At the time of conducting the focus groups and observations, however, the school perceived the situation quite differently – respondents expressed their dissatisfaction with the way in which the project of education integration of refugee pupils was designed and carried out. The feelings of being overloaded, unsupported, frustrated and exploited dominated in the teachers' narratives.

The small teaching staff was faced with numerous project-related responsibilities that were less of a burden for bigger schools. The already high proportion of domicile pupils from vulnerable groups and in need of additional educational support made the arrival of newcomers harder to cope with. Teachers' primary complaints concerned not students but the additional administration and obligations that came with participating in the project.

Young and enthusiastic school.   Members of the teaching staff described the school as an *open, friendly, warm-hearted*, pleasant and hospitable place. Talking about the process of refugee pupils' enrolment, the school pedagogue described the school as "prepared to try". She also noted how the school was devoted to the process, even to the extent that it occasionally paid more attention to refugee students than to domicile students, who, in turn, were also highly engaged in helping the newcomers in initial orientation and adjustment.

This school proved to be very successful in the process of inclusion of refugee children in formal education. Dissatisfaction with certain aspects of the process of refugee inclusion could be heard in the teacher's narratives, but the general self-assessment is that the school staff has paid a lot of attention to planning, preparation and structuring the activities. Considerable efforts were made in teaching Serbian language, thus providing an informal preparatory language course to the refugees. The school showed sensitivity to the needs of refugee students, made efforts to monitor students, demonstrated willingness to re-examine its first assumptions, and showed flexibility in designing learning opportunities and organizing the schedule for refugees so that teaching could be individualized and adjusted to their needs. The school recognized its role as the main source of socialization in the absence of systemic support, focusing, therefore, on languages and the practical skills needed for refugee students to cope with the new and unknown environment. Frustration with the lack of systemic support and the general disarray of the involved institutions, according to teachers, was something that staff had in common with other schools involved in this study, which will be elaborated further in the text.

(Surprisingly) Positive Experience

In the narratives of all respondents form all three schools the signs of a similar relief and positive experience could be heard.

Resilience instead of trauma.   Based on prior experiences with children affected by relocation and war, as well as the preparatory activities, the schools had a widespread expectation that the refugee students will arrive at school highly traumatized and that, at least in the initial stage of their integration, dealing with war and displacement trauma will be the priority. According to the teachers' narratives, this expectation did not prove to be grounded. Instead, teachers were faced with children who were seen as resilient and with no visible disruptive distress symptoms. The initial assumption was that the main efforts of the teaching staff would be directed to the socio-affective domain of students' functioning, and that their first tasks would be "to reach out to them", "to make them open up", and "to prevent counter-effects". Instead, they faced resilient and smiling youngsters. The students enrolling in schools in Serbia in the autumn of 2016 or Winter/Spring of 2017 were doing so on a voluntary basis, not as an obligation or requirement. Also, they had already spent several months on the road, out of school, was most probably perceived as a positive change by the refugee students. Although aware of these circumstances the schools were still surprised. According to the teachers, these students "considering all their suffering, were very nice, no matter how unexpected it might be", they "realized they found themselves among friends" and "that no one would reject them". This chiefly positive emotional state of the refugee students facilitated, in the opinion of the teachers, positive and pleasant teacher-student interactions.

Low expectation revised.   Teachers also reported that their initial low expectations regarding the students' motivation and readiness to spend time at school, and to be engaged in school activities and learning, proved to be unjustified: "We expected them to be less organized, less motivated to work, less interested. We thought that they came to school because they had nothing better to do, and not because they wanted to learn something". These negative expectations were, eventually, completely discarded. Children "wanted to learn", "they wanted knowledge", as teachers have reported. The children plead for homework, and the next day they would come to school asking for feedback. The teachers reacted quickly when they spotted their misconceptions and tried to respond to the expressed need for knowledge. Since pupils were willing to learn, "especially girls", and "were like sponges, they absorbed everything we gave them", teachers shifted the focus from social adaptation to helping the students gain the knowledge and skills that refugee students saw as useful.

Students' academic aspirations as inspiration for teachers.   Students' competence and diligence regarding school engagement, their discipline during school activities, often followed by expressing gratitude for the efforts made by teachers, were clearly visible. In general, students' academic aspirations were seen as motivating for teachers, so they were inspired to invest more effort in preparing materials and resources. Teachers formulated their own gains from this process as inspiration, greater challenges and a general feeling of satisfaction, feeling that they were "encouraged to give more". In some cases these behaviours served as a positive model for domicile students. On the other hand, refugee pupils were surprised by how teachers were "young and smiling". They saw the domicile students, especially the younger ones as "happy" and "in a good mood".

Positive peer interactions.   Peer interactions between domicile pupils and refugees were often seen as highly positive. In the narratives of internal experts, there was no mention of peer conflicts. Emphasis was placed on the way they facilitated positive relationships and understanding between refugee and domicile children. Before the arrival of refugee students, teachers helped domicile students comprehend the life circumstances of refugee students and the difficulties they had to go through with an emphasis on similarities: "It's like when you need to change school and to go to a new and foreign environment". They worked to develop the understanding that "it was not easy for them", and to place a clear expectation of domicile students to help in the adaptation of newcomers. After the refugees started attending classes, teachers encouraged them to share their experiences, so that domicile pupils could, once again, get a chance to better understand their friends' situation and personally relate. They also exchanged personal experiences and preferences, as well as cultural specificities. As a result, domicile children expressed the need to learn refugee students' language, and independently organized a humanitarian action (collecting clothing and footwear) for the newcomers. As a form of formal peer support, schools included members of the Student Parliament to participate in all inclusion-related activities from the first admission of new students.

Benefits for local students. Peer support was used both in teaching and in adjustment to school life (for example, domicile students were delegated as hosts with the responsibility to provide support to refugee pupils in their schooling). An example of a particularly successful practice was the assignment of responsibility to potentially "problematic" local students, thus turning them into an important peer resource. In one such instance, a student's desire to be at the centre of attention was satisfied by assigning her a role of "assistant teacher" in communicating with refugee students in classes. It is important to underline how exceptionally useful this process proved for the transformation of potential "troublemakers" among the domicile students into valued teachers' helpers.

The schools noted additional important benefits for domicile learners – the development of empathy, increased sense of personal value by helping others, "de-centration" from their own cultural and school practices, and the prioritization of the development of competences over and above the typical focus on school grades. Firstly, domicile students met people with different looks (for example, girls with covered heads), beliefs and lifestyles, and learned about different school practices (e.g. physical punishment of students), which contributed to understanding differences in concepts and values in social and educational systems. This, altogether, represented an important aspect of developing students' intercultural sensitivity. Additionally, according to the teachers, Roma students realized that they were similar to refugees in several respects: aside from similitude in physical appearance, some of them were from asylum seeker families that were returned from a European Union member state, and found themselves in Serbia as newcomers in an unknown country where they do not know the language and the culture of the people surrounding them. The experiences of domicile (mostly Roma) students similar to that of refugees' facilitated their understanding and acknowledging attitude, which led to better acceptance of refugee pupils in peer groups. Lastly, domicile students (especially Roma students in the dominantly Roma populated school) got an impetus to reorganize their priorities and change their perspectives regarding the importance of (formal) education. The importance of attaining competencies became emphasized instead of focusing solely on school grades, making the students rediscover the meaning of schooling: "You can lose everything and go to another environment – you always carry what you have learned with you".

Benefits for parents. These positive experiences of domicile students with newcomers contributed to their parents' more positive and agreeable reactions to the integration process. The preparation and positive experiences of domicile students in their first contacts with refugees ("these are boys like any other boys") were recognized as decisive factors in the later positive attitudes of parents to the fact that refugee students would be attending school with their children. The parents' responses to the school notice regarding inclusion were far better than the school anticipated. Some parents even expressed willingness to provide material assistance to the refugee pupils. Even though there were some occasional reports of parents' dissatisfaction, schools reported facing far less difficulties in this regard than they anticipated.

Teacher–(refugee) student relationship. One of the important aspects of the overall positive approach, as teachers saw it, was the relationship that they built with refugee students: "If we were not close to them, they would never trust us, and that could lead to additional problems"; "If we get to know one another, we get to cooperate better". Teachers made themselves available for students regardless of working hours in the school, if students were in need of assistance or if they just needed someone to talk to. Teachers gladly accepted this dependency believing it to be beneficial for the students as an aspect of socio-emotional support: "I think the most important thing for the students is the additional care that we provide them, the thing that is not related to the educational process – that someone is thinking about them". As we can see, the acceptance of personal responsibility for the process and the autonomous search for solutions to the problems they were experiencing was beneficial to the process of inclusion, especially if it was accompanied with sensitivity to and respect for cultural specificities: "If he/she feels secure, he will ask the translator to tell me what he/she needs". This sensitivity was also catalytic, helping boost flexibility in adapting the organizational and content aspects of the teaching process to the specific circumstances that were sometimes changing on a daily basis, such as responding to students' preferences regarding attending classes, reorganizing the regular school schedule in order to accommodate to the needs of the refugee students at some particular times, etc.

Cherished resources. What are the most valuable resources that were beneficial to the schools in this process? When it comes to the characteristics of the schools themselves, the first and mostly addressed resource were the teachers, professional associates and principals themselves and their proactive attitudes. The schools recognized the importance of their own efforts in planning, implementing and adapting activities needed for the process of refugee inclusion. Even in the case of the school with a small teaching staff, they heavily relied on personal strengths – independent preparation of materials, designing plans and their adjustment, coping with problems as they occurred and succeeding in resolving them by themselves. Additionally, in the school mainly attended by Roma students, the teachers relied on their experience and positive attitude towards working with culturally diverse students and students from poor socio-economic conditions, who may be neglected, abused or otherwise traumatized. Thanks to these previous experiences, they were eager to engage and dedicate themselves to the project with the aim of benefiting all the students.

Valuable external sources of assistance to these schools came in the form of translators hired by the project and many engaged volunteers. Since the refugee students were very heterogeneous regarding their knowledge of Serbian and English languages, the assistance of translators was essential. The translator played a valuable role, not just in the most practical sense, but also as a cultural mediator who helped teachers to understand and address the cultural specificities of the students.

Finally, schools could easily rely on some of their previous systemic experience: inclusion of refugees during the civil war in the former SFRY in the 1990s, a decade of integration of Roma students into formal education (2005–2015) and the implementation of inclusive education starting in 2009. Unsurprisingly the three schools drew mostly from their experiences of Roma integration and the skills for managing differentiation and individualization gained by using individual education plans.

As a conclusion of this section, we can say that teachers, professional associates and directors strived to use all available resources. Furthermore, they strived to think in terms of wellbeing, not just of refugee students, but of domicile students as well, and teachers themselves. However, there is another side to the medal. According to the respondents, barriers and stumbling-points that hindered the students' inclusion process did exist, some considered that they even prevailed, and the process of inclusion, the way that it was organized in, could not provide real benefits for neither the refugees nor the local students.

Weak Points

Narratives of school experts can be summarized in the following way as regards faced difficulties, barriers and areas for improvement.

Poor macro-level organization. Schools assessed an aggravating circumstance in the process of integration was the lack of a clear and coherent policy for refugee integration. This was visible through contradictory and delayed instructions that schools received regarding instructional aspects, student assessment, school administration, project evaluation arrangements, etc.; untimely notices regarding organizational aspects such as changes in student schedules, transport, or student safety; and general "on the move" decision-making which resulted in tasks for school practitioners with due dates "for yesterday".

In addition to such difficulties, a very negative experience of schools, gravely present towards the end of the school year, was the lack of basic necessities for newcomers such as food, clothing, transportation, and school supplies, signalling that the organization of support for refugee students was far from satisfactory. These necessities were provided at the beginning of the project, but there were no additional provisions later on.

The schools also identified less than adequate communication and coordination between the relevant institutions during the entire project – collective centres for refugees, the centre for social work, relevant state institutions and non-governmental organizations. According to school staff, these institutions and organizations asked for and offered services, "without consideration of the broader picture", i.e. the activities of other involved actors. Schools had to deal with numerous visits by interested officials, class observations by researchers from various institutions, which altogether disrupted the already out of the ordinary way the schools were functioning.

Finally, internal experts uniformly expressed a sense of general lack of support and assistance for schools, even by the institutions that they explicitly asked for support. Teachers complained that they needed guidance regarding instructional materials and procedures that they could apply in critical situations, but that they rarely received it. They were thus left to "learning by trial and error" in many situations, since they did not have persons whom they could call in need of help – an involved and interested mentor, an available counsellor, or informed coordinator.

Unexpected diversity among the refugee population. The second source of challenges identified by the school practitioners was the width and depth of differences among the refugee pupils themselves. There were many differences in terms of cultural characteristics and the educational background in the country of origin, the students' years of formal and non-formal education, level of competence in different school subjects. These differences were more substantial than expected by the schools. Students also differed regarding age, mother tongue, and mastery of English language, or occasionally Serbian. All of these, as well as the fact that schools had no guidance for an appropriate approach regarding initial assessment (of knowledge, competences, mastery of language, and many other school relevant characteristics) made it even more difficult to set clear criteria for the placement of the new students to the appropriate class grades in their new school. Teachers noted that instructions that were provided were not detailed enough and could not be easily followed. On the other hand, class-placement criteria had to consider both the characteristics of refugee students and domicile students, as well as the capacities of the school: sometimes, refugee students were much older or younger than their classmates and sometimes classes were already attended by students under IEP which made teaching more difficult. In many instances the schools also had to take into account the wish of several refugee brothers and sisters to be placed in the same classes. In these situations, schools were left to choose whether they would be satisfying one's emotional or educational needs, and opted for the former. Also, when there were too many Roma students in regular classes, refugee student would lack the opportunity to socialize with the Serbian majority which could, potentially, lead to a sense of being segregated.

The lack of a common language between refugees and the domicile population but also among the refugees was a substantial problem. The refugee students spoke English on a very basic level, while not all teachers felt competent teaching in English, and none of them were competent to teach students how to speak Serbian as a foreign language.

Additionally, there was a high degree of fluctuation in school attendance by the refugee students. This was mostly present in the school that enrolled the highest number of refugee students. Despite their willingness to tackle these unpredictable circumstances, teachers felt uncomfortable because of the frequent fluctuations of refugee students: "It's always inconvenient, we just get used to them and they go away, you do not see the end of that. Something just gets accomplished with one, then another enrols and we start from scratch". If we also take into account the problem of untimely notices mentioned above, we can see how perplexing the situation was for teachers. These challenges reflect the overall complexity and unpredictability of the situation of refugees on the international level.

Coping with students' nascent education needs. As already mentioned, instead of traumatized pupils requiring psychosocial support for integration in the school system and society, schools encountered resilient students in search of transferable skills that could be used outside Serbian borders. This surprised many teachers, but also posed a new demand – they needed to rethink the possible benefits of education and re-evaluate the longer-term meaning of knowledge. As the refugee students spent more and more time in schools, their interest shifted from socializing with peers to mastering computer sciences and mathematics, and learning English and German language. While teachers acknowledged the relevance of these nascent needs, accommodating them in regular daily school practice posed additional difficulties.

Dilemma between conflicting goals. An important circumstance raising concerns for school practitioners was the unclear status of Serbia in the migration of refugees from the Middle East across Europe. If Serbia retained the role of a transit country that it had had since the beginning of the refugee crisis, said the teachers, schools would have to adopt a support program during the limited stay of refugees passing through to the countries of Western and Northern Europe. On the other hand, a more permanent residing of refugees in Serbia would, according to teachers, require the design of a long-term program of integration into the Serbian education system and wider society and would imply systemic solutions and much greater systemic support for their implementation. Of course, in the evolving and changing European migration policy and attitude towards refugees, nobody can really answer this question. Nevertheless, the dilemma is present in the narratives of staff of all three schools, contributing to the general feeling of uncertainty and "chaos". In the words of teachers, "the system (meaning the Ministry of Education, Science and Technological Development) has to make up its mind, and only afterwards to allow children to enrol". Numerous relevant questions remained unanswered for teachers: Should the focus be on preparing refugees for further migration or for longer stays? Should teaching be focused on socialization or on learning? Should students be taught English or Serbian language, should they be thought Cyrillic or Latin script? And so on. Schools faced a huge discrepancy between the requirements for constant adaptation, flexibility and successful responding to unforeseen circumstances on the one hand, and their own need to be strict, clear, and in some sense "rigid", as required by the school system in Serbia, on the other. Schools needed support in dealing with such discrepancies and unstructured challenges.

Professional concerns of teachers. The experience of being overburdened was clearly stated by the teachers in their narratives. Firstly, they had to cope with teaching in a much more heterogeneous setting requiring a higher degree of instructional differentiation due to the heterogeneity of refugee students. Secondly, teachers reported that inclusion of refugee students into regular classes resulted in a need for additional time dedicated to the preparation of instructional materials. These materials now had to be adapted to the specificities of not just those domicile students that were educated based on IEPs, but also to the specific features of refugee students (regarding their age, mastery of English and/ or Serbian language, previous knowledge etc.). An additional problem was that the personal details of the refugee students were rarely known to the teachers in advance. Teachers described their working setting and additional requirements in this process as "working in a mine".

Teachers expressed concern on whether the quality of teaching could be maintained in a setting of such diversity. Lack of classroom assistance was also aired as a concern. This problem was especially stated by teachers who already worked with highly diverse student classrooms (students with IEPs, Roma and other minority students). Teachers needed provisions of customized instructional materials and textbooks that could be useful for non-Serbian speakers, as well as additional personal assistants as translators. All these pedagogical gaps, teachers felt, could consequently reflect on students' achievements in the final exam, as well as in the external evaluation of their institution.

Finally, teachers also questioned how long their motivation for working under such challenging conditions will last. Their fear of burnout and loss of motivation seemed to be partly also due to the fluctuations of refugee students. While at the beginning of the integration process the refugee students themselves showed progress and gave positive feedback, later on, as students were migrating further, teachers were left without the reinforcement for their efforts that usually comes from students who stay in the same school for a longer period. Teachers were also dissatisfied by and even surprised that the relevant stakeholders and participating actors showed no acknowledgment for teachers and their efforts. Teachers felt frustrated and abused as "free of charge labour" and stated how it was "unjust to only resort to their humanity" while no systematic and focused support was provided.

DISCUSSION, CONCLUSIONS AND RECOMMENDATION

We found the opportunity to peak into the experiences of schools that face a radically new situation highly enriching and meaningful. This opportunity allowed us to examine in detail a compelling education integration process as it evolved. We were able to create snapshots of attitudes and values of students and teachers which constituted the school environment against which the integration process developed, but which were also constructed around and influenced by the new experiences all actors in the schools acquired due to the unfolding integration process. We also observed first-hand how school staff, teachers, advisors, directors, teams, and external mentors to the schools processed and interpreted through their narratives their own experiences during the process. We witnessed their positive and negative surprises, dilemmas, concerns, expressions of feelings of pride and of abandonment before these experiences reached full articulation and official legitimacy or censoring. Based on this research and observations, we hope to be in a better position to draw recommendations and provide advice for future integration processes whether in Serbia or elsewhere, enabling integration-supporting projects to avoid some of the traps we identified and improving their impact and efficiency. In addition, we could look at the school change connected to the integration process from a somewhat wider perspective: observe how the typical barriers in integrating migrants play out when it comes to refugee children in Serbia and even further, examine what the collected experiences say about school innovation as such.

The main findings of this study shed light firstly on the positive experiences rising from the process of integrating refugee children. We found lower social distance towards refugee students than expected, suggesting that peer relationships between domicile and refugee students can play an important role in the integration of refugee students both in terms of their wellbeing and academic success. At the same time we did not find a significant difference of social distance towards the refugee students between the two domicile groups, Serbs and Roma – both groups displayed a similar attitude. The focus group discussions highlighted numerous examples of peer support, occurring as a spontaneous student-led activity or facilitated by the teachers. The very integration process also appears to have benefitted domicile students, as they found themselves engaging in new supporting roles and, according to the teachers, discovering the meaning and importance of education. It seems that the positive peer interactions between students could have a catalytic role in facilitating cooperation between refugee and domicile parents as well. Moreover, the self-assessed intercultural values, beliefs and goals of the teachers were found to be high, contributing to the general classroom climate of warmth, tolerance and acceptance towards the refugee students.

These findings corroborate the finding of the NESSE report (NESSE, 2008) about the mediating role of school culture and the school's level of interest to welcome new students from diverse backgrounds. The schools we worked with were indeed exceptional in their positive and welcoming attitude – they voluntarily applied for participating in the integration project, they were selected among twice as many applicants to pilot the activity and help develop models that would help other schools to embark on similar activities nationwide. They enrolled the greatest number of refugees in the first round, they stayed in the process even when faced with a lack of support, and they accepted the researchers and participated in the somewhat tedious research procedures with openness and good will. A good part of the credit for the positive outcomes should go for the project preparatory activities and work of the mentors, such as extending the focus of the project to include the preparation of domicile parents for the reception of newcomers from the refugee population, or designing the welcome activities and package for the refugee students' first visit to their future school. Of course, our research methodology does not allow us to extract the effect of each contributing factor. The message from our research is rather different – our findings highlight that with a little good will, interested schools with open-minded staff, motivated migrants and smart preparation of all parties, real change can happen, mutually reinforcing relationships can be constructed that can produce lasting benefits for both the refugees and the local children.

The focus group discussions identified another equally salient, unexpected and positive feature of the integration process that occurred in all three schools: the refugee students superseded all expectations of the school experts in respect of their psychological resilience, academic aspiration and demonstrated social skills, and hence in substantial ways reduced the scale of challenges the schools faced in opening their doors for the newcomers. This finding needs to be handled with due care. The refugee students' resilient and forward-looking approach was undoubtedly a positive sign, received by teachers with relief and joy, and had numerous beneficial effects on the overall integration process. The finding is also in line with the set of research (e.g. Pinson & Arnot, 2007) that finds war trauma a less pervasive phenomenon in the refugee population, juxtaposing instead other hardships the refugees face, such as living in poverty, lack of employment prospects, and discrimination as the most disturbing ones. Our findings at this early stage of the integration process did not record any from the list of mental health and psychological problems provided by Arnot and Pinson (2005) or researchers from Serbia (Vukčević Marković, Gašić, & Bjekić, 2017; Vukčević Marković, Gašić, Ilić, & Bjekić, 2017). Still, there is place for a word of caution. Seeking refuge from war is the kind of stress that can produce consequences with delayed onset, indiscernible immediately. Research on crisis intervention and continuous coping with war trauma (Arnot & Pinson, 2005; Vlajković, Srna, Kondić, & Popović, 2000) indicate that resilience can be the first but not the last response to stressful surroundings. Undergoing acute intense stress (as experienced fleeing from a warzone) coupled with a prolonged exposure to intermediate intensity stressors without any clear perspective for their alleviation (e.g. extended stay in collective refugee centers) can result in delayed signs of trauma. Therefore, from a long-term perspective it would be important to develop a strategy for monitoring the mental health of refugees and introducing at least some support programs that acknowledge the refugees' cultural explanatory models for mental distress (Neftçi & Çetrez, 2017).

Literature reviews highlight several further concerns, experiences and ideas typically discussed when integrating refugees, immigrants, asylum seekers that were not directly observed in the schools researched in Serbia.

The rich discussion about the best modalities for organizing language instruction for refugee students throughout Europe (e.g. European Commission, 2012; UNHCR, 2015; Kornhall, 2016) which surfaces as one of the most important integration topics, was largely absent in the schools we observed. The pilot schools organized language learning while children were immersed in the everyday activities of their school, as research has shown to be the most effective (Christensen & Stanat, 2007; Bartlett, 2015) and that it is unnecessary and undesirable to postpone academic teaching until students fully master the language of instruction (Nusche, 2009).

Unsurprisingly, foreign language learning was mentioned, options discussed, the teachers themselves even questioned their own competencies in this respect, indicating that both students and teachers were aware that the newly enrolled refugee students are only temporarily in the Serbian schools, and foreign language proficiency will help them more on the long run.

Another important integration strategy not directly tackled within our study refers to the inclusion of elements of the migrant community's culture, language, and traditions into the mainstream curriculum as an integration facilitator (Eurydice, 2009) and trauma-reducing measure (Neftçi & Çetrez, 2017), with some efforts put in order to make curricula more culturally sensitive (Bennett, 2001). Integration of specific cultural content is also important for the domicile community, since widening knowledge about the origin of new neighbours reduces fear and anxiety and prevent bias and stereotypes, as suggested by the research on "contact hypothesis" (Alport, 1954). Although the project schools received information on the culture, languages and traditions of the Middle Eastern refugees, as part of their training and as a small leaflet, teachers were still surprised by the width of diversity encountered in the classrooms, indicating that the obtained information was not sufficient.

Although widely recognized as an issue for the South East European education systems in general (INEE, 2010; Kovač Cerović, Vižek-Vidović, & Powell, 2010), and in particular as very important for early childhood care (NESSE, 2008), the involvement of refugee parents in the schooling of refugee children was, predictably, almost completely missing in the school experts' narratives. Parent involvement was also not addressed by the design of our study which involved only domicile students and the school experts. This missing link needs to be tackled.

In another way and for another reason, the focus group discussions and other qualitative data sources did not touch upon one of the main risks refugee students or students with an immigrant background face throughout several countries in Europe – education in separate, segregated schools for migrants, most often using a shortened, downgraded curriculum (e.g. Bartlett, 2015; NESSE, 2008). The risk of segregated education is painfully present and most researched with respect to the segregation of Roma students (e.g. Rostas, 2012; Kočić-Rakočević & Nagy, 2015). Building on the knowledge Serbia has acquired during the Decade of Roma Inclusion with the introduction of inclusive education, Serbia has developed and legislated a policy preventing segregation in education, and a comprehensive guidebook on desegregation and on preventing segregation has been developed. (Kovač Cerović & Luksić Orlandić, 2016). Refugee students were placed in schools and classes taking care to avoid their overrepresentation in any of the schools or classes. Segregation can increase as non-immigrant students tend to choose schools with fewer immigrant and disadvantaged students (Bloem & Diaz, 2007) and majority students start to leave a school with minorities, the so-called "white flight", turning it from regular to "ghetto school" (Rangvid, 2007). Indeed, during the first year of integrating refugee students in Serbia no events leading to segregation have been reported. However, the very fact that two of the three participating schools had a higher-than-average percentage of Roma students calls for careful monitoring of the composition of the student body in the schools which are candidates for future refugee intake and dispersed allocation of refugee students to mainstream schools coupled with busing. Methods to prevent education segregation of migrant communities can rely on the methodologies developed to prevent the segregation of Roma (Roma Education Fund, 2015), or other marginalized minorities.

Teacher sensitivity is another widely recognized factor of successful school integration of any marginalized child (OECD, 2016). Two major areas of teacher competencies are teachers' intercultural competencies and teachers' (high) expectation from their students. The findings of this study regarding the former are somewhat inconclusive. Teachers demonstrated a high level of intercultural values, beliefs and goals. This could have served as a rich source of motivation to embark on the task of integrating refugee students and to remain on track even in the absence of visible support. The "Survivor" school seems to have coped with the integration task the easiest, while the staff of the other two were more quick to air frustration. On the other hand, staff from all three schools scored lowest on the Self-regulation dimension of intercultural competencies. The difference in results between the scale dimensions reflects the fact that the inclusive education system reform in Serbia is still a very recent innovation, and while teachers' beliefs are supportive, their competencies to act accordingly through differentiated and individualized teaching are still developing and require more systemic support (Kovač Cerović, Jovanović, & Pavlović Babić, 2016). Hence, the current state of practice in the Serbian school system regarding inclusion in general renders the task of opening schools for refugee students considerably more challenging for even the most competent teachers.

On the more practical side, numerous logistical problems cited by the literature such as lack of placement capacity in the closest school, distance to school, lack of transportation, and/or lack of safety on the road (Bartlett, 2015; UNHCR, 2015) have been reported. The project staff and the mentors were heavily involved in negotiating and re-negotiating transportation schedules, provision of books and utensils, clothing, etc. and helping to prevent that the newly enrolled refugee students drop out of school because of such problems.

The three schools we focused on had many comparable experiences and articulated their successes and drawbacks often in similar ways. Nevertheless the differences in the school context, structure and know-how influenced the way the schools were responding to the challenges they encountered. Each of them responded to the unpredictable and unstructured situation in their own unique way and relied on their main strengths as the most important resource. The school "Flexible survivor" fully relied on their rich previous experiences in working with heterogeneous student populations, and easily adapted to changing circumstances as they came. Their readiness to connect with and devote to students' wellbeing highly facilitated the integration process. The school "Young and enthusiastic", on the other hand, drew on the high motivation of its staff, especially the young teachers. They conducted with great care all the necessary preparations and with excellent internal organization managed to successfully educate the first group of refugee students. The third school, "Frustrated and overburdened", as a school with a small number of teachers, cherished respect for each individual, relied on experiences in individualization and accepted overtime work in order to accomplish what is expected from a teacher – to be there for every child.

Our findings show relevance regarding school, local and national level policy making. The accounts of school staff and mentors in the focus groups provide a strong critical voice, pointing out the system divides between offices of education, social affairs, health, and refugee protection – divides often present with regards to other vulnerable groups in general, contributing also to early dropping out from schools (Kovač Cerović, Lakićević, Cenerić, Vainalanen, & Mladenović, 2013). More specifically, teachers and other school staff who participated in the focus groups highlighted their frustration regarding organizational and logistical uncertainties, lack of a clear strategy, lack of timely support or instruction and finally, student fluctuation. These objections, tapped into a more fundamental problem of schooling as such. They indicated the existence of a wide gap in requirements between the traditional school system on the one hand and the policy and practice of integration on the other. Schools by default necessitate good organization, regulations and predictability, while the mobility and uncertainty with respect to future status of the refugees renders the integration process itself unpredictable and constantly changing. The consequences of this gap are predominantly borne by the teachers – they reported that the permanent requests for thinking "on the go" and managing the teaching process in ever-changing circumstances without detailed structure or guidelines, started to make them feel as being "thrown in the fire" and burning out. Understandably, novel sustainable solutions need to be found to mitigate and prevent instances of teacher burnout and withdrawal or segregation and neglect of the refugee students.

However, the paradox might be even deeper: Education systems as such are tasked with preparing all students for the "unpredictable world of the future" where they will set out to solve the problems that cannot be anticipated at this time. This is exactly the kind of challenge schools are encountering here and now with the integration of refugees. For such future-oriented educational outcomes we need flexible schools, innovative teachers, open classrooms, and willingness to experiment. It is necessary for the system to support the development of these competencies.

Recommendations

There are several limitations to our research.

The voice of the refugees is not included due to the sheer technical difficulties in obtaining translators at the time the research was conducted; hence we can base our hypothesizing about their perspectives only on third party accounts. An additional round of encounters with schools and students should address this.

We did not distinguish between the schools' internal and external experts' opinions in the analysis. For the first account about the challenging, exciting and moving experiences, we felt it is better to cluster these accounts together; however, in further analysis they could be considered separately.

Our methodology did not allow us to explore in greater detail some of our interesting findings – for example, the large social distance of domicile students towards their Roma peers – as a first next step to further research on vulnerability, exclusion and inclusion, these findings would need to be taken into account.

Nevertheless, the experience of the schools from piloting education integration of refugee students from the Middle East collected through this study provides good basis for policy recommendations to other schools in Serbia and to the Serbian education system, but could also be relevant for other countries where social inclusion and education integration of refugees is taking place.

Provide better organization: procedures, inter-sectoral cooperation, mediator. One of the main recommendations pertains to better, more efficient, more timely and more relevant organization. Regarding the very process of integration, this would mean formulating the steps and clear procedures for the different aspects of the integration process (for example, for the initial assessment, class integration, monitoring development, compiling pedagogic evidence, etc.) through developing protocols, guidelines and trainings of main decision makers at local and regional level.

Another organizational aspect to be mended is inter-sectoral cooperation, which would ensure a more efficient flow of information and timely provision of support. Coordination and good planning is crucial for avoiding overlap of activities among different actors. One way to implement this based on international best practice is by expanding the role of the translator into a mediator and inter-sectoral coordinator. This coordinator could participate in helping the refugees overcome diverse barriers – linguistic, cultural and institutional, contribute to an initial feeling of security and familiarity, and enable them to communicate their needs. There is a relatively well-developed practice of including assistants and coordinators of immigrant origin, who in addition to providing support in learning can assume the role of mediator between local refugees and the wider community (NESSE, 2008). A program of Pedagogical Assistants is, in some countries such as Serbia, already well established for supporting the education of Roma in a very similar way (Daiute & Kovač Cerović, 2017), which opens the possibility to expand the current Pedagogical Assistants Program to assume this additional role.

Providing support to teachers for their teaching. Furthermore, the findings suggest that particular attention needs to be devoted to strengthening the capacity of and providing continuous support for teachers to work in a much more diverse environment created by involving refugee students. Teachers require instruction materials that are adapted to the linguistic, cultural and academic characteristics of the newcomers. Teachers also need training and professional improvement in the areas of differentiated teaching, intercultural instruction and appropriate response to signs of psychological and physical distress of students. Finally, it is crucial to encourage long-term motivation of teachers as the most important actors in this process through recognition of their role and introduction of a reward system. Also, as a special incentive for the school as a whole, external evaluation of schools should include indicators related to the quality of work with refugee students, as it is developed for inclusive education (Kovač Cerović, Pavlović Babić, Jokić, Jovanović, & Jovanović, 2016).

The measures listed above might attenuate teachers' worries about possible decrease in the quality of teaching as a consequence of having refugee students in the classes. Moreover, these measures can assume the role of "helping the helpers" strategies which aim to alleviate the stress of the helpers that directly interact with trauma-survivors (Kovač Cerović & Vulić, 2016). Working with refugee students sometimes requires significant emotional investment on part of the teachers, and renders the development of adaptive coping mechanisms a necessity.

Developing an external support network for the schools. An overwhelming experience of all internal school experts is that they lacked the support of "external supporters" in the integration process. Major school innovations, such as schools without violence, inclusive education, Roma integration, external examination, etc. were in Serbia usually disseminated and implemented with the help of external support networks whom schools could call, ask and rely on in case of any uncertainty. In the process of refugee integration a comparable size of support mechanisms was not set up. A better orchestrated system and strong co-operation between schools and external actors seems to be needed to help schools cope with the challenges in the course of the integration process.

Collaboration between internal (school) experts – teachers, school psychologists, pedagogical assistants, members of refugee support teams on one hand and external experts (school mentors and other experts focused on different aspects of the refugee students' needs) on the other hand could provide the level of professional support needed. The analysis of facilitators of inclusive education recently carried out on a sample of Belgrade schools (Pavlović Babić, Simić, & Friedman, 2017) provides additional support to this recommendation.

Furthermore, particularly useful would be to build further on the already established peer relationships, ensure the sustainability of the support provided by peers, and enrich the scope of peer to peer activities. Peer support can become an important bridge to creating a positive atmosphere also among the refugee and domicile parents. Peer support could be helpful not only for social adaptation but also for the academic advancement of migrant students. As we already saw, such peer interactions could produce benefits to domicile students as well. In previous experiences with refugees from former Yugoslavia, four types of intervention were most often used for supporting peer interactions between refugee and domicile students: tutoring and afterschool classes, extracurricular and recreational activities (including sports, youth clubs, etc.), psychosocial support programs, and summer and winter camps (Kovacs-Cerovic & Vulic, 2016). The appropriateness of these models for the requirements of the new situation should be explored.

A significantly richer connection of the school with the parents/guardians of migrant students, established either through visits of internal experts to the refugee camps or by "opening the door" of the school to parents is an important recommendation for the coming period.

Finally, a system for co-operation between schools and volunteers or non-governmental organizations active in the refugee camps where the students are living should be set up. Organizations that are already familiar with the cultural, family, educational and medical history of the refugee students as well as their current situation would be invaluable to the schools to provide initial detailed information on the pupils supported from their side as well. These organizations could also provide continuous support to the schools leveraging the expertise gained throughout the integration process.

***

We would like to close this chapter with a quick glimpse on a first unusual and unforeseen but successful use of our research about piloting refugee integration in Serbia during 2016/2017.

Šid, a small town in north-western Serbia near the country border, with a sizable refugee camp, offered the possibility for around one hundred children from the camp to enrol in school starting September 2017. The decision was made late, preparations were hasty, the five schools in the municipality did not get a training comparable to what the first cohort of pilot schools got, and of course, problems emerged almost immediately. The schools were instructed to organize parent meetings informing them about the decision and the modalities of enrolling refugee students in the schools, but they skipped this phase of preparation. Instead, they distributed to the students a leaflet with instructions how to welcome the refugees and how to acknowledge cultural differences. The leaflet arrived to the students' homes and as in the game of "Chinese whispers", the messages passed from the Ministry to teachers and students to parents were greatly misunderstood resulting in parents protesting against refugees being included in the same schools and classes with local children. The protests lasted for days, local parents did not allow their children to go to school, the Ministry intervened, conducted extensive discussions with the parents trying to persuade them to change their minds. A real breakthrough happened only when the team coordinating the first cohort of pilot schools was asked to convey their experiences with integrating migrants. This team asked us, the researchers, to prepare an easy to understand presentation on the experiences of the schools based on our research, which was in turn conveyed to the schools and parents. Understanding that there was no reason for fear and anxiety, and that the experience could be also positive, parents agreed to discontinue the protests and support the integration process. Three months after the incident, at the time of writing this text, Šid and its parents are not any more in the news – integration of refugees in schools became a normal everyday activity.

NOTE

[1] The research results described in this chapter were presented at the ECER 2017 Conference: Reforming Education and the Imperative of Constant Change: Ambivalent roles of policy and educational research, Copenhagen, August 22–25, 2017.

REFERENCES

Allport, G. W. (1954). *The nature of prejudice*. Cambridge, MA: Perseus Books.

Arnot, M., & Pinson, H. (2005). *The education of asylum-seeker and refugee children: A study of LEA and school values, policies and practices*. Cambridge: University of Cambridge, Faculty of Education.

Arsenović-Pavlović, M., Jolić, Z., & Buha-Đurković, N. (2008). Social closeness and features that Roma school children assign to Serbs. *Journal of Education, 2*, 165–174.

Bartlett, L. (2015). *Access and quality of education for international migrant children*. Background paper prepared for the education for all global monitoring report 2015, UNESCO, Paris.

Baumert, J., & Kunter, M. (2013). The COACTIV model of teachers' professional competence. In M. Kunter, J. Baumert, W. Blum, U. Klusmann, S. Krauss, & M. Neubrand (Eds.), *Cognitive activation in the mathematics classroom and professional competence of teachers: Results from the COACTIV project* (pp. 25–48). New York, NY: Springer.

Bennett, C. (2001). Genres of research in multicultural education. *Review of Educational Research, 71*(2), 171–217.

Bloem, N. S., & Diaz, R. (2007). *White flight: Integration through segregation in Danish metropolitan public schools*. Humanity in Action, Team Denmark.

Bloor, M., Frankland, J., Thomas, M., & Robson, K. (2001). *Focus groups in social research*. London: Sage Publications.

Christensen, G., & Stanat, P. (2007). *Language policies and practices for helping immigrants and second-generation students succeed*. Washington, DC: Migration Policy Institute.

Daiute, C., & Kovač Cerović, T. (2017). *Minority teachers – Roma in Serbia – narrate education reform*. Belgrade: Institute for Psychology.

Deardorff, D. K. (2009). Synthesizing conceptualizations of intercultural competence: A summary and emerging themes. In D. K. Deardorff (Ed.), *The Sage handbook of intercultural competence* (pp. 265–270). Thousand Oaks, CA: Sage Publications.

European Commission/EURYDICE/EUROSTAT. (2012). *Key data on teaching languages at school in Europe*. Brussels: EACEA P9 Eurydice and Policy Support. Retrieved December 7, 2017, from http://eacea.ec.europa.eu/education/eurydice

Eurydice. (2009). *Integrating immigrant children into schools in Europe*. Brussels: Eurydice Network.

Gibson, W., & Brown, A. (2009). *Working with qualitative data*. London: Sage Publications.

Ignjatović-Savić, N. M. (1995). Expecting the unexpected: A view on child development from war affected social context. *Psihologija, 28*(pos. br.), 27–48.

INEE. (2010). *Minimum standards for education: Preparedness, response, recovery*. New York, NY: INEE.

Kia-Keating, M., & Ellis, B. (2007). Belonging and connection to school in resettlement: Young refugees, school belonging, and psychosocial adjustment. *Clinical Child Psychology and Psychiatry, 12*(1), 29–43. doi:10.1177/1359104507071052

Kočić-Rakočević, N., & Nagy, A. (2015). *The benefits of early childhood education and desegregation: Case study of an educational intervention in the Konik camp in Montenegro*. Washington, DC: CIES.

Kornhall, P. (2016). Reception of newly arrived migrants and assessment of previous schooling: Peer learning activity in Stockholm Sweden 6–7 April 2016. Sweden: Ecorys.

Kovács Cerović, T. (2018, January). Education policies for Roma integration through narratives from the Roma pedagogical assistants in Serbia. In A. Mehendale & R. Mukhopadhyay (Eds.), *The right to education movements and policies: Promises and realities* (NORRAG Special Issue, pp. 131–134).

Kovač Cerović, T., Jovanović, O., & Pavlović Babić, D. (2016). Individual education plan as an agent of inclusiveness of the educational system in Serbia: Different perspectives, achievements and new dilemmas. *Psihologija, 49*(4), 431–445. doi:10.2298/PSI1604431K

Kovač Cerović, T., Lakićević, A., Cenerić, I., Vainalanen, R., & Mladenović, S. (2013). *Policy impact analysis: Providing additional support to students from vulnerable groups in pre-university education*. Belgrade: UNICEF Serbia.

Kovač Cerović, T., & Lukšić Orlandić, T. (2016). *Prevencija segregacije, razvoj inkluzivnih upisnih politika i desegregacija škola i odeljenja: Međunarodna iskustva i preporuke za praksu u Srbiji* [Prevention of segregation in education, development of inclusive school enrolment policies and desegregation of schools and classes: International experiences and recommendations for Serbia]. Beograd: Kancelarija Poverenika za ravnopravnost.

Kovač Cerović, T., Pavlović Babić, D., Jokić, T., Jovanović, O., & Jovanović, V. (2016). First comprehensive monitoring of inclusive education in Serbia: Selected findings. In N. Gutvajn & M. Vujačić (Eds.), *Challenges and perspectives of inclusive education* (pp. 15–29). Belgrade: Institute for Educational Research.

Kovač Cerović, T., Vizek-Vidović, V., & Powell, S. (2010). *School governance and social inclusion: Parent participation in life of schools in Southeast Europe*. Ljubljana: Center for Education Policy Studies, Faculty of Education.

Kovacs-Cerović, T., & Vulic, I. (2016). *Supporting education of refugee and migrant children and youth* (Working Paper Series No. 76). New York, NY: ESP.

Leutwyler, B., Petrović, D. S., & Jokić, T. (2018). The structure of teacher-specific intercultural competence: Empirical evidence on the 'Beliefs, Values, and Goals' dimension. *Psihologija, 51*(1), 107–126.

Matthews, J. (2008). Schooling and settlement: Refugee education in Australia. *International Studies in Sociology of Education, 18*(1), 31–45.

Mikuš Kos, A., & Huzejrović, V. (2003). Volunteers as helpers in war-related distress. *Intervention, 1*(2), 50–56.

Neftçi, N. B., & Çetrez, Ö. A. (2017). Resilience and mental health risks among Syrian refugees in Europe: A cultural perspective. *Acta Psychopathologica, 3*(5), 65.

NESSE. (2008). *Education and migration: Strategies for integrating migrant children in European schools and societies: A synthesis of research findings for policy-makers*. Brussels: European Commission.

Nusche, D. (2009). *What works in migrant education? A review of evidence and policy options* (OECD Education Working Papers No. 22). Paris: OECD Publishing. Retrieved from http://dx.doi.org/10.1787/227131784531

OECD. (2015a). *Education policy outlook 2015: Making reforms happen*. Paris: OECD Publishing. Retrieved from http://dx.doi.org/10.1787/9789264225442-en

OECD. (2015b). *Immigrant students at school: Easing the journey towards integration*. Paris: OECD Publishing. Retrieved from http://dx.doi.org/10.1787/9789264249509-en

OECD. (2015c). *Indicators of immigrant integration 2015.* Paris: OECD Publishing. Retrieved from http://dx.doi.org/10.1787/9789264234024-en

OECD. (2016). *Low-performing students: Why they fall behind and how to help them succeed.* Paris: OECD Publishing. Retrieved from http://dx.doi.org/10.1787/9789264250246-en

Panayotova, D., & Evgeniev, E. (2002). *Successful Romani school desegregation: The Vidin case.* Retrieved December 21, 2016, from http://www.errc.org/article/successful-romani-school-desegregation-the-vidin-case/1630

Patton, M. Q. (1990). *Qualitative evaluation and research methods.* London: Sage Publications.

Pavlović Babić, D., Simić, N., & Friedman, E. (2017). School-level facilitators of inclusive education: The case of Serbia. *European Journal of Special Needs Education,* 1–17. doi:10.1080/08856257.2017.1342419

Perry, L. B., & Southwell, L. (2011). Developing intercultural understanding and skills: Models and approaches. *Intercultural Education, 22*(6), 453–466.

Petrović, D. S., Jokić, T., & Leutwyer, B. (2016). Motivational aspects of teachers' intercultural competence: Development and psychometric evaluation of new scales for the assessment of motivational orientation. *Psihologija, 49*(4), 393–413.

Pinson, H., & Arnot, M. (2007). Sociology of education and the wasteland of refugee education research. *British Journal of Sociology of Education, 28*(3), 399–407.

Popadić, D. (2009). *Nasilje u školama.* Beograd: Institu za psihologiju.

Popadic, D., & Plut, D. (2007) Nasilje u osnovnim školama u srbiji – oblici i učestalost. *Psihologija, 40*(2), 309–328.

Rangvid, B. S. (2007). *School chioce, universal vouchers and native flight out of local public schools* (Working Paper No. 2007:3). Copenhagen: AKF, Danish Institute of Governmental Research.

Roma Education Fund. (2015). *Making desegregation work.* Retrieved July 3, 2017, from http://www.romaeducationfund.org/sites/default/files/publications/desegregation_toolkit__2015_web.pdf

Rosenthal, R., & Jacobson, L. F. (1968). Teacher expectations for the disadvantaged. *Scientific American, 218*(4), 19–23.

Rostas, I. (Ed.). (2012). *Ten years after: A history of Roma school desegregation in Central and Eastern Europe.* Budapest: Central European University Press.

Rostas, I., & Kostka, J. (2014). Structural dimensions of Roma school desegregation policies in Central Europe. *European Educational Research Journal, 13*(3), 268–281.

Rutter, J. (2006). *Refugee children in the UK.* London: McGraw-Hill Education.

UNHCR. (2015). *Education: Issue brief* (pp. 1–6). Geneva: UNHCR.

Vlajković, J., Srna, J., Kondić, K., & Popović, M. (2000). *Psihologija izbegliištva* [Psychology of refugee status]. Beograd: IP Žarko Albulj.

Vukčević, M., Dobrić, J., & Purić, D. (2014). *Study of the mental health of asylum seekers in Serbia.* Belgrade: UNHCR.

Vukčević Marković, M., Gašić, J., & Bjekić, J. (2017). *Refugees' mental health – 2017 research report.* Belgrade: UNHCR, PIN.

Vukčević Marković, M., Gašić, J., Ilić, I., & Bjekić, J. (2017). *Challenges and potentials of refugee chidren – 2017 data overview.* Belgrade: UNHCR, PIN.

Willig, C. (2008). *Introducing qualitative research in psychology.* Berkshire: Open University Press.

Zlatković, B., Petrović, D., Erić, M., Leutwyler, B., & Jokić, T. (2017). Self-regulatory dimension of teachers' intercultural competence: Development and psychometric evaluation of new scales. *Psihološka istraživanja, 20*(2), 199–200.

Tünde Kovacs Cerović
Department of Psychology, Faculty of Philosophy
University of Belgrade
Serbia

Sanja Grbić
Institute for Educational Research
University of Belgrade
Serbia

Dragan Vesić
Institute for Educational Research
Belgrade
Serbia

LAURE KLOETZER, MIKI ARISTORENAS AND
OULA ABU-AMSHA

5. "MY COURSE, MY LIFELINE!"

*Reconnecting Syrian Refugees to Higher
Education in the Za'atari Camp*

INTRODUCTION

Forced displacement reached an unprecedented level in 2014 – the highest since World War II. By the end of 2015, 65.3 million people were forcibly displaced as a result of persecution, conflict, generalised violence, or human rights violations (UNHCR, 2016a). In regards to higher education, while there has been no rigorous research thus far on the number of refugee students desiring and succeeding access to higher education programs, UNHCR estimates globally only 1% of refugee youth are able to access higher education (UNHCR, 2014). This translates to only 195,000 students accessing university although around 7.2 million refugee children and youth complete secondary education. This is especially problematic when considering the high levels of demand for Higher Education among refugee students. Displaced students are increasingly coming from countries with historically high enrolment rates. In pre-war Syria specifically, the university-level participation was 26% in urban areas and 16% in rural areas compared to 2015 where fewer than 6% were enrolled in higher education programmes with significant discrepancies between potential and actual enrolment statistics for Syrian students in Turkey, Lebanon and Jordan (UNHCR, 2015a). Of the more than four million Syrian refugees in the Middle East and North Africa, 450,000 are 18–22 years old and, based on pre-war enrolment rates, 90,000–110,000 are qualified for university as estimated by the Institute of International Education (IIE).

In this chapter, we will first discuss Higher Education (HE) for refugees, according to the existing literature. This overview will focus on aspirations of students, barriers to Higher Education, and coping strategies of students to overcome them. We will then present the Jamiya project and how it attempts to provide some Higher Education opportunities for Arabic-speaking students in the Za'atari Camp through a pilot IT (Programming in Java) program jointly run with Göteburg University. Jamiya's concept is to reconnect displaced Higher Education networks in order to fill the gap in provision. Along with displaced academics, Jamiya Project reconnects students with international universities, local NGOs in the Middle East and educational-technologists to provide blended and accredited university courses

© KONINKLIJKE BRILL NV, LEIDEN, 2018 | DOI:10.1163/9789004383227_005

with adapted language support. The Jamiya project has been running in Jordan, in the Za'atari camp and in Amman, in 2016.

From the very beginning, Jamiya has been designed as an education project and not as a research project. Therefore, it has been driven by concrete goals of providing HE within the camp. However, Jamiya's team engaged early on in a reflexive process of analysis of what was going on and how to improve the program. Following this reflexive track, we collected data, including interviews with participants, focus groups and online (WhatsApp) discussions. This data collection does not follow a rigorous research design, but it follows field opportunities, and the steps of the project design, implementation and evaluation. From the 35 initially enrolled students, 10 successfully graduated. This chapter will provide an analysis of some of the data collected in order to understand (a) students' aspirations with regards to HE, (b) barriers to HE in the camp, as expressed by the students themselves, and (c) emergent coping strategies to overcome these barriers, thanks to a dialogical analysis of data collected in the course of the project (focus group and interviews). Based on our understanding of the students' aspirations, barriers and emergent coping strategies identified in everyday interactions and follow-up interviews, we will finally discuss consequences for this kind of delicate and promising blended learning HE projects.

WAR ON HIGHER EDUCATION

While forcibly displaced populations are usually split into six main groups (camp-based refugees, urban refugees, internally displaced persons, asylum seekers, returnees, resettled refugees), we will focus on camp-based refugees in relevance to the education intervention to be discussed in this chapter. One third of the global refugee population is estimated to be living in camps, with Za'atari Camp in Jordan being one of the newest and fastest growing camps in the world. Za'atari Camp received 5000 new refugees each week in mid-2015.

The right to education and its interrelation with other human rights have been progressively established in humanitarian discourse, especially through the worldwide movement for *Education for All* (initiated in Jomtien in 1990 and reiterated in Dakar in 2000). Education is recognized as a priority in the rhetorics of the international community, as demonstrated by the goals set by the HCR: "By 2030, ensure that all girls and boys complete free, equitable and quality primary and secondary education leading to relevant and effective learning outcomes". In this view, education serves wide goals to protect the kids, guarantee their well-being and prepare their future. Among the recently defined Sustainable Development Goals defined by UNO, the fourth one is related to education: "Ensure inclusive and equitable quality education and promote lifelong learning opportunities for all". The presentation of this SDG reaffirms that education is a public good, a fundamental human right and a basis for guaranteeing full participation to social life and the realization of other rights. Despite this worlwide recognition, a close look at humanitarian action shows that agencies prioritize expenditure on food, water, shelter and health (Crea, 2016), and that funding promises are not fully transformed into efficient education resources. The issue of Higher Education specifically has been largely unaddressed in policy and scholarship (Dryden-Peterson & Giles, 2010), being the least prioritised by UNHCR in 2015 spending (UNHCR, 2015b). The international community is also realizing that within this context of uncertainty, long-term displacement and knowledge-based economies, a portable and adaptable university-level education is critical (Dryden-Peterson, 2010).

Consistent arguments towards providing a strong HE system include that (1) access to higher education provides strong incentives for students to complete studies at primary and secondary levels (Gladwell & Tanner, 2013; Robinson, 2011); (2) providing a 'university student identity' contributes significantly to the protection of older youth mitigating their risk of being drawn to violent or sectarian ideologies (Hart, 2008; Barakat et al., 2015); (3) HE increases professional opportunities and gender equity, as highlighted by El Jack (2012): "it enables refugees, particularly women, to gain knowledge, voice, and skills which will give them access to better employment opportunities and earnings and thus enhance their equality and independence" (El Jack, 2012, p. 19); and (4) higher education develops the human and social capital necessary for future reconstruction and economic development in refugee students' home countries (UNHCR, 2017; Barakat et al., 2015; Lorisika et al., 2015).

However, especially in refugee camps, engagement of public agencies with HE faces both practical challenges (more urgent needs have to be addressed first, like water, food, basic health, shelter, and primary education) and political challenges. As discussed by Laura-Ashley Wright and Robyn Plasterer in their studies of Higher Education in Kenyan Refugee Camps, "by failing to recognize the protracted nature of refugee situations in order to maintain this narrative of temporariness, donors restrict themselves from providing opportunities for learning and skills development beyond primary and secondary education" (2012). Barbara Zeus (2011) in studying encamped Burmese refugees in Thailand highlights three barriers to Higher Education prioritization for refugees: (1) Higher Education institutions are regarded as long-term operations whereas refugee camps are viewed as temporary, despite the fact that several have existed for multiple decades, (2) Higher Education is presumed as a part of a nation-state whereas refugees are 'nation-stateless' and (3) the trauma of war and conflict resulting in refugee dependence on external aid appears incompatible with the capability to cope with the challenges of Higher Education.

While there is limited research on refugee Higher Education, a general lack of Higher Education places in immediate host countries is clear (Lorisika et al., 2015). With needs of this magnitude, international scholar programs alone fail to meet the demand with applications exceeding available places by ratios of around 100:1 in most cases (Al-Fanar Media, 2015). A number of initiatives have emerged over the last decade ranging from small camp-based and host-community programs to large, theoretically unrestricted online learning platforms. As devising a universally applicable model is impossible given the unique contextual elements and changing populations and environments (CRS, 2010), the providers of refugee Higher Education fall into five categories according to a landscape review by Jigsaw Consult (2016): (1) physical presence among affected populations; (2) host community scholarship programs; (3) international scholarship programs; (4) online learning platforms; and (5) information sharing platforms.

In scientific literature, refugee students' barriers to education are primarily linked to restricted access to universities, a multidimensional reality mainly due to:

1. Cost. Unless participating in a program specifically designed for refugees or with fee reductions, refugee students are typically charged international student fees without government support (Watenpaugh et al., 2013; Refugee Support Network, 2011). Additionally the cost of living in Jordan, which is already higher than that in Syria, continues to rise (Watenpaugh et al., 2013).
2. Lack of documentation. It becomes nearly impossible for refugee students to enter foreign universities without the necessary paperwork and credentials. Lost exam certificates, academic transcripts, lack of recognition and identity or nationality requirements have resulting in students making life-threatening journeys back to their home countries (Dryden-Peterson & Giles, 2010; BHER, 2010; Lorisika et al., 2015).
3. Lack of available information on potential opportunities (Lorisika et al., 2015). This is exacerbated in urban areas where refugees are dispersed without central information points or communication portals and where there is an evident lack of coordination between providers (Dryden-Peterson & Giles, 2010).
4. Diverse schooling systems. In Jordan specifically, the focal country of this paper's research, Syrian students face compatibility constraints between degree programs with Jordanian Higher Education following the American model and the Syrian educational system following the French.
5. Language issues. Written and spoken English is often required and expensive and time-consuming to obtain (British Council, 2015).
6. Lack of available places. Some universities may give priority to their own national students.
7. Distance and/or restricted freedom of movement. Freedom of movement is also restricted for refugees living in camps, who are forced to stay in the camp, therefore unable to access local HE.

However, another barrier, which would deserve further investigation, is disruption. Without preparatory courses, successfully completing university-level programs in host countries is challenging even for those 'higher-education ready' students (Dippo et al., 2012; UNESCO, 2015).

Despite evident barriers to Higher Education, the few studies on Refugees Higher Education have presented interesting findings on student attitudes similarly reflected in this chapter. Returning to the research within Kenyan refugee camps, Wright and Plasterer (2012) found that refugees shared frustrations of conflict having disrupted their education and of the lack of transition opportunities for those who wished to re-enter schooling. As a result, these refugees described feeling idle and forgotten by the international community.

In terms of the importance of education to refugees, Jacqueline Stevenson and John Willott (2007) looked at those resettled in the United Kingdom and found that though their interviewees were apprehensive about entering the Higher Education environment due to fear of feeling isolated and finding teaching methods, reflective practices and participatory learning styles to be too difficult, "all of the individuals interviewed spoke about their high aspiration for themselves and their desire to use higher education as a route out of poverty and exclusion and as a means of establishing a better and more secure way of life for themselves" (p. 676).

Lastly, in an interesting study on refugee youth in Toronto, these aspirations are put into action when the authors find refugee youth persistently and resiliently employing tactical strategies to address common barriers and pursue educational goals. These strategies include seeking help and support from friends, seeking help from education-focused newcomer services, and asking questions from all available sources (Shakya et al., 2012).

THE JAMIYA PROJECT

The Jamiya Project is a UK-based organization, working on a model to deliver relevant and accessible education to refugees and asylum seekers. Jamiya Project's current focus is on Higher Education for Arabic-speaking refugees, having delivered its pilot course in Za'atari Camp and Amman, Jordan. The concept behind the project is to reconnect displaced higher education networks in order to fill the gap in provision. Realizing the potential of the Syrian higher education network that has been dispersed, displaced and disconnected with several thousand Syrian academics who have left the country, Jamiya aims to unlock the capacity, knowledge and skills of these academics to open up higher education opportunities for refugees. Along with Syrian academics, Jamiya Project reconnects students with international universities, local NGOs in the Middle East and educational-technologists to provide blended and accredited university courses with adapted language support.

The pilot course has been running in both Amman and Za'atari Refugee Camp from September 2016 to January 2017. The pilot course was a Bachelor course in Information Technologies called *Introduction to Programming in Java*, it was free and run in collaboration with the University of Gothenburg. It was developed by a team of Syrian and Swedish academics who worked to adapt material from an existing course at the University of Gothenburg for the local context and translate the material into Arabic so that it would be accessible to students.

Syrian nationals and Syrian Palestinians with Asylum Seeker status under UNHCR protection based in Amman or Za'atari Refugee Camp were eligible to apply through an online application form where they uploaded copies of any type of ID, proof of high school completion or former university studies in Syria and a minimal requirement of computer literacy.

The course was delivered in a 'blended-learning format' meaning online study was complemented with face-to-face lectures, seminars and group work. There is an increasing trend for blended learning, as recognized in Jigsaw Consult's landscape review, as the approach offers refugees who are not in a position to study outside their communities an opportunity to access high-quality international programs while being part of and supported by a local student community (Ferede, 2016). The online course content was primarily hosted on the Arabic Mooc platform Edraak (Queen Rania Foundation) and delivered using a combination of videos and screencasting lectures, required and supplementary reading material, exercises, individual assignments and a moderated discussion board. Displaced Syrian academics from Jamiya Project's network led the course remotely and also acted as mentors over WhatsApp and Skype to students through Jamiya Project's mentorship program. The face-to-face components were facilitated by local tutors at the NGO centres hosted by Jesuit Refugee Service in Amman and Norwegian Refugee Council in Za'atari Camp. There were initially two weekly sessions, increased to three after the first month, and aimed at helping students navigate the course and troubleshoot problems along with two block seminars lasting two full days each where students received lectures and engaged in classroom group work led by course professors.

Assessment was performed through online quizzes, individual assignments and a final exam, the course was graded on a scale of: Pass with Distinction (VG), Pass (G) and Fail (U). Students who successfully completed the course received a certificate from the University of Gothenburg stating that the course is the equivalent of 7.5 credits under the European Credit Transfer and Accumulation Scheme (ECTS).

From the 35 initially enrolled students, 10 successfully graduated. At the end of the course, Jamiya Project gathered 46 Syrian academics willing to contribute as mentors and matched 19 mentors with 22 students.

The Jamiya Project is first and foremost an education intervention and not a research project, with action-orientation taking precedence over research. Because Jamiya Project was not formed with research being the primary objective of the organization, data throughout the course was collected in an ad-hoc manner for the purpose of efficiently and continuously improving the impact of the model's delivery. That being said, members of the Jamiya team were strongly engaged in a design-based reflection process, and qualitative data were collected at key points throughout the intervention: beginning, middle and final course evaluations. Subsequently, numerous qualitative pieces of data (including three focus groups, 8 long interviews, short video interviews, and WhatsApp discussions) were collected and gathered into one central location where it could then be transcribed and translated for the purpose of analysis. The two goals with analysing relevant themes, or student gaps and needs, were to inform future Jamiya's interventions, and to contribute to the knowledge and information in the field of refugee Higher Education more broadly.

HIGHER EDUCATION IN THE CAMP IN THE EYES OF THE REFUGEE
STUDENTS: A DIALOGICAL ANALYSIS

The focus of our analysis in this chapter is on one focus group conducted in October 2016, one month into the *Introduction to Applied IT Java Course*. The focus group is lead by Jamiya Project's founder, Ben Webster, at the Norwegian Refugee Council (NRC) learning centre in Za'atari Camp, with the help of a local translator who is an employee at NRC. The participants of the focus group are three students who shall be referred to as S1, S2 and S3. The focus group has been recorded, transcribed, and fully translated. In this focus group, we will analyse the subjective experience of the students regarding the course, the barriers to study, and their coping strategies, as it is displayed in the discussion.

Focus Groups are linguistic data, and as such they allow for and require a close analysis of speech. They are also specific linguistic data with a strong social dimension, in which speech circulates among a number of subjects according to both the logic of their internal thinking, and the logic of conversation, shared assumptions, and collective construction of knowledge. As highlighted by Markova, Linell, Grossen, and Salaza-Orvig (2007), in focus groups, "participants think together and talk together and are stimulated in their thinking when listening to other people's ideas. It is as if the 'strange perspectives' of others (Bakhtin, 1986) stimulate individuals to mobilise their own potentials to develop new insights and associations, and recall those which they have encountered on previous occasions. Therefore the analysis of focus group data requires dialogical methodologies, in which utterances should not be analysed as static expressions of thinking, but dynamically, as ways by which participants perform an "active responsive understanding" (Volosinov, 2000) of on-going implicit and explicit conversations. In this view, focus groups are "socially situated interactions" (Markova et al., 2007), in which "meanings and contents of the participants' communicative interactions derive their significance from situations in which they take place as well as from many related and socially relevant phenomena" (p. 45). The analysis therefore aims to look at the focus group interaction as a web of interdependent sense-making and sense-creating in a socio-cultural space instead of a series of juxtaposed individual contributions (Markova et al., 2007). It seeks to understand the circulation of ideas – specifically how ideas are introduced, re-worked and developed and the resulting sequence of ideas between the three students, the researcher, and the translator taking into account that each individual is bringing his or her own experience and background which manifests itself in their language and arguments. To account for these social dynamics of dialogue in the focus group situation, we build on analytical tools, especially analysis of multivoicedness and the multivoiced Self, as described by Emma-Louise Aveling, Alex Gillespie and Flora Cornish (2015). Their three-step method comprises (1) identifying the voices of I-positions within the Self's talk, (2) identifying the voices of inner-others within the speaker's discourse, or voices attributed to others as direct or indirect quotes or even echoes, and (3) examining the dialogue and relationship between these voices (Aveling et al., 2015).

The Focus Group is also situated within the larger context of the everyday life of the camp, including its most concrete material, economical and political aspects, refracted through the individual subjectivities and activities of the participants, as it will soon become clear through the analysis. To take these dimensions into account, we follow Vygotsky's cultural-historical psychology on the relationship of thinking and speech. According to Vygotsky, "the structure of speech is not the simple reflection, as in a mirror, of that of thinking. So speech cannot put on thinking as a confection dress. It does not serve as an expression to a ready thought. By transforming itself into speech, thinking is reorganized and modified. It does not express itself but is realized in the word" (Vygotsky, 2013, p. 431). In the situation of the focus group, which takes place on a significant topic for them, and in a significant context (on the course, in the camp), the participants are not passively answering questions of the researcher, but they pursue their own activities as students and refugees, as the analysis will demonstrate. What they say cannot fully be understood without some analysis of what they do (or try to do) in this situation. Therefore, our analysis will also consider utterances as speech acts (Austin, 1962), in the pragmatist tradition, and follow the activity of the participants in the focus group. Speech here is conceived as a human activity and dialogue as a joint activity, through which conversational partners may pursue different goals and activities. Speech turns are simultaneously speech acts, but they cannot be analysed in isolation, as if they would bring independent topics or actions into the discussion and social space; they must be analysed in the process of development of the conversation, step by step, with meanings which might differ as the discussion proceeds, and in connection with the subjective activity of the people acting in and through dialogue in this situation (Kloetzer, 2008; Kostulski, 2011).

Camp Education in the Eyes of Refugee Students: A Multivoicedness Analysis

The two following tabs display an analysis of I-positions (Table 5.1) as well as Inner-Other voices (Table 5.2) expressed in the focus group.

Our first analysis, based on analysis of multivoicedness in the dialogue (Aveling et al., 2015) offers a subjective representation by the students of their situation and education, which can be represented as students in relation to their participation to Jamiya course, their work as "volunteer employees" in local NGOs, the camp situation, and the international community. It highlights the multiple I-positions of the students, and how the students relate to different Inner-Other voices, in the following way:

In relation to their education in the camp and in the Jamiya program, the students display a number of heterogeneous internal voices. They speak as human-beings, as Syrian citizens, as NGO employees, as students of Jamiya Project's Applied IT course, and as young adults in a refugee camp setting. The students present themselves as individuals with interests and "high aspirations" in connection to

Table 5.1. Analysis of I-positions in the focus group discussion

I-positions	Characteristics	Illustrative quotes
I (We) as NGO employee(s) enrolled in course	Bitter, constrained to the strict regulations of NGO employment and pressure, a barrier to study both directly (time) and indirectly, causing exhaustion	"My work lasts until 3 pm, and the time of the course is between 12 and 3, which means that I have to get permission for 3 hours… and deducing these three hours leaves me with only 3 work hours a day, it is as if I did not go to work and this means that I will have black points in my work in terms of attendance… My employers will tell me: you do not keep up… or you get a lot of leave permissions…" "Sometimes one of us comes to the session after his work, he is tired… we are considered as volunteer employees so we do not have any rights or incentives, and we are not easily allowed to leave work early" "At my work… everyday, I wait for my director to leave and I "sneak" to the course"
I (We) as student(s) in Jamiya course	A balanced view: positive but challenging	"We enjoy that we have an atmosphere allowing us to make friends… but we hope that the method of teaching by the doctors can be better at the right level" "I wish the course is more simplified… or in two stages for example… the course requires that we study hard as we've been told, and here the situation of the camp does not allow to study the quantity required from us" "It has been 6–7 years that we have interrupted studies, it is difficult to complete… I mean at this high level. One should have a high pace to continue" "We suddenly interrupted our studies, and we got back to study suddenly" "We have the will… we have a chance from nothing. Our studies were interrupted and we had a chance, which is our only hope. We are very eager to create and produce but the circumstances do not help… now this course is our only hope and we want to create something in it" "I do not have a computer in the house to applied what I learned" "There is another matter, for example, the professor gives us a homework and we have a full day to solve it… but the problem is that you go home there is no computer… sometimes you come to the course late because of the work, for example you arrive at 2 o'clock, you cannot follow on…" "I mean it at home you do not study because there are no devices… you can only read the theoretical (material) without application"

(Continued)

Table 5.1. Analysis of I-positions in the focus group discussion (Cont.)

I-positions	Characteristics	Illustrative quotes
		"Like my colleague has said, one should make an effort, but (suppose) you want to go home and study, but you don't have the right settings, as we said you do not have a computer, electricity or internet"
		"When I was at the institute I studied Java and C++ but it was very simple, but here I felt that I did not know anything…"
I (We) as university-age individuals in a refugee camp	Dark with a situation inhibiting their ability to study or achieve their larger aspirations, but full of hope for HE	"We have a lot of free time in the camp…we are in the situation of an emergency camp and people in this situation need more incentives to study… I hope that our study does not go down in vain… we hope to have more opportunities through this course"
		"We rely a lot on this program… we rely on it to open the way for us to complete university studies, but without your help and without no one supporting us, we will not get what we want… especially as we are in the position of the whole world knows it"
		"As for me I count on this session to give me the possibility to find a job in the future… or make me perhaps pursue my studies… but given the situation here… how can I complete my studies without being supported by anyone… especially I am in such a situation and within the Za'atari camp?"
		"We are trapped within a circle all failed… this is a real reality. We must succeed in this session"
		"I have been waiting for my future for 3 years and a half, I am waiting for the first step of my future since I came to the camp…"
I (We) as Syrians	Suspended lives, between the "damn war" and reconstruction	"If we return to Syria, we will be busy with reconstruction and the situation… as you know the situation in Syria… none of us will have time to pursue his studies"
		"Because of the damn war, we went out, and I could not pursue my studies. We left Syria and came to Jordan and this ended my chance to study. I have had some hope that made me apply for a scholarship in Egypt and I got a scholarship to study human medicine at the University of Ain. I did not have a chance to go to Syria. But due to financial constraints I could not go to Egypt"
I (We) as a human being	Like everyone else, has interests and has to try hard	"Tell him that we are people with high aspirations and hopes"
		"I was dreaming that I was study informatics… I want to study informatics – anything that concerns the computer, especially hacking programs…"

Table 5.2. Analysis of inner-other voices in the focus group discussion

Inner-Other Voices	Characteristics	Illustrative Quotes
NGOs (employers)	Dictatorial	"they do not allow you to leave the workspace"
The course	Omnipotent messiah figure	"the course came to satisfy my desire… and to increase my skills in electronics… allowing us to make friends… we have a lot of free time and the course allows us to fill it"
		"we rely on it to open the way for us to complete university studies"
		"I would say this course is like First Aid"
		"the course requires that we study hard as we've been told, and here the situation of the camp does not allow to study the quantity required from us"
The (camp) situation	Black hole	"the environment in general does not allow… small caravans (the houses), there is (always) noise… young children (meaning: children at home making noise)"
		"As I told you, within the settings of the Za'atari camp, and we all know what it is, it is an emergency camp, this is impossible to happen without help"
		"the professor asked you to make a HW and you are willing to solve it. You want to solve it and eager to produce something… but the problem is that you go home and write on paper, but the paper doesn't return any result"
The international community	Presence with the power to help but not necessarily doing so	"without your help and without no one supporting us, we will not get what we want… especially as we are in the position of the whole world knows it"
		"the help of the donors…the help from the university… help us to make our way to study at the university"
		"how can I complete my studies without being supported by anyone… especially I am in such a situation and within the Za'atari camp?"
The other Syrian refugees (incl. potential students)	Argument to continue with the program	"people in this (camp) situation need more incentives to study…they need something to encourage to that…"
		"Consider us as a (first) experience, but try to give an opportunity to others or (even) let us retake it if we fail"
Current course "doctors"	Too complex	"the explanations of the doctors that are very very high level and the density"

(Continued)

Table 5.2. Analysis of inner-other voices in the focus group discussion (Cont.)

Inner-Other Voices	Characteristics	Illustrative Quotes
The local IT mentor	Very relevant and helpful	"Mr. H. says 2 words explains to us a bit we fully understand" "Without H. we could since long close the computer and leave (laughs)" "Mr. H. is an essential reason for the success of the course… one or two words from him and we understand all what is said" "If we succeed – god willing – I am talking about myself – I want to offer my success to Professor H. because he really helped us"

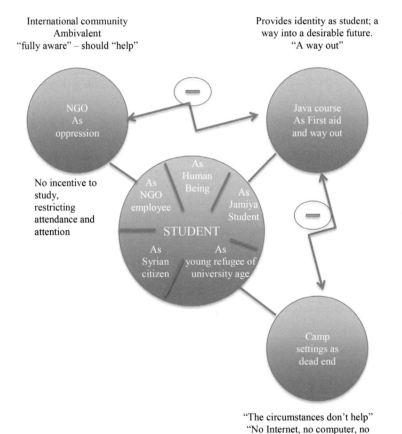

Figure 5.1. Overview of the dialogical analysis of multivoicedness multiple I-positions

humanity by describing interests and passions and hopes as any person may possess, such as a knack for computer hacking. As Syrians, the students refer to their previous residence nondescriptly and mainly as a predominantly in causing tension with current educational pursuits, the war that prevented study university completion, and the hypothetical inability to study due to reconstruction once they return, if they return. In identifying as students of the Applied IT course, they provide a balanced perspective yielding both positive feedback on the course along with course-specific challenges mainly around content-level and practical working conditions (no Internet, no computer, working hours). Because students are aware this focus group was conducted for the purpose of evaluating Jamiya's course and because they are conversing directly with somebody whom they identify as the course provider, this balanced view is to be expected and is discussed deliberately and methodologically by the students as evidenced at the beginning of the focus group when one student attempts to give positive comments in order to compensate for the negative comments that had been previously discussed in this unsolicited comment: "Most of us talk about negative aspects... but there is also something much much more positive than negative aspects... the negative ones may be very light...". Lastly, the perspective drawn from most often is that of a university-age camp refugee. When students speak about themselves from this perspective, there is a melancholic pessimism whereby students refer to their helpless state and hopeless situation unequivocally inhibiting their ability to study or achieve larger aspirations. Consider this excerpt from one student: "I have been waiting for my future for three years and a half, I am waiting for the first step of my future since I came to the camp...". This student is describing a feeling of stagnancy and entrapment compounded by prevention of study as a refugee student in the camp.

NGOs as Restrictive Employers

The intrusion of the NGO employer's voice in student discourse is striking. The three students participate to the course in parallel to their working life as "volunteer employees". They all work "for a symbolic amount of money" either in NGOs or in community-driven associations (here, at the Mosquee), all of them with children (in relation to health or education of children). The timing of the IT course was constrained by Za'atari's situation, with inflexible opening hours of the host learning centres, due to both safety reasons, and to the fact that the employees of the learning centre live far away from the camp. Therefore, there is a time conflict between working hours and participation to the course. In the focus group, first, we see the internal voices of the students identifying themselves as and speaking from the position of NGO employees or, in some cases, NGO volunteers. The tone of the students is indisputably bitter, constrained by the strict regulations of NGO employment. This resentful tone is illustrated in the narrative of one student, "sometimes one of us comes to the session after his work tired... we are considered as volunteer employees so we do not have any rights or incentives, and

125

we are not easily allowed to leave work early". The pressure of their engagement with NGOs ultimately poses a barrier to studies both directly in conflicting with course provision time and indirectly in causing exhaustion not conducive to study. The restriction of students' employment is heard early on in the discourse in the following excerpt: "they do not allow you to leave the workspace… my employers will tell me: 'you do not keep up'… or 'you get a lot of leave permissions". Here, his employers, local NGOs he refers to later in the dialogue, are directly quoted as reprimanding and pressuring students to not take any absences from work. The result of this interaction is predominantly oppression as students within the focus group and referenced peers are prohibited from engaging fully and freely with the course due to employment pressures. There are some instances when the students exhibit a form of resistance to this oppression, a student at one point mentions waiting for employers to leave and subsequently "sneaking" out of work. Regardless, the voice of the NGO as employers never takes on a flexible or forgiving tone.

The Za'atari Camp as a Deadend, Hopeless and Failure Situation

Participation to the course also strongly conflicts with the settings of the Za'atari camp. The circumstances of Za'atari Camp – often referred to as "the situation" resemble a dead end, preventing the students from fulfilling their studies. Consider one student's narrative: "as I told you, within the settings of the Za'atari camp, and we all know what it is, it is an emergency camp, [study] is impossible to happen without help". Students present details about the practical impediments only when the translator suggests that the researcher may be unaware of some aspects of their situation. They then explain what is lacking to study, place, time, calm, computers, Internet, and what they call "incentives" (we hypothesize that they refer to future opportunities that would support their active engagement with the content of the course despite their difficult material situation). But usually, students re-emphasize the idea of the camp as a dead end to the audience, assuming that everyone is well aware of how oppressive the settings of the Za'atari camp are, and concluding that these settings are preventing them from studying on their own.

The Course as "First Aid" and Lifeline

The course, as it appears in student narratives, embodies a chance, a reason to reconnect to HE and complete university studies, a "hope or reason to allow us to study again", a "reason to have one's brain work again", but above all, it is conceived as a "way out" of a hopeless situation. It is compared to "first aid" and can be best described as a lifeline, having impact of the participants' identity as students, and opening a potential future, especially because it is delivered from outside the camp, from a Swedish university, therefore allowing for outside the camp and international connection and recognition.

The International Community as an Ambivalent Reality, between Fear of Abandonment and Wish for Help

There is an inner-other voice found continuously throughout the students' dialogue that can be broadly characterised as the international community, whose help the students are seeking, which in one instance is identified as "donors" or "universities" by one student. The researcher is also often included in this category when students directly address him asking for his support or for his continued delivery of the course. This inner-other voice of the broader international community appears to be fully aware of the refugee camp situation, often with the capacity to remove or at least alleviate their hardship, as perceived by the students, but seems not to be acting on this awareness. Consider students' call to the researcher: "without your help and without no one supporting us, we will not get what we want... especially as we are in the position of the whole world knows it". As the students continuously called for the help of these "others", it is clear that though the international community is not resisting the pleas of the students, it appears to be ambivalent. Because this conversation involves three students of an education intervention at Za'atari Refugee Camp in direct dialogue with the perceived provider of this educational opportunity what's important to note is the powerful intention and deliberation behind the students' messaging. Their message to the researcher, perceiving him to be one of these "others" with the resources to help them, is strategically crafted and political in nature entrenched in emotional pleas. Despite the researcher's attempts to separate himself from the university or funders throughout the discourse, the students address him directly in association with this international community, making their position clear that this course and this educational opportunity must continue as evidenced by one student direct request to the researcher, "we hope you do not abandon us". This focus groups takes place at the beginning of the Jamiya program, and the mere fact that the students' emphasis on the continuity of the course is unmistakable this early on in the intervention and ceaselessly integrated within a dialogue is extremely striking.

How Refugee Students Try or Fail to Overcome Barriers to HE in Camp

Complementing this dialogical analysis of the voices present within the focus group and their relations, we can identify in the content of the focus group barriers to effective study expressed by the students, as well as emerging coping strategies.

Barriers

It is important to note the barriers to education students discuss in their discourse especially in light and in comparison to common literature regarding challenges in refugee education. While the course, as education delivery in this context is most often perceived, provides a necessary social atmosphere and topics in line with

127

students' interests and skills, there are contextual barriers Jamiya Project's students faced. As often cited in the existing, though limited research, the material constraints including lack of internet access, lack of electricity, and lack of devices (computers) are clearly problematic for any education delivery with an online component. The crowded and noisy camp environment not conducive to study does not facilitate the independent study culture required for academic preparation outside the classroom. And, crucially, the gap and interruption in education and studies, without preparatory course, leaves the students with difficulties in content and general course manageability with which they struggle to cope. Additionally, time and its dimensions and implications in a camp setting are important to consider: the lack of material resources result in "wasted time" when students are unable to apply programming assignments effectively at home, and inflexible time caused by employer-driven hours directly affect course attendance, accessibility and psychological state when attempting to study.

Coping Strategies

Upon further investigation of the above barriers students faced throughout the delivery of Jamiya Project's Applied IT course, project members discovered a series of coping strategies students utilized in order to allow them to re-engage with their higher education especially following this gap of up to seven years since the last time they were involved in some sort of study. We were also led to look at where and how students were engaged with learning outside of the classroom since provided platforms like Edraak were not being used.

Following a workshop of Jamiya Project team members with the objective of reflecting on and discussing coping strategies that arose throughout the course from individual discussions with students or observed student behaviour, we found that strategies students employed were focused around three central themes; social support from instructors, social support from peers, and outside educational resources provided through independent Internet research.

Students sought out social support from their tutors evidenced by instances they would call Mr H. on their phones outside of classroom times or even meet with him in person. Ad-hoc gatherings of some students at the tutor's home were organized. In addition to the tutor, students also reached out to remote professors for assistance, by posting questions on the WhatsApp group, and expecting the online professor to provide the answers. WhatsApp was largely used as a support educational technology, through discussions with professors or within students.

Additionally, we found peer support to play a large role in student behavior throughout the course. One female student (from Amman group) cited finding social support from "the girls" with whom she was able to gather with physically outside of classroom times. Students cited instances of private lessons with peers when they encountered barriers in the learning material. Peer encouragement was evident in the course WhatsApp messaging thread.

In a rather unexpected way in the Syrian educational student-institution interactions, in mid-course, students from both groups in Amman and Za'atari reached out to the coordinator of the course, to express their concerns about the general lack of commitments in the group and suggesting to take actions and to provide more structured activities and homeworks with deadlines and grades to help them and their peers better navigate the content that started to become more difficult. We think these communications have a very strong purpose and can be considered as a coping strategy with a high sense of social responsibility. Formerly, Syrian students did not easily take such actions as they were not really expected to speak out and not necessarily heard by the Syrian educational institutions.

Outside educational resources provided through independent Internet research were also mentioned by students as an important tool in helping support their studies. This especially came in the form of online videos researched for additional information and explicit examples of work related to their programming assignments.

When asked to pinpoint what exactly was helpful from peer and tutor social support or outside research, students continuously cited the re-interpreting or deciphering of material. Peers or external professors with whom students had relationships were able to re-phrase the assignment questions and content students found confusing. An important thing to note was the reliance and the aspiration of immediate feedback from peers, external advisors, and even from WhatsApp which was a frequented channel of communication between students and between instructors. Feedback to questions and concerns is provided as quickly as possible through these channels that students are already using outside of the classroom, more so than the unfamiliar course mandated channels, i.e. the course discussion forums.

A deep follow-up interview with a student from Amman who brilliantly succeeded in the course exams, although she has failed in the previous evaluation, was conducted to better understand her coping strategies. This interview was conducted by skype by the third author, fully translated and transcribed. This student also provided a handwritten list of the most important elements which contributed to her success, which looks as follows:

- The last day teacher explanation of the first exam questions.
- Extensive and long search on the net to understand the material, and watching all the videos of an independent YouTube Java course (150–300 short videos) more than once.
- Explanations of Professors.
- Learning the principles of programming through private tutoring with another student.
- Studying the material from the platform and watching the videos many times.

This student, a Palestinian Syrian, explains that she studied until baccalaureate but couldn't pass the exam for family reasons. Then she got married, and she explains: "I did not think about studying again… but since the baccalaureate when I did not succeed… my dream was to complete my studies. All my siblings have studied… Not only that. The study is beautiful in general… I had a great desire to continue. But the circumstances did not help me and myself I did not succeed in the baccalaureate. I kept in mind that I wanted to study". She is a caregiver for 3 children and her mother, and therefore can study only "after they sleep… Sometimes after 10 or 11, until I finish my work, then sit down to study at night". In the interview, these difficult conditions seem counterbalanced by social support, especially family support. Although it is not clear whether her husband and children supported her, they don't prevent her from studying: "All the people at home were repeating java java". In complement to this, she does not have a rich social life in Jordan, and therefore manages to save time to study. She comments this point very explicitly: "What encouraged me to study here is that you have time to be filled. Even though there was work pressure with the kids and at home and even with my mother… but you still have time because there is not much socialization (*social life*)". Social support from the third researcher, who is also the pedagogical advisor and coordinator for this course, also played an important role for her: "whenever I felt weak I reminded myself that you trusted me, and that one should not betray the trust put in him". She describes feeling lost during the course, and highlights the importance of feeling supported in these circumstances: "The situation was difficult… I used to get in and get out of the session feeling that I do not understand anything! I felt lost… Even Professor M… I used to tell him I do not want to go back and continue, I wanted to withdraw… He used to tell me: No! You should come back and keep going!". Then she began searching through the Internet for all terms and ideas that she did not understand. "I started to look on the Internet so I can understand – I searched for everything". However, this process was time-consuming and exhausting. "I was very lost and I had a strong desire to drop out and my determination was falling down and I was telling myself I no longer wanted to pursue… I do not know… I am able to do nothing… this is how I felt". The tutor supported her a lot: "at the end of every lesson I go out and say I do not want to go back!! He kept saying: No… You have the capabilities you should return… This was happening after every lesson!". Beyond searching intensively over the Internet, even translating parts of material from English, comparing Arabic and English terms, understanding better the course thanks to alternative methods of the professors and tutors (like drawings or skype conversations), and requiring the help and private tutoring of other students, In order to succeed she had to be able to understand what was expected from her in the exam: "I did not understand what is required in the question, so Mr. A. (*another professor*) only read the question and then explained to me: for example, with this word they mean such…, and with this one they mean such… and in this way you directly get the answer and you understand it… this helped me a lot in the end". As a conclusion, she adds: "I searched a lot on the net […] if the one of us was not searching by himself and learn, whatever assistance you have, you will not be able to succeed… To understand any point… For instance, those video clips with Abdullah Eid, they were about 300 YouTube clip. I watched all of them, and I had to re-watch all of them once or twice and sometimes three times to understand everyone of them and apply it and even sometime until I write it... I worked very much on that and it helped me so much".

This interview brings very interesting additional elements, including strong personal determination to succeed and get any help available, need for quick feedback on points which are unclear, importance of video material on the Internet, and need to understand the job of being a student and the logic of exam questions to be able to pass the exam. However, further work would be much needed to better understand (1) at what point during the learning process do students develop coping strategies or fully realize there is a need for a change in study behaviour, (2) a ranking of which coping strategies were their preference and which were most frequented and (3) an analysis of how these rankings are related to accessibility. Additionally, further research is needed to understand why some students were unable to successfully complete the course and if and why they were unable to avail of the above-mentioned coping strategies.

DISCUSSION: WHAT THEN? TALKING TO THE FUTURE

Coming back to the focus group discussion, our dialogical analysis highlighted the subjective experience of some participants to the Java course regarding Higher Education in the refugee camp and their situation as students in the Jamiya program, based on heterogeneous voices expressed in the discussion and their relations. However, what is striking in this discursive piece is the consistency of the students. From the very beginning of the discussion, they introduce the topic that is critical in their eyes: the role of this Java course in connecting their study, which has to overcome significant barriers, with future opportunities.

First Extract of the Focus Group

S1:   Most of us talk about negative aspects... but there is also something much much more positive than negative aspects... the negative ones may be very light... I am talking about myself – I was dreaming that I study informatics... I want to study informatics – anything that concerns the computer, especially hacking programs.

Researcher: Hahaha

S1:   I am a villain... So the course came to satisfy my desire... And to increase my skills in electronics... Also a nice thing that we enjoy that we have an atmosphere allowing us to make friends... We have a lot of free time in the camp and this course allows us to fill it. But we hope that the method of teaching by the doctors can be better and at the right ("known") level... And that there are more incentives... We are in the situation of an emergency camp and people in this situation need more incentives to study… they need something to encourage them do that… I hope that our study does not go down in vain. We hope to have more opportunities through this course. And here I mention an information that is out of the scope of our current talk is that most of us have left university studies interrupted. We rely a lot on this program, I mean the "Java course", we rely on it to open the way for us to complete university studies, but without your help and without no one supporting us, we will not get what we want, especially as we are in the position of the whole world knows it.

Researcher: without the help of whom?

S1: the help of the donors… the help from the university… help us to make our way to study at a university, not just to do this course… not only to take a certificate in Java language and then stay at home.

S2: After the Java material we have taken, is there a follow-up?

This discussion happens at the beginning of the focus group. The way in which the students frame their request for a follow up is very striking, as it is directly connected to the conditions of the camp in a political tone: "We rely a lot on this program, I mean the "Java course", we rely on it to open the way for us to complete university studies, but without your help and without no one supporting us, we will not get what we want, especially as we are in the position of the whole world knows it". Talking to the researcher in the context of the first evaluation of the Java course, this student adopts a political phrasing and talks simultaneously to another hidden addressee, which is supposed to stand behind the researcher, which is the international community, the donors, the university – any powerful entity outside the camp. Talking within the camp, he talks from a camp perspective to people outside the camp to request for help.

Second Extract of the Focus Group

This topic of the meaning of the course for future life is kept during the whole discussion. It appears later in the focus group with a rhetorical tone:

S1: We are indeed dependent on this course. We have followed courses before now… But we did not count on any of them that they give us something or give us a motive forward… As for me I count on this session to give me the possibility to find a job in the future… Or make me perhaps pursue my studies… But given the situation here… How can I complete my studies without being supported by anyone… Especially I am in such a situation and within the Za'atari camp? In Aristotle's statement:

Translator: Oh really! You want to cite Aristotle!? (Everyone laughs)

S1:   (continues, kindly ignoring the exclamation of the translator) Aristotle says: You have to succeed in a failed society... We are trapped within a circle all failed... This is a real reality. We must succeed in this session. [...]

S2:   For us, as my friend said... All the opportunities for study so far are cut off... This scholarship or course is the reason for our return to the study seats. In Syria, we reached the baccalaureate stage, but we did not have a chance to continue. [...] The grant (*meaning the course*) was as a hope or a reason to allow us to study again

S1:   I would say this course is like First Aid... I was inspired by that "picture" (*Probably pointing to some poster*)

S2:   Now, in Jordan, there is no chance to continue studying. If we return to Syria, we will be busy with reconstruction and the situation... As you know the situation in Syria... None of us will have time to pursue his studies... You can say that we attach many hopes to the scholarship (means the course). And we hope you do not abandon us... Not only one Java course! But continue.

In the discussion, personal success in study and life seems impossible without external help, due to the camp conditions: "How can I complete my studies without being supported by anyone... Especially I am in such a situation and within the Za'atari camp?" The Aristotle's quotation supports this political vision that the camp is a trap, "a circle all failed", a sad reality that can be overcome only with external help. The intervention triggers another student's engagement into the discussion, pointing at the emergency of their situation, trapped between the lack of opportunities for study in Jordan and the impossibility to study back to Syria. The message is clear: "Do not abandon us. Continue".

An analysis of the dialogical activity of the three students in this focus group shows the consistency of their actions: they take advantage of this discussion space, or tribune, to talk to the world and deliver a simple and critical message: don't let us down. We need you. We need help to reconnect to our study – i.e. to our future.

CONCLUSION

In this chapter, we conducted dialogical analyses of some data collected during the evaluation of the Jamiya project, which offered in autumn 2016 a course on Introduction to Sofware Programming (Java) at the University Level to refugee students from the Za'atari camp in Jordan. The analysis sheds light on some important dimensions of the subjective experience of the students in relation to Higher Education in the camp. It allows us to understand part of their aspirations, barriers to study as they are experienced on an everyday basis, and coping strategies to overcome them. This analysis adds to our understanding of barriers to refugee education, including higher education, in camp situations. In particular, it highlights the difficulties faced by students who, as they say, "suddenly interrupted their studies, and suddenly got back to them". Most importantly, the analysis shows the consistency of the dialogical activity of the three students in this focus group. From the very beginning to the last seconds of this interaction, they take advantage of the tribune offered by the discussion space around the project evaluation to call for help and support. They simultaneously talk to the visiting researcher present in Za'atari, and to the external others beyond him. The international community, including "donors" and "universities", receives here a very clear message: "don't let us down".

REFERENCES

Al Fanar Media. (2015). *Strengthening delivery of higher education to Syrian refugees* (Workshop Report). Retrieved October, 2015, from http://www.al-fanarmedia.org/wp-content/uploads/2015/12/Al-Fanar-media-workshopreport.pdf

Austin, J. L. (1962). *How to do things with words: The William James lectures*. Cambridge, MA: Harvard University Press.

Aveling, E. L., Gillespie, A., & Cornish, F. (2015). A qualitative method for analyzing multivoicedness. *Qualitative Research, 15*(6), 670–687.

Bakhtin, M. M. (1986). *Speech genres and other late essays* (V. W. McGee, Trans.). Austin, TX: University of Texas Press.

Barakat, S., & Milton, S. (2015). *Houses of wisdom matter: The responsibility to protect and rebuild higher education in the Arab world*. Doha: Brookings Doha Center.

Crea, T. M. (2016). Refugee higher education: Contextual challenges and implications for program design, delivery, and accompaniment. *International Journal of Educational Development, 46*, 12–22.

Dippo, D., Orgocka, A., & Giles, W. (2012). *Feasibility study report: Reaching higher: The provision of higher education for long-term refugees in the Dadaab Camps, Kenya*. Toronto: The Borderless Higher Education for Refugees Partnership/York University.

Dryden-Peterson, S. (2010). *Barriers to accessing education in conflict-affected fragile states: Afghanistan*. London: Save the Children.

Dryden-Peterson, S., & Giles, W. (2010). Introduction: Higher education for refugees. *Refuge, 27*(2), 3–10.

El Jack, A. (2012). "Education is my mother and father": The "invisible" women of Sudan. *Refuge: Canada's Journal on Refugees, 27*(2), 19–29.

Ferede, M. (2016, May). *Virtually educated: The case for and conundrum of online higher education for refugees* (Global Education Monitoring Report). Paris: UNESCO.

Gladwell, C., Hollow, D., Robinson, A., Norman, B., Bowerman, E., Mitchell, J., Floremont, F., & Hutchinson, P. (2016). *Higher education for refugees in low-resource environments: Landscape review*. London: Jigsaw Consult.

Hart, J. (2008). Displaced children's participation in political violence: Towards greater understanding of mobilization. *Conflict, Security, Development, 8*(3), 277–293.

Kloetzer, L. (2008). *Analyse de l'homélie de la messe dominicale: développement de l'activité langagière et conflits de métier: la part de dieu, la part de l'homme* (Doctoral dissertation). CNAM, Paris.

Kostulski, K. (2011). *Formes et fonctions psychologiques des réalisations langagières* (Document de synthèse pour l'Habilitation à diriger des recherches). Paris: CNAM.

Lorisika, I., Cremonini, L., & Safar Jalani, M. (2015). *Study to design a programme/clearinghouse providing access to higher education for Syrian refugees and internal displaced persons* (Final report). European Union/PROMAN.

Marková, I., Linell, P., Grossen, M., & Salazar-Orvig, A. (2007). *Dialogue in focus groups: Exploring socially shared knowledge.* London: Equinox Publishing.

Robinson, J. P. (2011). *A global compact on learning: Taking action on education in developing countries* (Center for Universal Education at Brookings). Washington, DC: Brookings Institution.

Putnam, R. D. (1995). Bowling alone: America's declining social capital. *Journal of Democracy, 6*(1), 65–78.

Schindler, K. (2010). *Social capital and post-war reconstruction: Evidence from northern Mozambique.* Berlin: German Institute for Economic Research.

Shakya, Y. B., Guruge, S., Hynie, M., Akbari, A., Malik, M., Htoo, S., Khogali, A., Mona, S. A., Murtaza, R., & Alley, S. (2012). Aspirations for higher education among newcomer refugee youth in Toronto: Expectations, challenges, and strategies. *Refuge: Canada's Journal on Refugees, 27*(2), 65–78.

Stevenson, J., & Willott, J. (2007). The aspiration and access to higher education of teenage refugees in the UK. *Compare, 37*(5), 671–687.

UNESCO. (2015, May). *UNESCO-EU Jami3ti higher education initiative: Mapping of higher education needs and opportunities for Syrian refugees.* Jordan: Survey Report.

UNESCO. (2017). *The UN decade of educational sustainability* (Online). Retrieved from http://en.unesco.org/themes/education-sustainable-development/what-is-esd/un-decade-of-esd

UNHCR. (2012). *Education strategy, 2012–2016.* Geneva: UNHCR.

UNHCR. (2014). Retrieved from http://www.unhcr.org/en-us/statistics/country/556725e69/unhcr-global-trends-2014.html

UNHCR. (2015a, July). *Higher education considerations for refugees in countries affected by the Syria and Iraq crises* (Education Brief). Geneva: UNHCR. Retrieved from http://www.unhcr.org/uk/protection/operations/568bc5279/higher-education-considerations-refugeescountries-affected-syria-iraq.html

UNHCR. (2015b, December). *UNHCR says most of Syrians arriving in Greece are students.* Geneva: UNHCR.

UNHCR. (2016, September). *Missing out: Refugee education in crisis.* Geneva: UNHCR.

UNHCR. (2016b). *Projected global resettlement needs 2017.* Geneva: UNHCR. Retrieved from http://www.unhcr.org/uk/protection/resettlement/575836267/unhcr-projected-global-resettlementneeds-2017.html

UNHCR. (2017a). *Figures at a glance* (Online). Retrieved from http://www.unhcr.org/en-ie/figures-at-a-glance.html

UNHCR. (2017b). Syria refugee response: Inter-agency information sharing portal (Online). Retrieved from http://data.unhcr.org/syrianrefugees/regional.php

Watenpaugh, K. D., Fricke, A. L., & King, J. R. (2013). *Uncounted and unacknowledged: Syrian refugee students and scholars.* Jordan: Institute of International Education.

Watenpaugh, K. D., Fricke, A. L., & King, J. R. (2014a). *The war follows them: Syrian university students and scholars.* Lebanon: Institute of International Education.

Watenpaugh, K. D., Fricke, A. L., & King, J. R. (2014b). *We will stop here and go no further: Syrian university students and scholars.* Turkey: Institute of International Education.

Wright, L. A., & Plasterer, R. (2012). Beyond basic education: Exploring opportunities for higher learning in Kenyan refugee camps. *Refuge: Canada's Journal on Refugees, 27*(2), 42–56.

Zeus, B. (2011). Exploring barriers to higher education in protracted refugee situations: The case of Burmese refugees in Thailand. *Journal of Refugee Studies, 24*(2), 256–276.

Laure Kloetzer
Institute of Psychology and Education
University of Neuchâtel
Switzerland

L. KLOETZER ET AL.

Miki Aristorenas
Jamiya Project
London, UK

Oula Abu-Amsha
Jamiya Project
London, UK

TATJANA ATANASOSKA AND MICHELLE PROYER

6. AUSTRIAN PERSPECTIVES ON REFUGEE STUDIES

INTRODUCTION

In 2015, Austria hosted the third-most number of refugees with regard to population size. Many of these refugees have stayed in Austria, and many have obtained their positive asylum decision. During the 2015–2016 school year, Austrian schools were challenged by a higher influx of students with a refugee background than the years before and after. For the young people themselves, even two years after arrival, the situation and their educational situation can still be challenging.

Traditionally, compulsory schooling in Austria ends after nine school years or at age 15. This makes it quite difficult for older students to enter the schooling system as a place is somewhat dependent on the goodwill of the school. For older youths, if schooling is possible, then it usually happens in adult education, in German courses, or in courses in preparation for a school leaving certificate (Atanasoska & Proyer, 2016).[1] Transition throughout the schooling time can be an obstacle for young people with a refugee background (see Proyer, Atanasoska, & Sriwanyong, 2017).[2]

In this chapter about Austria, we present a varied look at the situation for young people with a refugee background. To achieve a broad view, the two main authors invited nine co-authors to contribute their views and results with regard to the educational situation of refugee youth. We grouped the contributions into two fields of interest:

- Part 1: Language Learning and Young Learners – Language Classes, Schools, and Beyond
- Part 2: Higher Education and Labour Market – Student Involvement and Beyond

PART 1: LANGUAGE LEARNING AND YOUNG LEARNERS – LANGUAGE CLASSES, SCHOOLS, AND BEYOND

In the first study Verena Plutzar focuses on the experience of migration and flight and its influence on identity and life in the new country.

Language Learning among Students with a Refugee Background[3]

In this short contribution,[4] I (Verena Plutzar) reflect on migration and language teaching, focusing on how forced migration affects language learning and showing

© KONINKLIJKE BRILL NV, LEIDEN, 2018 | DOI:10.1163/9789004383227_006

how language teaching can respond. My considerations arise from many years of language teaching practice in a shelter house for refugees, my academic studies on language teaching in intercultural groups, and my reception of psychoanalytic theories of migration and exile. When I started to teach groups of refugees in 1991, I experienced that the answers my academic education could provide were insufficient for my work reality. What helped me instead were psychoanalytic theories on adult immigrants and refugees which perceive migration as a process with significant and persistent impacts on identity (Akhtar, 1999).

Migration as Mourning Process

Instead of focusing on the technicalities of teaching, I had to learn that migration is a process of mourning, experienced as more or less grievous. One must proceed with it so that a new identity can be formed. This new identity 'will be reflected in a remodeled self-representation that incorporates selective characteristics into the new culture that have been harmoniously integrated or that prove congruent with the cultural heritage of the past' (Volkan, 2017, p. 6). Psychoanalysts state that voluntary and forced emigration link to culture shock, losses, and struggle for adaption. They also go beyond the definition of trauma as direct personal experience of a severely distressing event like Becker's concept of abscondence as sequential traumatization (Becker, 2006, p. 193f.). In this notion, trauma contains more: the experience of peace being destroyed by war as well as the destruction itself, the arms as well as the lack of food, the loss of family members as well as the memory of torture, the uncertainty if it is possible to stay as well as to return, the voicelessness as well as the economical dependency, and the lack of privacy in shelter houses as well as the lack of intimacy. And it contains waiting. I will focus now on two aspects that I find to be particularly relevant for teaching: waiting and voicelessness.

Waiting.   The waiting of asylum seekers differs from a common daily experience. Fritsche (2012, p. 377) refers to 'existential waiting' when she states that the active forces one is exposed to are powerful and yet incomprehensible. The orientation towards an uncertain future hinders the living of a meaningful time structure. The lack of predictability restricts one's capacity to act. In this limbo, inner resources are trapped. The waiting time thus cannot be utilized for language learning as matter of course, and this situation does not necessarily end by the granting of asylum. Becker calls this phase the sequence of 'chronification of the provisional status'. He differentiates two stages which can, but do not have to, follow each other. The first stage is adaption to the circumstances which are estimated to be provisional. This makes it easier to defend the old identity. In the second stage, the situation is accepted and a forthcoming return is not expected. This facilitates integration but involves a more decisive breach of identity. In their course, both stages depend on locally given opportunities rather than on the sheer willingness of the refugees.

Voicelessness. The loss of the familiar language(s) and the need to acquire a new language, to the extent that a self-directed life is again possible, is another key experience of refugees as well as migrants. León and Rebecca Grinberg (1989) showed that language is a highly vulnerable area where defence mechanisms play a major role. Voicelessness demonstrates more than anything else the loss of the previous identity as it intensifies helplessness and loss of control already triggered by the experience of migration. In addition, it can foster regression or evoke aggression. Language teaching must escort persons during this particularly sensitive phase of radical change in a way that learners can find voice in their new language. Refugees' language learning is inextricably linked to the reorganization of a stable self-representation, in line with a positive reliable self-concept which is accepted by the new environment.

Meaningful Teaching

Teaching learners undergoing profound changes due to forced migration cannot be expected to happen in the same way as teaching exchange students. As the language taught, along with the situation, was not freely chosen, instructions must open doors and establish affiliations with the new language and ideally the new surroundings. Learners need to build a relation to the new language itself. This can be realized through understanding and expression. Teaching refugees and migrants requires engaging the learners in meaningful activities so that they can use the new language to explore and express their present situation as well as their ideas, interests, and topics of concern. All their languages have to have a part in their learning process as they are the point of departure relating to both identity and knowledge. García (2017) points this out perfectly well regarding adult refugees, while García and Kleyn (2016) show how this happens with multilingual students in schools. Their case studies demonstrate impressively how learners' affiliation to the new language can be developed by organizing classroom activities around what learners know and what they already are able to do. It is not surprising that in some case studies arts play an important role: poetry, music, and pictorial arts trigger emotions and affiliation and can be linked to the self in many ways. Artistic expression makes a language course a place where the new language has a chance to become part of one's inner self. This is only possible if the courses are provided in a trauma-sensitive way, where the course can be experienced as a safe place, attendance is voluntary, and expected progression is not directly related to the number of lessons passed. Furthermore, assessments by tests which are oriented on common frameworks and are prescribed by law have proven to be counterproductive. Instead, the growing independence of learners and the increasing means of expression should be taken as benchmarks to measure progress and to follow up with language learning goals.

The next contribution focuses similarly on the need for 'free minds' for successful learning. Thomas Fritz outlines results from an international interview study about the situation for young migrants, where results are transferable to the situation for young refugees.

What Young Migrant Learners Need Is Not Only Language Education[5]

Introduction. We see that young migrant learners are motivated but at times find it hard to learn. They seem to be distracted but 'If only their minds were free'.

What do young migrants and especially displaced persons need when they come to our countries; is it the language spoken in the country or is it something else? In a European project, a team of researchers and adult educators interviewed 15 people and the results of the interviews were neither surprising nor exceptional.

The migrants first need stability. This means family and friends, a secure residence status, and realistic perspectives. They need to know how their families back home are doing, when they will be able to join them, and so on. They need to make new friends, and to build and regain trust in order to achieve the above-mentioned stability. Only then can they start learning with all their attention and start building their new careers.

Methods and Data

In the framework of a European-funded learning partnership named 'Enabling and empowering young adult migrants to fully participate in society' 15 interviews were carried out with migrant learners in three European cities: Gothenburg, Cologne, and Vienna. The interviewees' ages ranged from 15 (6) to 30 (5) and over 30 (4), and consisted of 9 male and 6 female learners.

The interviews were carried out using an interview guideline produced by all project partners jointly. Some interviews were carried out in Swedish, some in German, and some in English. Unfortunately, the financial means did not allow interviews in the learners' first languages.

Following are some statements that highlight the necessity for stability and a feeling of safety that young displaced learners need to free their minds and to start learning successfully.

There are several aspects of this category to be observed if we take a closer look at the interviews. A young female migrant reports about her coming to Austria and being moved around the country with her parents. This is a result of the relocation policy in Austria. Her journey from Chechnya involved multiple stops in different countries.

We lived in Poland for 10 months and then Slovakia, that's what it is called I think, there about a week or so and we went to Kirchberg, there is a bed and breakfast, like, and there we lived for a year. And then to Wagram, there we lived about three or four months and then again to Traismauer. And there we were for two years, And then to Melk we went and there also one and a half years and here for five years in Vienna. I hope that is it. (AT-B2)

The journey via two countries – and two languages – to Austria took quite some time. The interviewee is not even very certain what the countries were called, a fact that could have affected – or still might – her legal status as refugee, as her narration does not conform with assumed patterns (Blommaert, 2106). As a child during this long journey, her schooling, if any, was interrupted. After having arrived in Austria, the constant movement continued; she mentions five different venues. This permanently being on the move is a concrete threat to schooling, as she mentions herself:

Yes, I do not want any more [e.g. moving around] because of school. Each time I have to go to a new school. Everything is new. That is so difficult. (AT-B3)

We certainly cannot infer from this one interview how asylum policies foster or hinder educational careers and hence, perhaps, integration,[6] but taken as an individual example, we see that for B, schooling was made very difficult. This is why she was in a Second Chance Training course for secondary school leaving exams at the time of the interview. Apart from demotivation, these procedures or mishaps cost valuable time in the process of education and finding a place in society as is always demanded by policymakers.

A different aspect of the category stability is the legal status that refugees have in a certain country and the lack of legal rights and opportunities this entails. GER-E mentions that she/he has no residence permit.

I have no proper residence permit. Every six months I have to renew my residence permit. You can't do anything with a temporary residence permit. And so for a long time goes on and I have no more hope. I see no future with this temporary residence permit. (GER-E1)

A temporary residence permit means that GER-E1 cannot get a proper job, as there is no security that he/she will still be available in six months. It also means no opportunity for an apprenticeship or a long-term educational programme or other trainings and no long-term rent or loans, and hence no integration.

But the stress and the feelings of obligations do not cease even after permanent residence permits have been granted:

When you get a permanent residency permit, you straight away feel like you have to build something to integrate yourself to the society. (SW-T16)

The lack of stability is present in many interviews, but a completely different aspect of stability also is mentioned in some of the interviews. Stability here means safety, freedom, and a choice of opportunities, as the following quotes clearly show.

Freedom. This is very, very important for me, I had no freedom in Iran. Here there is real freedom. This is great. (GER-E20)

To feel calm… to start over… and to leave all problems there… It's important to feel at peace. (SW-T1)

Education

Education is a major issue for young migrants. Very often they have lost precious time by migrating to the country they are in at the moment. Due to the allocation policies in place in most countries, migrants end up in places where there are facilities to live, but sometimes these places do not offer any educational opportunities, as S mentions.

First it was a bit difficult as we were in a small village and there was no school and no German classes. (AT-S25)

In other cases, education that already has been successfully completed is not recognized in the receiving countries, an issue that is similar in all European countries and is in stark contrast to the oft-mentioned need for more qualified people (Gächter & Smoliner, 2010). Lack of certainty and information as well as very long periods of waiting for qualifications to be recognised are a major obstacle for many young, highly qualified migrants.

I would like to know what kind of German university degree equals the degree I already have. (GER-G12)

Lost or hard-to-retrieve documents from universities in countries where wars are raging stop young people from continuing their academic careers.

I would like to continue with my studies, and I have read the law. If I want to become a lawyer, I need to be a Swedish citizen. I shall apply for Swedish citizenship, and after that I want to find a job. (SW-U1)

Work and Job Perspectives

Work perspectives are characterised by two features. One is continuity, i.e. going on doing the job they had before they had to migrate, as expressed by SW-T3.

My wish is to return to my profession, even if it means to start from the beginning. But everything good will come. (SW-T3)

The second is the drive to help others who are going through the same procedures they themselves had to undergo. Ri. states that he wants to work as a lawyer to help people on their way to a secure country, to support them with legal advice.

And I want to work like this. I help these people when they come to Bulgaria, then Slovenia, and then come to Vienna or Germany. They need help and want to do it like that. (AT-Ri27)

To conclude, I would like to quote S. on being part of society:

I: It sounds as if you feel like a part of this society…

S: Well, we all are, aren't we? Important or less important, we all play our parts, don't we? As an electrician, you are part of a construction, each one in his own profession. A small part, but you do. (GER-S8)

Although Thomas Fritz mentions education especially with regard to higher education, Daniela Marzoch, Ilija Kugler and Karoline Iber tell more about an initiative by the Vienna University Children's Office, where young refugees are offered the possibility to learn and develop their knowledge, and to continue to pursue their wish to enter higher education later on.

UniClub – Guiding Refugee Minors on Their Educational Path UniClub[7]

Introduction.   This section is a reflection on the practical approach of UniClub, and it describes how UniClub acts as a model regarding the inclusion and education of refugees. We will discuss the impact this project has on young refugees, university students undertaking a teaching degree, and Austrian society. Furthermore, we will give an insight on how we try to support young people with a migration and/or refugee background on their way to higher education.

Structure.   UniClub was formed to guide young people between the ages of 13 and 19 who express a keen interest in university but whose parents have never attended universities in Austria. Starting out as a diversity initiative by the University of Vienna, the idea was to promote social inclusion within the educational system. About 300 young refugees are registered at UniClub.

The project itself is part of Vienna University Children's Office, an independent non-profit organisation linked to the University of Vienna and experienced in establishing innovative projects around outreach activities and science engagement for young people. A strong collaboration with the Centre for Teacher Education at the University of Vienna makes it possible to work with a large group of volunteers, all students of the university. Their work as volunteers is integrated in the curriculum at the University of Vienna. Students have the chance to professionally reflect their work on an academic level within a university setting and gain ECTS credits. About 200 students, most of them future teachers, have volunteered at UniClub between autumn 2015 and summer 2017.

UniClub activities are led by a team of professional youth workers, who also are responsible for the conceptual development of the project. They are supported by the management of the Children's Office and by a psychologist specialised in trauma therapy. The project is funded by the government, donors, and the University of Vienna, and is free of charge for the young people who attend.

UniClub as an inclusive project.   Responding to the refugee situation in Austria in fall 2015, the concept of UniClub was extended to focus on the needs of young refugees. Young people who were forced to leave their home countries often wish to continue their education, some with the aim to attend university. However, building upon their previous interests and educational careers plays out difficult.

The challenges they face vary depending on their age, educational background, life story, and current situation, but there are four main ideas which almost all the teenagers have expressed:

- We want to improve our language skills, and we need support to meet the challenges of school.
- We need a place to meet and to study without distractions.
- We want to learn and experience new things and visit new places.
- We need support to study at university one day.

UniClub attempts to address those needs. The project is based on three main pillars, which are linked to each other:

1. First there is LernClub, open twice a week for three hours in the afternoon. It provides learning stations for about 35 students at the same time. LernClub offers a room with computer workstations, a workshop, and a quiet learning room; supportive learning material is at the students' disposal. Here, young people can study, do their homework, or prepare presentations. Up to 10 volunteers are present at all times for individual support. LernClub also provides the chance to socialise, meet friends, and exchange thoughts and ideas with the volunteers. After finishing their school work, many of the young people are happy to stay behind and take part in German and English lessons or various workshops prepared by volunteers.
2. To support our students even more, we established 1:1 learning support, the so-called StudyBuddy programme. This forms the second foundation of our project and offers continuous learning support throughout the school term. Volunteers and students usually meet for about two hours once a week and work on assignments and homework at UniClub. Because of the individual support that students receive, they can progress much quicker. Our volunteers get continuous support by our project team. We also provide psychological support if need be. Around 60 StudyBuddy couples were active during the summer semester 2017.
3. Additionally, UniClub offers workshops at the University of Vienna or excursions to various places like museums, science labs, etc. The activities take place twice a month and follow the interests of our young people, giving an insight into aspects of Austrian society, history, and geography. Young people get an impression of different scientific fields and gain knowledge of the university system.

The students of UniClub.   The young people that form UniClub join the programme on an entirely voluntary basis. They are not referred to us by any teachers or parents, and they solely attend because they want to learn and are seeking help. Their enthusiasm in learning as well as their energy and interest is highly inspiring.

Moreover, their way of interacting and sharing skills makes the atmosphere of learning at UniClub unique.

All our students have a migration background; many of them came to Austria as refugees in 2015. Aged between 13 and 19 years, they face different challenges. Some students were about to graduate secondary school in their home countries. In Austria, they are not given the chance to enter the regular educational system because of their age or a lack in language skills. Some of them go to school, are fluent in German, but need to work on their technical vocabulary to improve their grades and continue their school career. They face an ever-increasing workload, and the support these students need is extensive. Almost all the students show a clear lack of information and knowledge of the educational system in Austria.

UniClub offers them the chance to confront their individual needs, working as flexible and as open minded as possible. Apart from our learning support, UniClub helps students in many other ways. Information about school systems and further educational programmes is offered. Our team tries to find school or work placements, gives information on leisure activities, and sometimes also helps in other matters not directly linked to educational questions. Based on the relationships that have been built over time, our team members are able to act as advisors when individually approached. Hence, counselling and guidance also are part of our work.

University students as volunteers. Inclusion in the educational system is a key element for the participating young people, but UniClub offers a unique opportunity for teacher training students to experience inclusion first hand as well. Most of them are studying to become secondary school teachers. Upon completion of their studies, their prospective students and colleagues will be able to benefit from the skills gained during their work placement at UniClub. Moreover, they can take their gained experiences back into the university setting and share them with their professors, teachers, and fellow students.

Their positive feedback, interest in the topic, and the fact, that they participate on a voluntary basis show that the idea of an inclusive school system, and therefore an inclusive society, is an important learning field within the curriculum. They will go on sharing and promoting this concept among the groups previously mentioned and Austrian society.

We strongly believe that through their work with UniClub they will be able to draw from their experiences of inclusion and exclusion within our educational systems and make appropriate changes to their future teaching style.

Conclusion. Supporting students on their path towards higher education is the main goal of UniClub. To achieve this goal, it is important to work on a flexible, individual basis and to listen to the needs of the young people.

UniClub is a place that works towards a more inclusive society. With the help of student volunteers, UniClub is in a position to support young people on their way to higher education. UniClub acts as an example where refugees and migrants can get support to achieve higher goals and where future teachers get inspired to make schools more inclusive.

In the UniClub project, support to students with a refugee background is given beyond schooling time, in the afternoon. Another project which is presented by the project leader Susanne Binder and Ilija Kugler shows possibilities of how volunteer educational support can be included in schools directly.

Intercultural Mentoring Supports Kids with Refugee and Migration Background in Schools[8]

Mentoring as an action to promote integration. In the project 'Intercultural Mentoring for schools'[9] students with a migration or refugee background visit a classroom once a week. The pupils see the mentors as role models and persons they can trust. Through the support of the students, the children and teenagers gain positive learning experiences, which boost their motivation to be more engaged in school. The additional support and attention that mentors provide in their classrooms promote the children's self-confidence and feeling of self-worth!

Special focus on children from refugee families. In the 2017 school year, 35 mentors worked in 25 schools in Vienna and St. Pölten; approximately 90 children from refugee families were in the mentoring classes.

Because of the high demand for Arabic-speaking mentors, the search for people with those skills was intensified in autumn 2016. The idea was that these mentors would support Syrian and Iraqi children in the classrooms. Currently, 11 mentors who came to Austria as refugees are part of our team. They are from Syria, Iraq, and Kirgizstan, and either are college educated or have a professional background in pedagogic work. Unfortunately, most of them had their educational or professional career interrupted because of war and/or flight to another country. In Austria, their main focus shifted towards learning German, but they all have one thing in common: They want to be part of the Austrian society and hone their language skills through contacts and participation! Mentor B. described it as follows:

> When I came to Austria, many people supported me. That kind of support I would like to pass on to the children in the classrooms.

It is not only Syrian colleagues who are working with children and families who sought refuge in Austria. We were able to expand our team with two Farsi-speaking mentors. Many of the children who travelled to Austria also spent a certain amount of time in Turkey and learned Turkish. So, our Turkish-speaking mentors also are successful in communication with kids who arrived recently in Austria as mentor F. mentions in her report.

> One child in the classroom comes from a refugee family, who understand very little. But because he has spent some time in Turkey, he speaks

Turkish. Therefore, I or the other Turkish speaking children can help him or translate.

Through our monthly meetings, all our mentors gain specific knowledge regarding flight and asylum. Therefore, many mentors are especially motivated to support children who experienced flight. Mentor M. talks about his motivation.

For me personally it was very important to contribute and help with the situation that arose in Austria in summer 2015. Because of those events, I realized that not only the Austrian state could do something, but also the whole society. That was also the reason for me to switch schools. For me it is very new to work with children who came to Austria as refugees, but I am sure that I can learn a lot through the experiences that I'll make in the coming months.

Oftentimes, the mentors intervene when it comes to interpersonal situations, e.g. when children bother each other, when they showcase aggressive behaviour, or when conflicts arise in the classroom. In these situations, it shows why mentors are role models. For example, a Syrian mentor helped a girl the same way as an older brother would by organizing a circle with chairs for the Arabic-speaking children so they could talk about the conflict in Arabic. The children had the opportunity to talk about this situation and discuss a solution in their native language. Generally, the children like to talk to the mentor and tell him many things about the class.

Mentor R. describes how much the seven children from refugee families profit from his weekly presence. On the one hand, he tries to show them facets of Austrian society and on the other hand, he works with the pupils on individually composed worksheets. These sheets are very popular among the pupils and are even demanded by them. This kind of learning success strengthens their self-awareness and motivates them to do more.

The presence of our mentors is especially appreciated in alphabetisation courses in schools. In these courses, the challenge is to teach children with different language skills and ages. Additionally, there is a lot of fluctuation in those courses, which means that the teachers permanently must adjust to new children. Mentor M., who works twice a week in a middle school in Vienna, said:

The alphabetisation course consists of seven children right now. All of them came as refugees to Austria (from Syria, Afghanistan and China). Their ages vary between 8 and 15 years. The challenges are the different levels of schooling, which they have received in their home countries (some learned to read and write, others not) and the psychic and environmental situation of the children. Most of them are living with their families, two in Austria by themselves and life in a flat for unaccompanied minors. Especially one pupil needs special care and psychological support. His behaviour stands out, he disrupts class, provokes and threatens other pupils, can't concentrate or sit for too long.

The mentor can support the pupils individually in this situation:

> When it's the two of us (teacher and mentor) then I can notice that we are advancing, and everyone has something to do. Otherwise, the other pupils wait the whole hour to read one sentence.

One teacher from a middle school in the 2nd district in Vienna is very happy about her Syrian mentor, because he serves as a role model for the Syrian teenagers in their alphabetisation course and works as a translator for the parents. This makes it easier to follow classes and advance. The teacher also appreciates that the mentor has a 'similar teaching' style and a lot of experience teaching.

Arabic-speaking mentors often are engaged with the parents. Sometimes they are invited to parent teacher meetings or they translate. Even though the parents are very happy about the translations, for one mentor it was quite a challenge and uncomfortable because she had to tell the parents some negative things about their child. Our Syrian Mentor H. describes that 'sometimes he is the only option to communicate with the parents'.

Some pupils – of course not just the ones from refugee families – can have their self-esteem enhanced through the empathy and additional attention that they receive from the mentors. Mentor K. remembers how she felt ashamed when she didn't speak German well enough as a child. One of the children in her classroom had that same feeling of shame. After discovering that, she specifically worked with him because he spoke very quietly, he was very withdrawn. After a couple of months, she described the following development:

> O. (from Kuwait) changed with time. He was more engaged and eager to ask questions. He is much more open towards the other children and is not ashamed to talk. I think that he changed because I showed interest in him as a person and in his home country. He now has the feeling that somebody supports him when he has a problem.

But other children from refugee families, who are very motivated from the beginning and are learning German incredibly fast, also can profit from the individual support from our mentors. Sometimes they need support in very specific aspects. Ö. provides one example from a Viennese primary school.

> In this semester, I have worked quite regularly with one girl from a refugee family. Even though she isn't quite fluent in German, she understands everything quickly. Her knowledge of math is fantastic, but this semester she had a lot of issues with fractions. I tried to explain each fraction to her through drawings. After numerous examples, she managed to fill out every work sheet and was able to do fractions.

Talking with the mentors can be a relief for the children because they can talk about their worries and problems, especially when it comes to fleeing from their home. Mentor T. describes the following situation:

Some children are looking for a one-to-one chat with me and tell me about their worries, which are quite significant with one 9-year-old girl. At my last visit in the classroom, the girl took me aside and told me that her family won't be able to go back to their home because she saw a picture on Facebook how children are being killed in her city.

Positive impact also can be seen with teachers, especially when stereotypes can be deconstructed. At one school, where 'most Afghan pupils are seen as unwilling and unable', one of our mentors worked with two Afghan boys and tried to change this image.

From the beginning I noticed, that the teachers have no hope in children form refugee families. I hope that I was able to change that image through my work.

Resume. In a newspaper article from June 26, 2017, Martina Fürpass, the chief executive officer of the Intercultural Centre Vienna, emphasises that Buddy systems promote integration. Through the personal relationship, exchange can happen, mutual understanding can grow, and new members of society get in touch with Austrian society. The mentoring programme shows this on different levels, too. The empathy and individual support that the children receive through the mentors help them greatly in school; the teachers appreciate the extra support and time that our mentors invest; and in the end, the mentors profit as well. The mentors who had to flee their home countries especially can engage with children in the Austrian school system and learn a lot about their new home and society. This makes them participants and not just receivers of aid. And we assume participating in society as one of the main aspects of integration.

PART 2: HIGHER EDUCATION AND LABOUR
MARKET – STUDENT INVOLVEMENT AND BEYOND

While Part 1 showed glimpses into the specific situation of young people with a refugee background and projects that support these young people, the authors in Part 2 aim to change possibilities in higher education and the labour market. With regard to the teaching profession, teachers in Austria want and wish further education and support for teaching refugee students in their schools. On the other hand, refugee teachers – this means people who were teachers in their home country prior to their flight to Europe – would in many cases want to continue working in their profession.

Gottfried Biewer, Linda Kreuter, Jekaterina Weiß, and Michelle Proyer report from the initiative to support on-site schooling in refugee camps. In some countries, schooling in refugee camps is part of the schooling system. In Austria, this was a very unusual and new idea to offer school places for refugee children and was undertaken only for two years.

Education of Children with Forced Migration Background through the Lens of Supporting University Students[10]

The inclusion of primary and secondary school students and unaccompanied youths with a forced migration background, including experiences of violence and trauma, is a challenge at the institutional and individual level (Dursun & Sauer, 2016; UNHCR Österreich, 2016). The large number of children of compulsory school age with a forced migration background who arrived in late 2015 and in the first months of 2016 in Austria evidenced within a few months the need for fast and temporary solutions. Due to Austrian legislation and different from other countries, every child aged 6–15 living in Austria must receive instruction. Although the Vienna School Board promotes an inclusive way of education in regular schools, neighbourhood schools did not feel capable of including all those in large habitations of refugees. Thus, temporary classrooms were established in refugee camps, despite the inclusive approach to the school system of the Vienna City government and the school administration. Although Vienna had experience in refugee education in the time of the post-Yugoslavian wars in the 1990s, the current situation could not build on previous knowledge.

The contribution describes and analyses the emergence of new educational structures through the lenses of almost 50 university students during four semesters, who were part of this new structures during two semesters. They worked in the emerging structures from the beginning, in a double position as supporters and researchers.

The project documented a rare situation in educational research. It showed the very beginning and end of a new educational institution with children who had just arrived in a new country, parents who were feeling strange in a new environment, children from different countries who entered school after the interruption of their education process, teachers who were not trained for the new challenges, and classrooms which had to be established and newly equipped. As the students worked from the very beginning in the education sector of the refugee habitation, their reports documented the emergence of new institutional structures and their development for almost 18 months and beyond in two different refugee camps, which worked independently from each other.

The classes started not in the beginning of the school year, in September, but in February or April, some months or weeks after the students' arrival in Austria. Topics of research of the bachelor degree theses were, for example: reasons for the flight from the perspective of Syrian and Iraqi parents, the situation of preschool-age children, the structure of teaching in the classrooms, linguistic and cultural aspects of language acquisition, social development and sources of tensions, mode of communication among children, and trauma and secondary traumatisation. Research covered different perspectives on the paradox between inclusion and exclusion in a protected space. The methods used were diverse and depended on the specific research topic. They included observation and participant observation; interviews with teachers, social workers, and parents; document analyses; and surveys.

The majority of children were from Syria, Iraq, Iran, and Afghanistan; others were from Somalia and Chechenia. The classrooms in the refugee habitations were the first educational setting they entered in Austria. Due to the pedagogical concept of the Vienna City School Board, the learning of spoken and written German was one of the main topics, as it was regarded as a prerequisite of initiating further learning processes. Beside the German-speaking classroom teachers, there were native-language teachers who spoke Arabic and Farsi and helped facilitate learning processes in the beginning. Groups of children with the same mother tongue were formed and nonverbal communication tools were used in the beginning. Shifting language codes during a conversation followed, and after some months later, children among the different national groups could communicate in German.

Some student theses examined different topics of social development in the classrooms. At first there were groupings among the different nationalities, languages, genders, and ages, with processes of exclusion and inclusion and tensions among the different groups. These groupings dominated the pedagogical work at the beginning of classroom activities, and tensions among the groups were visible. These phenomena existed in all four school classes. During the process of observation, these structures dissolved to some degree as new rules of grouping emerged.

Interviews with parents of an Arabic-speaking university student focused on the motives for the flight to Europe. The wish for a secure life for their children, the option of educational development, and the unsatisfying living conditions and development conditions were the main reasons the parents said they left Syria, Iraq, and neighbouring countries, especially Turkey.

Experiences in their home country and during the flight brought traumatic injuries for a number of children of all ages. The theory of 'sequential traumatic experience' (Plutzar, 2016; UNHCR Österreich, 2016) describes the ongoing process in the country of arrival: the disappointment in the new environment, which does not fulfil expectations; the longing for the home country; fear about the situation of relatives in the country of origin; and uncertainty about the future. These topics were not only described in the parents' narratives, but they were visible in the children's' behaviour. The consequences of trauma are well described in the reports of practical experiences as well as in some theses with a number of descriptions of children in the refugee habitations from preschool age to youths.

In the meantime, both refugee habitations were closed, and the children attended regular classrooms in regular schools in Vienna. The challenge of inclusion for children with a refugee background remains but in an inclusive educational environment. The temporary character of this form of schooling was clear from the beginning. Nobody wanted to establish permanent refugee classes. Some of the investigations of the students also addressed the processes during this time from a few months up to more than one year, and the educational provision which was available in this extraordinary situation. The main focus on learning the language of the country of arrival, with additional teachers speaking Arabic or Farsi, facilitated the educational process.

Compared to other countries, the legal situation of children at the age of compulsory schooling (e.g. 6–14/15 years) is clear. They have the right to get instruction if they live in Austria, independent from their nationality and their legal status.

The reports and bachelor theses reveal the insufficient education situation of preschool children and young persons beyond the compulsory school age of 14, who get no appropriate education provision in the Austrian educational and vocational system.

Since 2015, many teachers in schools throughout Austria experienced that their classes and schools became highly diverse, with students from very different backgrounds attending school together. Teacher education should provide opportunities to prepare future teachers for the heterogeneous reality of Austrian schools. Tatjana Atanasoska reports one of the initiatives to include the topic of 'refugees and schooling' into teacher education for secondary schools.

Including the Topic of Asylum/Refugees and Schooling into a Given BA-Teacher Education Curriculum[11]

For my part in this chapter, I want to present shortly how my life as a researcher in the field of refugees and schooling influenced constructively my life as teacher educator. Since autumn 2016, I have offered two pro-seminars in the BA-curriculum of teacher education at the University of Vienna which focus on the situation of refugee children in secondary schools. A comparative perspective is the special focus of one of the seminars, as we analyse and compare possibilities of the school systems in different countries regarding newly arrived refugee students. Both seminars are positioned in the fourth term, in Module 4 'Prerequisites, courses of development and consequences of teaching'[12] of the educational studies (which consist of 40 ECTS in the BA programme, see Universität Wien, 2016ab).

The topics of diversity with its different aspects (language, culture, ethnicity, religion, etc.) has been part both of the curriculum of diploma studies, but also in the bachelor and masters programs. The topic 'refugees' has not been offered to teacher education students before. The year 2015, with a great number of refugees arriving – and staying – in Austria was, for me personally, the beginning of my research and my teaching engagement with this specific group of pupils. For me, it was clear that my research and teaching experience with migrant pupils gives me a good basis, but is clearly not enough for developing and teaching a specific pro-seminar about refugees and schooling. Therefore, the first half of 2016 was dedicated to a research project with Michelle Proyer from the Department for Educational Science:

- We interviewed young refugees that were between 15 and 21 years old and had been living in Austria/Vienna for at least one year.
- The interview focused on their educational pathways and experiences especially in Austria but also before their arrival.[13]

Alongside the research and many volunteers, I started teaching German as a second language to refugees in September 2015, which later led to teaching of German and Mathematics for refugees who could not attend school in their home countries. As a teacher educator, it was important to have my own teaching experiences with this group of pupils before I send my students to similar teaching experiences. For me, it was clear that a seminar about 'refugees and schooling' cannot only be a theoretical seminar, where we – I as a tutor and the students – stay in a place where we 'know the rules', but where the students should get the possibility to gather practical experiences with learners who came to Austria as refugees. In some cases, this means a big challenge for students who have had limited practical experience in teaching and often only taught in whole-class regular school settings up to then.

The practical possibilities are conducted with the help of different institutions, projects, and non-governmental organizations in Vienna, where the students from my pro-seminars have the chance to work pedagogically with children, youth, and young adults.

- UniClub (see earlier in this chapter) offers teaching and leisure activities for youth who came as refugees to Austria. The students can engage themselves as StudyBuddys (teaching one-to-one), learning buddies (teaching a small group), or offer leisure activities (crafting, sports, excursions, etc.)
- PROSA offers courses in German as a second language and courses that lead to the compulsory schooling certificate.[14] Students can engage themselves as team teachers in the courses (together with the course instructor) or as learning buddies in preparation for final exams.
- The Integrationshaus has a long tradition of providing support to refugees. The students of my pro-seminar engaged themselves as StudyBuddys and helped participants of the German courses with their further language development.
- The "Projekt Nightingale" is offered by Kinderfreunde Wien and is part of the bigger projects that exist in several cities and countries in Europe. The aim is to offer valuable leisure activities for young children (with a migrant background, not only refugees) to foster their social development and integration. Students choose to engage themselves very actively as their studies are aimed at an older age group, but this specificity is seen as the special strength for their own teacher development to have had the opportunity to work with younger children.
- The "Interkulturelles Mentoring" project (see above) offers support for teachers in multicultural and multilingual classes in Vienna and Lower Austria. The project is quite popular, so only a small number of my students were part of this. Here, students support a specific teacher with a specific class of pupils in a specific school once or twice a week, either in a whole-class setting or teaching a small group of pupils (depending on the situation in the school).
- Amnesty International Austria (AI Austria) offers a short version of a human rights workshop training for interested students. These students then go to schools

and hold workshops about 'Refugees and Human Rights'. During the preparation of these workshops, students develop new didactic ideas for the workshop which can be used by AI Austria for future workshops.

Some of the pedagogical work is in the field of teaching (teaching of German, but also of different subjects), which, of course, gives students a highly appreciated possibility of gathering teaching experience. Still, other pedagogical possibilities (activating children and youth in their leisure time) are assessed very positively by the students themselves.

Together with AI Austria, I had a very special cooperation for these pro-seminars. One part of obtaining a positive mark consists of producing a very short video (maximum of three minutes) about the topic refugees and schooling. This was done in groups of 3–5 students. AI Austria supported us with information and help with regard to copyright questions.

Students have to write reflections about their experiences in their practical activity, they produce a video which we watch together (seminar attendees, friends, family, and the involved institutions/projects/NGOs are invited) at our video-evening, and they do two group discussions about their experiences. These experiences could have been obtained either during the seminar or outside the seminars; this makes no difference for the group discussion.

For the group discussion at the end of the seminar I ask for volunteers for an audio recording for my research. Only this group will be audio recorded, but the manner of the group discussion is the same for all groups. The transcript of the audio is used in my evaluation research using content analysis (Mayring, 2014). The group discussions are not moderated, which is a difference to traditional group discussions (see Flick, 2016). The students are led through the group discussion with six questions that I give them beforehand. These questions lie face-down on the table and therefore are not visible to the students. After 8–10 minutes of discussion per question, the group may uncover the next question. Therefore, all students know the leading question almost simultaneously, and the group conducts and organizes the discussion by themselves.[15]

I planned a slight adaptation for the pro-seminars for autumn 2017. In the reflections, I often read that students were confronted with a problem and they tried a solution, both of which they described. As I see this approach regularly with students, the next term will include action research methods (for a summary, see Cohen, Manion, & Morrison, 2007) to encourage them to focus more deeply and 'research-wise' on their problem solving and its effectiveness with regard to their practical pedagogical work with children, youth, and young adults with a refugee background.

As mentioned previously, it is not only Austrian teacher students who want to be prepared for diverse Austrian classrooms. Refugee teachers also aim at working in diverse Austrian schools. Yet, there are obstacles for these teachers to be able to enter the highly regulated profession of teachers in schools. Michelle Proyer and Gertraud Kremsner present the first possibility for refugee teachers in Austria to start their path into re-entering the profession in the new country.

Displaced Migrants' Inclusion in Education: Experiences from Developing a Course for Former Secondary School Teachers[16]

Introduction. The entrance of a large number of people with a refugee background into European territory during the summer of 2015 was source of political debate and civil society's engagement and upheaval, and bore the necessity for further developments of educational services. Right away there was a clear-cut focus on the provision of German classes, regardless of quality. The narrative was quite clear: After an often-welcoming arrival, people with a refugee background were to learn German. Afterwards, one was to see and assess their future professional or educational routes. More often than not, gaining a language-level beyond the introductory A1 and A2 according to the Common European Framework of Reference for Languages (Council of Europe, 2001) sometimes took years as the facilitation is managed by the Public Employment Service Austria that overlooks the provision budget and regulates necessities. On the other hand, at times the number of affordable classes simply was too limited. Parallel provision of training or further education is out of the question before the respective group reaches the 'magical' hurdle of passing the B2 exam, which is not only required for many jobs and further trainings and programs, but also for enrolment in universities at bachelor's level.[17] This mirrors many open questions in relation to further integration into European society, more precisely in this case, Austrian society. What happens after the newly arrived group has reached an acceptable German level? Does this process lead to automated integration (in contrast to discourses in other contexts, 'inclusion' rarely is mentioned) and the chance to go back to where one stopped in the country of origin?

In the case presented: Are former secondary school teachers after the fulfilment of the necessary German level, in the case of (compulsory secondary) schools C1,[18] simply able to apply in Austrian schools?

These introductory words are necessary to approach the development of the certificate course Basics of Educational Studies for Displaced Teachers, piloting in September 2017 at the University of Vienna, and the associated challenges. The number of refugees having obtained formal professional training is still subject to assessment. Due to many arriving at the same point and a lack of capacity or possibilities to coordinate and standardise the categorisation of professional backgrounds, intending to approach a specific group proved subject to many challenges. In the following we introduce the case of former secondary school teachers.

Inventing a course to enable former teachers to re-enter their profession. Following a query of the UNHCR, a small research initiative stemming from the Department of Education and the Center for Teacher Education started to assess whether the University of Vienna was to offer any opportunities for former secondary school teachers as a couple of other universities in Germany, the United Kingdom, Sweden, and Australia do. As time and means were limited, the first 6 months focused on identifying members of this group. As contact with the Public Employment Service Austria initially could not be established, NGOs providing education and housing were contacted. This led to the identification of initially 10 teachers and later more than 30. In the beginning, monthly meetings were used to get to know the teachers and their current living conditions and to enable exchange and not the least empowerment among the participants.

The assessment of the group with fluctuating members – coordinated through a WhatsApp–group – included monthly meetings during which teachers introduced themselves and their aspirations. The main findings of the initial open assessment were:

- Two-thirds of the group was mostly made up of Syrian male teachers, followed by male teachers from Iraq, and one male teacher from Afghanistan. Initially only one women and no teachers from Iran could be contacted.
- Almost all the teachers had studied only one subject and had not received formal educational training.
- The majority of teachers had taught Arabic language or English.
- The urge to immediately return to one's former profession was imminent.

These findings and the fact that Austria is facing a lack of teachers in selected (particularly science-related) subjects, led to an application with the Ministry of Europe, Foreign Affairs and Integration's annual call for integration projects. Initially, the application focused on an MA-postgraduate course in the area of inclusive teaching. Due to cuts in the funding and a reassessment of employment prospects, however, this was changed into a certificate course covering the pillar of educational training in the Austrian teacher education curriculum that is depicted in Table 6.1.

Table 6.1. Scheme of educational training in Austria[19]

Scientific Theory		Basics of Educational
Subject 1	Subject 2	Studies
70–80 ECTS	70–80 ECTS	
Elective range: 10 ECTS		(including 8 ECTS
Subject Didactics		school practice)
Subject 1	Subject 2	
15–25 ECTS	15–25 ECTS	
(including 1 ECTS school	(including 1 ECTS school	
practice)	practice)	
Total: 100 ECTS	Total: 100 ECTS	Total: 40 ECTS

The Certificate Course

Basics of Educational Studies for Displaced Teachers   The course mirrors the third pillar depicted in Table 6.1. It unites theory and practice and supports the entry of former teachers with a refugee background. Twenty-three participants from five countries fulfilled the entry requirements and succeeded in an assessment that was developed in conjunction with the Viennese School Authority and the job centers of Vienna and Lower Austria. The course started in September 2017 but due to the high administrative demands, data continuously collected can only later be analysed and published.

   The question to be worked on in the near future is whether the course is the next step in integration or so much more?

The authors of this chapter believe that collaboration in the context of education of people with a refugee background is key, which is why we chose to invite diverse authors representing personal and institutional engagement. Although all authors in this chapter contribute to a picture about the situation in Austria, there is the limitation that almost all of the presented projects/results are centred in Vienna, with some reaching out to the federal states near Vienna (especially Lower Austria). Still, this panopticum can shed light on activities in practice and in research that are conducted by different actors in Austria. This chapter shows one of many possibilities of collaboration in the field of young people with a refugee background and education. We believe that this kind of professional and personal exchange of different actors in the field can improve the situation for young people in education and with regard to other important questions of building a life in a new country. As one interviewee in Fritz' texts mentions – we all are part of the society, and we all want to be part of society.

ACKNOWLEDGEMENTS

This chapter contains sections contributed by Gottfried Biewer (Department of Educational Sciences and Centre for Teacher Education, University of Vienna, Austria), Susanne Binder (Project Intercultural Mentoring, University of Vienna, Austria), Ilija Kugler (Vienna University Children's Office/UniClub and Project Intercultural Mentoring, University of Vienna, Austria), Thomas Fritz (Lernraum Wien/Department of German, University of Vienna, Austria), Gertraud Kremsner (Centre for Teacher Education and Department of Educational Sciences, University of Vienna, Austria), Linda Kreuter (Department of Educational Sciences, University of Vienna, Austria), Jekaterina Weiß (Department of Educational Sciences, University of Vienna, Austria), Verena Plutzar (Educational Advisor, Department of German, University of Vienna, Austria), and Daniela Marzoch (Vienna University Children's Office/UniClub, Austria), and Karoline Iber, Vienna University Children's Office, Austria.

NOTES

[1]   A detailed account with regard to schooling possibilities for young people with a refugee background can be found in Atanasoska and Proyer (2016). The publication was a result of an interview study conducted in Vienna in 2016.

[2]   The situation in Austria is juxtaposed with the very difficult situation for refugee students at the border of Thailand. Also, a European perspective is sketched.

[3]   This section was contributed by Verena Plutzar.

[4]   For a more detailed exploration, see Plutzar (2016).

[5]   This section was contributed by Thomas Fritz.

[6]   In this chapter I use the term integration to describe a process much wanted by some policy makers responsible for migration and asylum policies although we are aware that integration is a very opaque and politically loaded concept that is highly controversial. We use it nonetheless in contexts where we do attempt to address issues that are on the above-mentioned policy makers and are part of the everyday discourse on migration and asylum.

[7]   This section was contributed by Daniela Schier and Ilija Kugler.

[8]   This section was contributed by Susanne Binder and Ilija Kugler.

[9]   The project, funded by BMEIA and Büro für Diversität St. Pölten, receives support from the Institute for Social and Cultural Anthropology, Vienna University; see further information at http://www.univie.ac.at/alumni.ksa/iku-mentoring/

[10] This section was contributed by Gottfried Biewer, Linda Kreuter, Jekaterina Weiß, and Michelle Proyer.

[11] This section was contributed by Tatjana Atanasoska.

[12] German original: 'Voraussetzungen, Verläufe und Folgen des Unterrichts'.

[13] This research has hitherto led to three publications: Atanasoska and Proyer (2016), Proyer, Atanasoska, and Sriwanyong (2017), and Atanasoska and Proyer (2017).

[14] This corresponds to the school leaving certificate after 8 years of compulsory schooling, obtained at the age of 14–15 years.

[15] A linguistical analysis is planned which can show specific characteristics for this special form of group discussions.

[16] This section was contributed by Michelle Proyer and Gertraud Kremsner.

[17] https://slw.univie.ac.at/en/studying/admission-procedure/knowledge-of-german/ [2017-08-15].

[18] According to §4/2 of the "Landeslehrer-Dienstrechtsgesetz", the law for Austrian teachers, professional competence also includes sufficient knowledge of written and spoken German, which teachers have to prove. For teachers in compulsory schools, the school board of the respective federal state requires a proof of C1.

[19] Source: https://ssc-lehrerinnenbildung.univie.ac.at/fileadmin/user_upload/SSC/SSC_PhilBild/Lehrer InnenBildung_LA_Bachelor/BA_Curriculum_ABG_20160627.pdf [2017-08-15].

REFERENCES

Akhtar, S. (1999). *Immigration and identity. Turmoil, treatment and transformation*. Northvale, NJ: Jason Aronson.

Atanasoska, T., & Proyer, M. (2016). Bildung mit und innerhalb von Grenzen – Herausforderungen für Flüchtlinge jenseits des Pflichtschulalters am Beispiel heterogener Schule und bildungsbezogener Übergänge. *SWS-Rundschau, 3*, 442–446.

Atanasoska, T., & Proyer, M. (2017). "Wenn man will, kann man das schaffen". Wünsche und Herausforderungen im Bildungsalltag von Jugendlichen mit Fluchterfahrungen – Einblicke und Gedankenanstöße. *Schulverwaltung aktuell, 4*.

Becker, D. (2006). *Die Erfindung des Traumas – Verflochtene Geschichten*. Freiburg: Edition Freitag.

Bildungswissenschaftliche Grundlagen für Lehrkräfte mit Fluchthintergrund. Further information on the course (German). Retrieved October 5, 2017, from https://www.postgraduatecenter.at/lifelong-learning-projekte/corporate-programs/bildungswissenschaftliche-grundlagen-fuer-lehrkraefte-mit-fluchthintergrund/

Binder, S., & Kössner, E. (Eds.). (2014). *Erfahrungen teilen – Vielfalt erleben. Interkulturelles Mentoring und Mehrsprachigkeit an österreichischen Schulen*. Münster: LIT Verlag.

Blommaert, J. (2106). *New forms of diaspora, new forms of integration* (Tilburg Papers in Culture Studies, Paper 160). Retrieved August 30, 2017, from https://www.tilburguniversity.edu/upload/ba515695-257b-4dd0-b030-b52a158c7a42_TPCS_160_Blommaert.pdf

Bundesgesetz vom 27. Juni 1984 über das Dienstrecht der Landeslehrer (Landeslehrer-Dienstrechtsgesetz – LDG 1984); consolidated version 2017-08-15. Retrieved August, 15, 2017, from https://www.ris.bka.gv.at/GeltendeFassung.wxe?Abfrage=BundesnormenandGesetzesnummer=10008549

Cohen, L., Manion, L., & Morrison, K. (2007). *Research methods in education* (6th ed.). London & New York, NY: Routledge.

Council of Europe. (2001). *Common European framework of reference for languages: Learning, teaching, assessment*. Cambridge: Cambridge University Press. Retrieved August 15, 2017, from https://www.coe.int/t/dg4/linguistic/Source/Framework_EN.pdf

Dursun, A., & Sauer, B. (2015). In whose best interest? Exploring unaccompanied minors' rights through the lens of Migration and Asylum processes (MinAs). *National Report Austria*. Retrieved October 10, 2017 from http://www.minasproject.eu/files/2014/10/A6_National-report-AT.pdf

Flick, U. (2016). *Qualitative Sozialforschung: eine Einführung* (7. Aufl.). rororo Rowohlts Enzyklopädie.

Fritsche, A. (2012). Zeit. Macht. Flüchtlinge. Und Flüchtlinge machen Zeit? Konzeptionen biografischer Zeit im Asylkontext. *SWS-Rundschau, 52*(4), 362–388.

Fritz, T., & Donat, D. (2017). *What migrant learners need: The linguistic integration of adult migrants: Some lessons from research* (pp. 163–168). Berlin: De Gruyter Mouton in cooperation with the *Council of Europe*.

Gächter, A., & Smoliner, S. (2010). *How well does education travel? Education and occupation with and without migration*. Vienna: ZSI.

García, O. (2017). Problematizing linguistic integration of migrants: The role of translanguaging and language teachers. In J.-C. Beacco, H.-J. Krumm, D. Little, & P. Thalgott (Eds.), *Linguistic integration of adult migrants: Some lessons from research* (pp. 11–26). Berlin: De Gruyter.

García, O., & Kleyn, T. (Eds.). (2016). *Translanguaging with multilingual students: Learning from classroom moments*. New York, NY: Routledge.

Grinberg, L., & Grinberg, R. (1989). *Psychoanalytic perspectives on migration and exile* (N. Festinger, Trans.). New Haven, CT: Yale University Press.

Mayring, P. (2014). *Qualitative content analysis: Theoretical foundation, basic procedures and software solution*. Austria: Klagenfurt. Retrieved January 12, 2017, from http://nbn-resolving.de/urn:nbn:de:0168-ssoar-395173

Plutzar, V. (2016). Sprachenlernen nach der Flucht. Überlegungen zu Implikationen der Folgen von Trauma und Flucht für den Deutschunterricht Erwachsener. In *OBST, 89, Flucht. Punkt. Sprache* (pp. 109–132). Duisburg: Universitätsverlag Rhein-Ruhr.

Proyer, M., Atanasoska, T., & Sriwanyong, S. (2017). Forces in non-linear transitions: On the impact of escape on educational pathways in young refugees' lives. In H. Fasching, C. Geppert, & E. Makarova (Eds.), *Inklusive Übergänge. (Inter)nationale Perspektiven auf Inklusion im Übergang von der Schule in weitere Bildung* (pp. 211–228). Ausbildung oder Beschäftigung.

UNHCR. (2016): *Flucht und Trauma im Kontext Schule. Handbuch für PädagogInnen* (Online). Retrieved from http://www.unhcr.org/dach/at/services/publikationen/bildungs-und-trainingsmaterial/flucht-und-trauma-im-kontext-schule

Universität Wien, Senat der Universität Wien. (2016a). *Allgemeines Curriculum für das Bachelorstudium zur Erlangung eines Lehramts im Bereich der Sekundarstufe (Allgemeinbildung) im Verbund Nord-Ost. Stand*. Retrieved August 20, 2017, from https://senat.univie.ac.at/curricularkommission/curricula/#c497224

Volkan, V. D. (2017). *Immigrants and refugees: Trauma, perennial mourning, and border psychology*. London: Karnac.

T. ATANASOSKA & M. PROYER

Tatjana Atanasoska
Centre for Teacher Education
University of Vienna
Austria
and
Teacher Education
Bergische Universität Wuppertal
Germany

Michelle Proyer
Centre for Teacher Education and Department of Educational Sciences
University of Vienna
Austria

WAYNE VECK, LOUISE PAGDEN AND JULIE WHARTON

7. CHILDREN SEEKING REFUGE, ASSIMILATION AND INCLUSION

Insights from the United Kingdom

INTRODUCTION

This chapter aims to elucidate the social and educational significance of distinguishing assimilation from inclusion for children who, having been uprooted from their homes, continue to confront an unnecessarily cruel world. 'Arguably, the response to asylum-seeking and refugee youth', Pinson and Arnot (2010, p. 248) contend, 'provides one of the greatest tests of social justice for any educational system'. In this chapter we address the complexities of this test by way of examining the pressures on schooling to assimilate children seeking refuge into existing school structures without pausing to consider the ways these children might be included.

We are concerned here with two forms of assimilation. In pursuing this analysis we take our lead from the work of Zygmunt Bauman. In his writings, Bauman points to a significant distinction between processes of assimilation determined by the goals of modernity and processes formed within what he (2005a, 2013) names 'liquid modernity'. The first is an active process that can see children new to the UK and seeking refuge within it forced, both to fit into fixed structures and practices, and to confirm to established values and social norms. The second process is characterised, not by what happens to people, but precisely by the absence of activity on, attention to and concern with them. This form of assimilation occurs, for example, when children seeking refuge find themselves left alone, abandoned, and thus with little choice but to adjust themselves to fit into a society of indifferent individuals. We name the former, *assimilation into the given*, and the latter, *assimilation into indifference*.

Due, Riggs, and Augoustinos (2016, p. 1287) usefully note that it 'is important to consider the broader social context of schools in addition to the learning experiences of students with migrant or refugee backgrounds'. It is within this broader context that we witness the ways the term refugee or asylum seeker can conjure up the image of the 'stranger' – someone unfamiliar to us in appearance or way of life. Bauman's (2016a) book, *Strangers at our door*, examines what has been described as the 'migration crisis' (p. 1), and emphasises the complex attitudes that this 'crisis' has given rise to. Despite the moral panic and feelings of fear that has spread across Western societies in recent years in relation to mass, forced migration, Bauman

(2016a, p. 2) suggests these same societies may be reaching a point of 'refugee tragedy fatigue'. This chapter explores these shifting attitudes to immigrants in the UK, incorporating nationalism and xenophobia, and their consequences for children seeking refuge in the UK. We go on to address the role of schools that have been awarded the status of 'Schools of Sanctuary' in countering assimilation and promoting the inclusion of these children.

LEARNING FROM SCHOOLS OF SANCTUARY

Alongside Bauman's thinking, the analysis that follows is illuminated by illustrative examples and insights from the Deputy Head and the Headteacher of a School of Sanctuary in the south of England, along with the reflections of a regional co-ordinator for the Schools of Sanctuary, again in the south of England. The Schools of Sanctuary organisation promotes the commitment of schools to be a 'safe and welcoming place for all, especially those seeking sanctuary' (Schools of Sanctuary, 2017). The Deputy Headteacher offered the following explanation of what it means for a school to gain recognition as a School of Sanctuary:

> The initiative is based on the three principles, and the first is learning what it means to be seeking sanctuary, the second is embedding that within your curriculum, your extra-curricular activities, and the third is to share your vision and your achievements. So they're three quite simple principles that you can interpret in different ways. It's not a set way in which you have to run the initiative across your schools.

Reflecting on the influence that this framework can have on inclusive values in schools, a regional co-ordinator for the Schools of Sanctuary organisation explained that schools 'take different sort of steps to building welcome... So it's a question of raising awareness, which is one of the key areas of our work going into schools'. The Schools of Sanctuary (2017) website outlines how the Framework they offer to schools can help to create 'a sense of safety and inclusion for all', alongside developing an 'understanding of what it means to seek sanctuary'. Concluding her research into the ways in which secondary schools promote inclusion, McCorriston (2012, p. 185) notes that a 'community approach to education for refugees and other marginalized groups... is a successful way to meet the educational needs of these vulnerable groups'. The Schools of Sanctuary Framework represents a significant way in which this strategic approach practice is put into practice. As the regional representative from Schools of Sanctuary stated, 'I think what inspires some of us to the cause is the revolution of generosity out there... British people are welcoming'. The Schools of Sanctuary movement attempts to cultivate this generosity to ensure that children seeking refuge in the UK are educated and welcomed in inclusive schools.

On the surface, at least, such values-led work is underpinned by the UK's 2006 *Education and Inspection Act*, which outlined the duty to report on schools' approaches to promoting community cohesion. In guidance to legislation the message is advanced thus: 'Different types of schools in different communities will clearly face different challenges and globalisation means both that the populations of schools are often more diverse, and that they might also change at fairly short notice' (DCSF, 2007, p. 1). Significantly, community cohesion is no longer a part of UK schools' inspections, nor does it fall within the official remit of school governors (although community relationships are to a lesser extent). The duty to report on community cohesion was repealed in the UK's 2011 *Education Act* (please see Section 154 EIA 2006).

In our interviews we explored the concept of inclusion and the various ways the school attempts to embed its inclusive values. Moreover, we examined together how the school was supported to be inclusive and considered the many challenges it encounters in its attempt to realise its inclusive values in its practices. We were keen to use an inclusive approach to our research to ensure that our participants were involved as 'people who may otherwise be seen as subjects for the research as instigators of ideas' (Walmsley & Johnson, 2003, p. 10). In an effort to secure this participation, the interviewees were given the initial questions we had in mind in preparation for the interview and, once the interview was underway, supplementary questions were asked in order to 'probe discussion and follow ideas' (Savin-Baden & Howell Major, 2013, p. 359). As the interview progressed answers were given freely and spontaneously and our time together resembled a 'normal conversation' (Savin-Baden & Howell Major, 2013, p. 371). The interview was recorded and then transcribed to allow for the thematic analysis of the findings. This allowed us to focus on the participants and their responses to our questions (Burton & Bartlett, 2009). The emerging themes related to tensions between exclusion, inclusion and assimilation. The interview also allowed for an initial exploration of the Schools of Sanctuary Framework (Saks & Allsop, 2013).

ASSIMILATION INTO THE GIVEN

Bauman (1995, p. 2) depicts 'the strategy of assimilation' under modernity as being concerned with 'making the different similar; the smothering of cultural or linguistic distinctions, forbidding all traditions and loyalties expect those meant to feed the conformity of the new and all embracing order, promoting and enforcing one and only measure of conformity'. If we begin with the expectation that other people should have similar life histories to our own, similar careers and similar interests, then acceptance of difference may be replaced with an attempt to eradicate difference. The quest here is to ensure that we all become one and the same, identifiable as part of the same group. In modern society this process occurs in a twofold fashion, since the same society that creates the stranger by way of distinguishing a person as 'other', an 'outsider', can then work upon this person, to reshape and recreate them to fit into the mould named, 'One of us'. The assimilated are, therefore, under the conditions of modernity, twice produced – they are at once a by-product of the actual and symbolic borders others have produced, the boundaries they have established to clearly distinguish what is 'normal' from what is to be deemed 'strange', *and* they are a direct product of the efforts of others to transform them. Bauman (2005a, p. 305) suggests that 'it is the gardener's attitude that best serves as a metaphor for modern worldview and practice'. It is the role of that gardener state to determine 'what kind of plants should, and what sort of plants should not grow on the plot entrusted to his care' and to guarantee that all plants conform to or are assimilated into 'the desirable arrangement' it has envisioned (Bauman, 2005a, p. 306). In what follows, we examine processes of assimilating people into what is given within any society in relation to children seeking refuge and schooling. We consider: first, Brexit and its consequences; second, the power of language to exclude; and, finally, attitudes to persons seeking sanctuary.

Brexit and Hostile Attitudes to Immigrants in the UK

What, then, are the pressures on UK schools to assimilate rather than to include children seeking refuge? It is hardly possible to answer this question without reflecting on the enormous importance of what is commonly referred to as Brexit. 2016 saw the people of the UK vote in a referendum to determine levels of support for the country remaining within or exiting from the European Union (EU). 51.9% of those who voted did so in favour of leaving the EU. In March 2017, the process of exiting the EU was initiated by the UK government, with 30 March 2019 set as the date for the completion of this process. One way of appraising the consequences of this decision can be found in the difference between the UK's responsibilities to persons seeking refuge within and out of the EU. As a member of the EU, the UK has to adhere to Dublin III Regulation, which ensures that refugees have the right to be reunited with members of their extended family members. In contrast, under the UK's current policy, this right does not extend beyond parents and their children. This has particularly obvious and stark implications for orphans seeking refuge in the UK. Thus, Mike Penrose, Executive Director of Unicef UK, observed, in an interview with the newspaper, *The Guardian*, 'Brexit could risk the ability to get children fleeing war and persecution to the safety of their close family in the UK', before going on to conclude: 'Now is the time for the UK government to broaden its own rules and ensure the protection of unaccompanied refugee children' (Elgot, 2017).

The dominant message of the campaign to leave the European Union was encapsulated in the title of their website, 'Vote leave, take control'. The website insisted: 'We can control immigration and have a fairer system which welcomes people on the basis of the skills they have, rather than the passport they hold'. In a continued effort to motivate voters, the site maintained:

> If we stay in the EU, immigration will be out of control. Nearly 2 million came to the UK from the EU over the last ten years. Imagine what it will be like when new, poorer countries join.

What was overlooked by this rhetoric was the fact that in 2015 over 1.2 million British people lived outside the UK in the EU, with over 300,000 British people living in Spain alone (United Nations, 2015).

The five yearly monitoring report by *The European Commission against Racism and Intolerance* (ECRI), (established by the Council of Europe, as an independent human rights monitoring body that specialised in questions relating to racism and intolerance) states:

> There continues to be considerable intolerant political discourse focusing on immigration and contributing to an increase in xenophobic sentiments. Muslims are portrayed in a negative light by certain politicians and as a result of some policies. Their alleged lack of integration and opposition to "fundamental British values" is a common theme adding to a climate of mistrust and fear of Muslims. (ECRI, 2016, p. 9)

There are, of course, many strategies employed by politicians, and some of these strategies serve to exacerbate difference and intolerance rather than embrace inclusion and understanding. In particular, there has been a proliferation of connections drawn between migrants and the rise of terror. As Bauman (2016a, p. 31) records, the Hungarian leader, Orban, has said that 'all terrorists are migrants' and has built a wall in order to keep out the 'stranger', thus creating what Bauman has terms the 'reciprocity of causation'. Bauman (2016a, p. 35) illuminates the consequences of such otherisation, noting that 'once they have been cast in the category of would be terrorists, migrants find themselves beyond the realm of, and off limits to, moral responsibility... and outside the space of compassion and the impulse to care'. In the UK, the language is more subtle. The Conservative party's manifesto for the 2016 national election included a section on 'Bringing Britain together', which focused on controlling immigration, integrating divided communities and defeating extremists. However subtly packaged and delivered, such associations between immigration and terrorism ensure that, in Bauman's (2016a, p. 44) words, 'governments... endorse the popular security panic by focussing on the victims of the refugee tragedy instead of the global roots of their tragic fate'.

Reflecting on Brexit and its consequences, the Headteacher of a School of Sanctuary noted, 'It's a bit of a cliché now but definitely some of the parents feel more comfortable making comments that would've been regarded as 'beyond the pale' a year or so ago'. A stark example of hostility to immigrants in the UK was given by a Deputy Head of a School of Sanctuary in England:

> There was a horrible event yesterday. We had all the classes move up a year group and had next year's Reception class come in and one of our new parents was walking in with her son for his first day at school, [and] just round the corner some big guy got in her face, shouted out, 'Al-Qaeda', and then reappeared with a baseball bat in his hands shortly afterwards... and I was – maybe it goes on a lot and people just don't say – but I was horrified.

This horrible and horrifying example of violence represents the dreadful extreme of the violence that accompanies the rejection of person entirely otherised. Indeed, in order to do away with strangers, the modern state engages in two, quite distinct exclusionary practices. First, strangers are assimilated; they are, that is, worked upon in order to fit them into dominate social norms and values. Second, there is the strategy of direct and violent exclusion where, in order to maintain what is perceived to be the 'norm', difference is not assimilated but banished into ghettos or out of the boundaries of the state. "Selecting, marking and setting aside the 'fringe of abnormality' is", Bauman (2012a, p. 78) maintains, 'a necessary concomitant of order building and the unavoidable cost of an order's perpetuation'. Thus understood, refugee camps might not be a stepping stone to safety, but a way of containing all the 'undesirables' and preventing them from disrupting order in a society imagined to be orderly.

The Language of Hostility and Assimilation

The word, 'refugee', has its origins in the English language in the Huguenot diaspora. The word refugee originates from the French word *réfugié* (Oxford Living Dictionary, 2017); this, in turn, comes from the verb *se réfugier*, which means 'to take shelter or refuge' (Collins Dictionary, 2017). The Huguenots, a group of French Protestants, were the first to be categorised as refugees as they fled from oppression in their homeland.

Wittgenstein (1975, pp. 17–18) describes 'the craving for generality' as 'the tendency to look for something common to entities which we must commonly subsume under a general term'. The signifiers 'refugee' and 'asylum seeker' are, for example, used in everyday discourse as interchangeable and generalisable terms. However, in practice they will be employed in many different and distinct ways. The definitions of 'refugee' and 'asylum seeker' vary greatly at a local, national and international level and the events that have caused people to seek sanctuary away from their homes differ in their nature. Hence, Goodwin-Gill and McAdam (2007, p. 15) consider the single word 'flight' and its multiple meanings thus: 'The reasons for flight may be many; flight from oppression, from a threat to life or liberty, flight from persecution; flight from deprivation, from grinding poverty; flight from civil war or strife; flight from natural disasters, earthquake, flood, draught, famine'.

Roger Slee (2011, p. 48) connects 'times of recession' to 'the rapid metastasizing of racism and the loathing of the immigrant, refugee and disabled people'. Certainly, in the UK, austerity has brought real degradation in the life conditions of the poor, the ill, the disabled and the elderly, but caught within these categories there are real people to whom we might respond. And yet, all the time the other person is contained within the category, austerity and its accompanying cuts can remain something that happens, not to the other person to whom I am responsible, but a mere category of individual. People living in poverty can find themselves frozen in one of a whole host of derogatory stereotypes contained on the front pages of tabloid newspapers, adults with impairment in fixed ideas about ability, and elderly persons in images of old age that arise in opposition to abstract fantasies about youthful potency. Young people labelled as 'having SEN', poor persons, persons with impairments and elderly persons can, in these ways, be rendered invisible. The same, of course, is true for the immigrant.

Garthwaite (2011, p. 370) sees, in accounts of illness and disability, advanced in the media,

> echoes of the 'undeserving' and 'deserving' poor, implying that people labelled workless are 'undeserving' if they do not at least seek paid employment, regardless of the quality and calibre of the work available. On the other hand, the 'deserving' poor are those who are making an effort to find work and see this as their responsibility to society regardless of how fruitless their search might be.

A parallel language resounds through much discussion of immigration in the popular press in the UK, where the deserving immigrant is distinguished from the undeserving immigrant. Indeed, in their manifesto for the 2016 national election, the Conservative party's vowed to reduce the number of asylum claims made in this country and welcome those most in need, rather than those 'young enough and fit enough' to make it to Britain. Thus, Lister and Bennett (2010, p. 88), reviewing the attitude of UK politicians from 1997–2010, maintain:

> Like New Labour, Cameron's Conservatives understand the power of language. They deploy it skilfully to represent the problem of poverty and its causes and solutions in ways which place the main responsibility on the individual and on communities rather than on government.

Further examples of the craving to generalise in relation to refugees can be found in the UK media. Khosravinik (2010) undertook a critical discourse analysis of the language used to describe refugees, asylum seekers and immigrants in the British press. 'Throughout all the text analyses', Khosravinik (2010, p. 11) notes, "terms used to refer to 'people who have moved out of their countries and entered the UK' seem to vary in terms of the degree of associated negativity". Thomas and Loxley (2007) describe how labelling can exacerbate power relationships that are unequal with the person who has assigned the label being able to exert an element of control over the person who has been labelled. The combination of 'opportunistic politicians' and the media more generally, ensures the 'continual linking of these young refugees to gang violence' and so 'perpetuates another layer of socio-political exclusion that is largely unsubstantiated'. In sum, as a consequence of our generalising tendencies, refugees are seen as a homogenous group, the 'otherness' of this group, their assumed strangeness, reduces them to a set of essences that accentuate their difference.

It is thus crucial that we recognise the ways in which our understanding of the terms and labels we use depend on the meanings we ascribe to them and also on the environmental context in which we employ them at any given time. In this way we might learn how to respond to a child seeking refuge as something more than an excluded other, a unit in a category, and witness who the child is becoming and not to what they have been reduced to. It is a question of addressing potential that can be given no definitive name, the potential to participate in the world and make an unforeseen and unforeseeable difference to it.

Understanding Hostile Attitudes to Seekers of Refuge

Bauman (1995) elucidates two ways in which the immigrant as a 'stranger' can be viewed. For those who live outside of impoverished neighbourhoods or 'ghettos', the stranger can be viewed as an exotic other, someone who can offer them something different – a unfamiliar meal or a useful service. But for those who live in close proximity to the stranger, marginalised and trapped in their own powerless and lack of freedom, the stranger might come to be viewed as a threat.

It now seems difficult to avoid the conclusion that a desire to curb freedom of movement across national boundaries, to take control of the borders and to tighten immigration controls encouraged people to vote in favour of leaving the EU. For example, the town of Boston, in the UK's east midlands, voted 75.4% in favour of leaving the EU; according to the Telegraph (2016) a UK newspaper that is politically on the right, the town has struggled to integrate the large numbers of eastern European immigrants. Other areas with similar results were also largely in the same geographic area of Britain and they experienced similar growing levels of unemployment amongst lower socio-economic groups, along with increasing numbers of immigrants. However, the areas with the highest percentage of 'remain' votes were (unsurprisingly) Gibraltar, followed by Lambeth. This is significant since, despite its high levels of immigration, Lambeth has 'a strong local economy means people aren't as fearful of rising European migration' (Dunford & Kirk, 2016). What this suggests, immediately, is that levels of economic flourishing inform attitudes to immigration. Brexit might, then, be heard as a cry, not simply against increasing immigration, but more broadly against social inequality. As Bauman observes, for the deprived and marginalised, 'the British referendum was the rare, well-nigh unique chance to unload their long accumulated, blistering/festering anger against the establishment *as a whole*' (original emphasis, 2016b).

Bauman (2016a) describes this growing group of people who voted to leave the EU as the 'precariat'. The precariat, Bauman (2016a) suggests, responds to the arrival of an unwanted social group with a lower social standing as something of a saving grace, a means to 'redeeming their human dignity and salvaging whatever is left of their self-esteem' (p. 13). At the same time, 'the arrival of a mass of homeless migrants stripped of human rights' (Bauman, 2016a, p. 13), confronts them as a threat. Indeed, the very presence of the newcomer, the stranger, can speak, 'irritatingly, infuriatingly and horrifyingly, of the (incurable?) vulnerability of our own position and the endemic fragility of our hard-won well-being' (Bauman, 2016a, p. 16). For one living in perpetual economic insecurity, the stranger can bring to mind just how close one is to being exposed as strange.

Asked how the children's families responded to the school becoming a School of Sanctuary, the Headteacher recalled:

Our School of Sanctuary [launch] was due in the referendum running so it was a very sensitive time so we had to think very carefully about how we were selling the message and ironically we'd got to stage a big celebration assembly the day the result of the referendum was announced and it was just the strangest atmosphere, the assembly, the scene, the kids were all sat there singing songs about a better tomorrow and some of the parents were sat very arms folded looking very disapprovingly. It was the strangest, strangest thing.

'In the postmodern city', Bauman (1995, p. 10) observes, 'the strangers mean one thing to those for whom "no go areas" (the "mean streets", the "rough district") means "no go in", and those to whom "no go" means "no go out"'. Could it be that what distinguishes the views of some teachers from that of some parents is that where the stranger represents an opportunity for the former, to the latter this same stranger holds up a mirror to precariousness that perpetually loams over their lives? The school's Headteacher recorded the most illuminating of incidents:

When we had Ofsted a year ago and the inspectors were talking to some parents and one of the questions they asked was, 'Is the school welcoming?' And the comment that came back from one of the parents was, 'Yeah, if anything it's a bit too welcoming.

It might be that this difference between those who can welcome the newcomer, seeking refuge with open arms and those who feel drawn to defensiveness corresponds to the distinction Bauman (1995, p. 11) draws out between those for whom the world is 'an adventure park' and those for whom it is 'a trap'.

ASSIMILATION AND INDIFFERENCE

If a child seeking refugee can be seen as a site of difficulty, a problem to be fixed, then there is also the possibility that, in what Bauman (2005a, 2005b, 2013) calls 'liquid times', the same child will be meet not with hostility but with indifference. It is Bauman's view that, while modernity was governed by the vision of a perfectly harmonious society, "the current 'utopia' of hunters" is essentially "'deregulated', 'privatized', and 'individualized'" (Bauman, 2005a, p. 310). In postmodern, liquid times, then, the included are precisely those people for whom the absence of a solid ground is a chance to glide and the excluded those for whom it is a condemnation to stumble. Thus, Bauman writes:

Individuality' stands today, first and foremost, for the person's autonomy... [it] means that I am the one responsible for my merits and my failings, and that it is *my* task to cultivate the first and to repent and repair the second. (original emphasis, Bauman, 2005b, p. 19)

So where the modernist project was to assimilate the stranger into the assumed natural and given order of things, the postmodern or 'liquid' project of assimilation involves the paradoxical project of making the stranger conform to non-conformity, to fit into a way of life characterised precisely by the absence of well-trodden paths to walk along. The task here is not, then, to assimilate the other into a given order but into a world without order.

The Absence of Political Commitment to Immigrants in the UK

Before refugee children can be included into or assimilated within schooling in the UK, they must first, of course, be welcomed across the UK's borders. According to the British Red Cross (2017), there are an estimated 118,995 refugees living in the UK or 0.18 per cent of the total population (65.1 million people). This is estimation, based on the previous year's successful asylum applications, fails to account for any person who came to the UK illegally nor does it include those people staying on beyond a failed application. In terms of unaccompanied minors, in 2016 3,175 children sort asylum in the UK, which was a similar number to 2015 (Refugee Council, 2017). However, this is a stark increase from the previous year which had 1,945 applications and only 1265 in 2013 (Refugee Council, 2017). Consequently, applications for asylum from unaccompanied minors have more than doubled in just three years. The vast majority of these were minors were aged 16 and 17 (65%), with only 8% less than 14 years of age 2013 (Refugee Council, 2017).

However, further statistics, published by the *House of Commons* (Hawkins, 2017), are more telling of the UK's commitment to persons seeking refuge when the UK's immigration figures are compared to those of other EU countries. The UK granted 9,900 of 31,100 asylum applications in 2016 (a 31.8% approval rate) (Hawkins, 2017, p. 16), while France granted 28,800 of 87,500 applications (a 32.9% approval rate) and Italy granted 35,400 of 89,900 applications (a 39.4% approval rate) (Hawkins, 2017, p. 16). Significantly, the following EU countries were more than twice as likely as the UK to approve applications:

- Austria granted 30,400 of 42,400 applications (a 71.7% approval rate);
- Germany 433,900 of 631, 200 (68.7%);
- Netherlands 20,800 of 28,900 (72%);
- Spain 6,900 of 10,300 (67%); and
- Sweden 6,900 of 10,300 (67%) (Hawkins, 2017, p. 16).

Also crucial to our understanding of political commitment (or its absence) to the welfare of persons seeking refuge in the UK is a potentially significant amendment to the 2016 UK *Immigration Act*, tabled by Lord Alf Dubs, and now known as the 'Dubs Amendment'. This amendment, now law, as Section 67 of the Act and spoken of, in general public discourse, as the 'Dubs scheme', guarantees the safety of *some* children seeking refuge in the UK. The amendment, in Section 67 of the Act, states:

The Secretary of State must, as soon as possible after the passing of this Act, make arrangements to relocate to the United Kingdom and support a specified number of unaccompanied refugee children from other countries in Europe. (UK Parliament Act, 2016, p. 60)

However, despite a commitment to provide refuge for 480 lone children, a mere 200 children arrived in the UK in 2016 and not a single child has been transferred in the first 6 months of 2017 (Travis, 2017).

How can we account for this limited political commitment to the acceptance of refugees and what are its consequences in relation to the schooling of children seeking refuge in the UK? Slee's (2011, p. 38) diagnosis of 'collective indifference' in contemporary Western societies provides a useful way to begin to articulate an answer to these questions. Such societies are characterised, according to Beck (2002, p. 135), by processes that lead to 'the subjectivization and individualization of risks and contradictions', and this 'means that each person's biography is removed from given determinations and placed in his or her own hands'. Bauman (2007, p. 60), observing the same trends, notes:

[I]n our hedonistic and thoroughly individualized society... loving care for others for the other's sake is disparaged as leading to detestable "dependency" and so to be avoided at all cost, while taking responsibility for the other's well-being tends to be condemned as an imprudent limitation of freedom to go where pleasurable experiences beckon.

Such individualism is perpetuated in UK schools whenever schooling becomes valued as a means to external, economic ends, whenever it becomes difficult not 'to think of knowledge production and consumption after the pattern of fast food, prepared rapidly and eaten fresh, hot, and on the spot' (Bauman, 2005a, p. 316). The consequences of this reduction of learning to consuming are significant, since there is no better preparation for taking up a place in a society of indifferent individuals than being in a classroom of indifferent learners.

Indifference to Uniqueness: Assimilation and Deficiency Views of
Children Seeking Refuge

In 2005, the UK's Home Office published *Integration matters: National strategy for integration*, in it the inclusion of refugees in the UK was firmly connected to language acquisition and employment. In response to this approach to the integration of refugees, Pinson, Arnot, and Candappa (2010, p. 54) write:

The decision to include only refugees in integration programmes symbolically deepened the exclusion from which asylum seekers already suffered. In effect the message to schools from the Home Office was that only some of their students needed to be integrated, to be prepared for a national model of democratic citizenship or for membership of a local community.

In other words, a division is created: it is "them" and not "us" that are in need of integrating. Dada (2012, p. 153) emphasises the role that schools have to play not only as education providers but also as 'a gateway for leading a new and peaceful life and being part of a wider community'. He writes that language acquisition is vital for communication and for studying and that education can lead to employment. He also stresses the importance of adequate resourcing by Local Authorities to allow schools to provide appropriate support. McCorriston (2012) supports this view by stressing the importance of extended services such as Ethnic Minority Achievement Services (EMAS) supporting schools with the inclusion of children who are seeking asylum or who have refugee status. Such measures are, of course, essential features of the inclusion of children seeking refuge, but they do not in and of themselves constitute a guarantee of inclusion. Indeed, what is missing in such technical approaches is a 'school approach to social inclusion' that incorporates the "'the whole child' rather than specific educational needs" (Pinson & Arnot, 2010, p. 256). This means that embracing a merely specialist, additional needs based approach, to the inclusion of children seeking refuge risks ignoring a primary need of all children – one that is, nevertheless, especially acute in those children who have been uprooted from their homes – the need to find a place where one can belong within the world.

In her investigation into the experience of six male adolescent refugees as they began their education in London, Hastings (2012, p. 337) discovered how 'a whole school attitude to refugee children which allows them to feel confident to identify themselves as refugees'. This confidence to announce where one has come from is secured only once one feels oneself to be welcomed, to belong to – as opposed to being assimilated into – a concrete and shared space. Gillies and Robinson (2013), drawing on the findings of a study of young people at risk of being excluded from inner-city London schools, outline a quite different experience. They note how 'a contemporary preoccupation with notions of personal development and emotional learning', one that constitutes an 'apparently progressive and inclusive agenda', has resulted in 'a highly regulatory framework, ordering the ways in which teachers and pupils are expected to experience and express care' (Luff & Gillies, 2013, p. 42). Laurent (2013, p. 40), too, observes the painful irony that has seen a policy focus on 'values education and social and emotional learning' lead to 'highly regulated professional caring' at the cost of 'a school-wide focus on pedagogical care'. When our care for, and the education we offer to, children seeking refuge is seen as synonymous with the meeting of established needs in particular individual children, caring and educational relations can become delimited and the potential commonality between those receiving this care and education and others can be obscured.

ADDRESSING HOSTILITY AND INDIFFERENCE: INCLUSIVE VALUES AND PRACTICES

Writing over twenty years ago, Bauman (1995, p. 14) contended that 'there is a genuine emancipatory chance in postmodernity, the chance of laying down arms, suspending border skirmishes waged to keep the stranger away, taking apart the daily erected mini-Berlin walls meant to keep distance and to separate'. Of course, this 'emancipatory chance' has passed and the borders stand firm, more fortified than ever. The chance was not taken and exclusion and assimilation remain. And yet, Bauman stands firms in his belief that the gardener's vision of a perfectly harmonious landscape, which guided the governance of modern societies, has come to be replaced by "the current 'utopia' of hunters", which is essentially "'deregulated', 'privatized', and 'individualized'" (Bauman, 2005a, 310). In other words, the defining state has lost its capacity to define, the gardener has left the garden, and the opportunity awaits us to allow persons designated as strangers to grow as they are, and not as some bureaucrat would have them grow. What is required first of all to understand our need for strangeness and the stranger. Might schools of sanctuary have a role to play in this process?

The Deputy Head of a School of Sanctuary reflected:

> One of the things that's really made a difference in achieving becoming an inclusive school and a School of Sanctuary is just being really clear in articulating our values. And the children, well they're really proud of them, but it's a new thing for them to think and talk about values and apply them to different situations.

Booth (1999) argues that all involved in schooling share a responsibility to address how our schools might change, how they may become places that are worthy of the inclusion of *all* young people. This suggests a move from viewing 'some learners as a focus for inclusion and a group apart' to seeing all students 'as part of the diversity that includes us all' (Booth, 1999, p. 165). Asked about individualised attention to children seeking refuge, the Headteacher of a School of Sanctuary responded:

> I think the best thing to do is just make sure that you've got the culture where whatever's right for that child if they want to talk about it then they know they'll be listened to with a sympathetic ear for that or if they want to access support in more of a low key way then that's fine as well.

There is a subtle and important irony at work here: the rejection an individualised approach – where needs are looked upon as 'special', as evidence of individual deficiency – in favour of a whole school approach actually enables teachers to address the unique needs of all their children. This is the case for no other reason than this approach, as the Headteacher illuminates, promotes deep listening, that is, listening to the child for the person they are now and for the person they are becoming, and not for what they have been through and what they are categorised as being. Asked how they welcome children seeking sanctuary, the Deputy Headteacher response conveys the significance of such careful attention to the uniqueness of all children:

> We respond in the same way that we would welcome anyone to the school: to make sure that they feel safe, that they understand who everybody is, where everything is that we have a really good understanding of who they are as a

person what their needs might be and new children are always paired up with somebody in a classroom and we try if possible if there's another child who is from the same part of the world or speaks the same language, to be paired up so that they have that kind of comfort too.

Inclusion stands, then, in contrast to a specialist approach to children seeking refuge, one that focuses merely on additional needs and deficiency. Schools of Sanctuary suggest that what is lacking in this approach – with its blinkered focus on what is lacking in the newcomer to the UK and to the school – is an acknowledgement of what this newcomer can contribute to the school and to the world beyond the school.

Rutter and Jones (2001, p. 3) observe that in there may be the risk that the 'refugee child' is viewed as a 'problem' in UK schooling, that the pressure on resources and the ever-present possibility of a school inspection may contribute to less than an inclusive welcome for a newly arrived child. 'Put an unheralded, non-English speaking refugee child into that classroom teacher's classroom on a wet, cold February morning', Rutter and Jones (2001, p. 3) maintain, 'and a camel's-last-straw reaction may seem understandable'. And yet, Rutter and Jones (2001, p. 3) insist that a child seeking sanctuary or a child granted refugee status may bring 'a range of opportunities and perspectives that can enrich the learning and understandings of everyone working there'.

However, the contributions that children seeking refuge might make should not, we contend, be delimited to their ability to share insights into the culture, geography and history of the land they have been forced to leave. This would be to risk degrading these newcomers to a particularly exotic species of the Stranger. On the contrary, the child seeking refuge, the newcomer, is new to the school and new, also, to the world. To include this child is to welcome and to celebrate a uniqueness that is entirely their own and which is becoming still in accordance with the child's growing ability to make a difference to others. The Deputy Head of a School of Sanctuary expresses how we might begin to address such otherising by way of encouraging reflection on and compassion for the experiences of others in the following reflections:

> We've made welcome bags recently for refugees and asylum seekers that are new to the city and it really made the children think about how would they feel if they were in that position, and what would they want to be in the bag, what would help to make them feel welcome, and their ideas were fantastic, really good. I think it's opened their eyes to different experiences and different challenges around the world and it's really helped them to show their empathy towards others.

Such values-led practices open up the possibility that inclusive communities might be created where persons enable, and in turn allow themselves to be enabled by, others.

CONCLUSION

In this chapter we have argued that the inclusion of children seeking refuge into schools stands in direct opposition to assimilation. In an inclusive school, we have contended, not only are children's individual histories, experiences, culture and faith celebrated, but attention is given to the distinct and unique characters of all children. In developing such inclusive schools, schools in the UK have turned for guidance to the Framework advanced by the UK's Schools of Sanctuary organisation. In these schools, teachers, support workers, other professionals and parents work together to elude a deficiency approach to the education of children seeking refuge so they might prepare all the children within their school for a flourishing life in an inclusive community.

REFERENCES

Bauman, Z. (1995). The making and unmaking of strangers. *Thesis Eleven, 43*(1), 1–16.
Bauman, Z. (2005a). Education in liquid modernity. *Review of Education, Pedagogy, and Cultural Studies, 27*(4), 303–317.
Bauman, Z. (2005b). *Liquid life*. Cambridge: Polity Press.
Bauman, Z. (2007). *Society under siege*. Cambridge: Polity Press.
Bauman, Z. (2012). *On education: Conversations with Richard Mazzeo*. Cambridge: Polity Press.
Bauman, Z. (2013). *Liquid modernity*. Cambridge: Polity Press.
Bauman, Z. (2016a). *Strangers at our door*. Cambridge: Polity Press.
Bauman, Z. (2016b, July 22). Bauman: History repeats itself: We are coming back to the small, tribal states (An interview with Helena Celestino). *Political Critique*. Retrieved from http://politicalcritique.org/world/2016/bauman-history-repeats-itself-interview/
Beck, U. (2002). *Risk society: Towards a new modernity* (M. Ritter, Trans.). London: Sage Publications.
Booth, T. (1999). Viewing inclusion from a distance: Gaining perspective from comparative study. *Support for Learning, 14*(4), 164–168.
British Red Cross. (2017). *Refugee facts and figures*. Retrieved from http://www.redcross.org.uk/What-we-do/Refugee-support/Refugee-facts-and-figures
Burton, D., & Bartlett, S. (2009). *Key issues for education governors*. London: Sage Publications.
Collins Dictionary. (2017). *Se réfugier*. Retrieved March 6, 2017, from https://www.collinsdictionary.com/dictionary/french-english/se-réfugier
Dada, J. (2012). Refugees and education in Kent in England. In L. Demirdjian (Ed.), *Education, refugees and asylum seekers* (pp. 151–165). London: Continuum.
Department for Children, Schools and Families (DCSF). (2007). *Guidance on the duty to promote community cohesion*. London: DCSF.
Due, C., Riggs, D. W., & Augoustinos, M. (2016). Diversity in intensive English language centres in South Australia: Sociocultural approaches to education for students with migrant or refugee backgrounds. *International Journal of Inclusive Education, 20*(12), 1286–1296.
Dunford, D., & Kirk. A. (2016). Revealed: The most eurosceptic and europhilic areas in the UK. *The Telegraph*. Retrieved from http://www.telegraph.co.uk/news/2016/06/24/revealed-the-most-eurosceptic-and-europhilic-areas-in-the-uk/
Elgot, J. (2017). Refugee children 'could be separated from their families after Brexit'. *The Guardian*. Retrieved from https://www.theguardian.com/uk-news/2017/aug/04/refugee-children-could-be-separated-from-their-families-after-brexit
Garthwaite, K. (2011). 'The language of shirkers and scroungers?' Talking about illness, disability and coalition welfare reform. *Disability and Society, 26*(3), 369–372.
Gillies, V., & Robinson, Y. (2013). At risk pupils and the 'caring curriculum. In C. Rogers & S. Weller (Eds.), *Critical approaches to care: Understanding caring relations, identities and cultures* (pp. 15–17). London: Routledge.
Goodwin-Gill, G., & McAdam, J. (2007). *The refugee in international law* (3rd ed.). Oxford: Oxford University Press.

Hastings, C. (2012). The experience of male adolescent refugees during their transfer and adaptation to a UK secondary school. *Educational Psychology in Practice, 28*(4), 335–351.

Hawkins, O. (2017). Asylum Statistics: Briefing Paper (Number SN01403). *House of Commons.* Retrieved from http://researchbriefings.parliament.uk/ResearchBriefing/Summary/SN01403#fullreport

Home Office. (2005). *Integration matters: National strategy for integration.* London: Home Office.

Khosravinik, M. (2010). The representation of refugees, asylum seekers and immigrants in British newspapers: A critical discourse analysis. *The Journal of Language and Politics, 9*(1), 1–28.

Laurent, U. (2013). Revisiting care in schools: Exploring the caring experiences of disengaged young people. In C. Rogers & S. Weller (Eds.), *Critical approaches to care: Understanding caring relations, identities and cultures* (pp. 30–41). London: Routledge.

Lister, R., & F. Bennett. (2010). The new 'champion of progressive ideals'? Cameron's conservative party: Poverty, family policy and welfare reform. *Renewal: A Journal of Social Democracy, 18*(1–2), 84–108.

MacDonald, F. (2017). Positioning young refugees in Australia: Media discourse and social exclusion. *International Journal of Inclusive Education, 21*(11), 1182–1195.

McCorriston, M. (2012). Twenty-first learning: The role of community cohesion in refugee education. In L. Demirdjian (Ed.), *Education, refugees and asylum seekers* (pp. 166–189). London: Continuum.

Oxford Living Dictionary. (2017). *Refugee.* Retrieved March 6, 2017, from https://en.oxforddictionaries.com/definition/refugee

Pinson, H., & Arnot, M. (2010). Local conceptualisations of the education of asylum-seeking and refugee students: From hostile to holistic models. *International Journal of Inclusive Education, 14*(3), 247–267.

Refugee Council. (2017). *Children in the asylum system.* Retrieved from https://www.refugeecouncil.org.uk/assets/0004/0485/Children_in_the_Asylum_System_May_2017.pdf

Rutter, J., & Jones, C. (2001). *Refugee education: Mapping the field.* Stoke on Trent: Trentham Books.

Saks, M., & Allsop, J. (2013). *Researching health: Qualitative, quantitative and mixed methods.* London: Sage Publications.

Savin-Baden, M., & Major, C. H. (2013). *Qualitative research: The essential guide to theory and practice.* London: Routledge.

Slee, R. (2011). *The irregular school: Exclusion, schooling and inclusive education.* London: Routledge.

Travis, A. (2017). UK has not taken in any child refugees under dubs scheme this year. *The Guardian.* Retrieved from https://www.theguardian.com/uk-news/2017/jul/19/uk-not-taken-any-child-refugees-dubs-scheme-this-year

UK Parliament. (2016). *Immigration act.* London: UK Parliament. Retrieved from http://www.legislation.gov.uk/ukpga/2016/19/pdfs/ukpga_20160019_en.pdf

Walmsley, J., & Johnson, K. (2003). *Inclusive research with people with learning disabilities: Past, present and futures.* London: Jessica Kingsley.

Wittgenstein, L. (1975). *The blue and brown books.* London: Blackwell.

Wayne Veck
University of Winchester
Winchester, UK

Julie Wharton
University of Winchester
Winchester, UK

Julie Wharton
University of Winchester
Winchester, UK

ABOUT THE CONTRIBUTORS

EDITOR

Fabio Dovigo (PhD) is Professor for Inclusive Education and Organisational Research Methods at the University of Bergamo. He is co-ordinator of International Relations and Erasmus+ Programs at the Department of Human and Social Sciences. His research interests include research methods in education and organisation, inclusive education, and mediation and coaching. He edited *Special Educational Needs and Inclusive Practices* (Sense Publisher, 2016).

AUTHORS

Oula Abu-Amsha is a Syrian Computer Science and Applied Mathematics Professor. She started her activities in refugee education in 2014 working with the World Bank education team. Since December 2015, she is the academic adviser of Jamiya, leading the development of courses and support services specifically designed for Syrian refugee students. She is currently a visiting scholar at the School of Engineering and Business of the Canton of Vaud, and at the University of Teacher Education of Lucerne, Switzerland.

Miki Aristorenas holds a Master degree (Ed.M.) in International Education Policy from the Harvard Graduate School of Education. Miki has worked on international and US policy projects with education non-profits in and outside of the United States, with the Swedish Education Ministry, the Department of Education in the Philippines and English language centres. She has been engaged with the Jamiya Project since 2016.

Tatjana Atanasoska has been a research assistant at the Centre of Teacher Education at the University of Vienna, but is now a research assistant at the Bergische Universität Wuppertal. Her main topics include a broad range of questions regarding migration and (secondary) schooling, with a special focus on education for young refugees. Her didactical focus is on German (as a second language) and language education.

Benjamin Braß is a research associate at the faculty for primary school pedagogy of Koblenz-Landau University, Germany. He teaches classes in primary school pedagogy and social studies and science teaching and he manages the GeKOS project. His research interests include teacher professionalization, video-based teacher education programs and pedagogical observation.

Henrik Bruns (PhD) is a research associate at the faculty for primary school pedagogy of Koblenz-Landau University, Germany. He is responsible for the evaluation and accompanying research of the GeKOS project. His research interests include pedagogical professionalization, evaluation methodology, quality management, organizational pedagogy and pedagogical theory of action.

Heike de Boer (PhD) is professor for primary school pedagogy and social studies and science teaching at the faculty for primary school pedagogy of Koblenz-Landau University, Germany. In 2015, she has established GeKOS, a mentoring programme for refugee children. Her research interests include teacher professionalization, cooperation between institutions in teacher education and school development, classroom interaction and pedagogical observation.

Sanja Grbić (MSc) is a doctoral student and teaching assistant at the University of Belgrade, Department of psychology, awarded with national scholarship for the best doctoral students in Serbia. She participates in research projects at the Institute for Educational Research and her professional interests include attachment and self-concept in adolescence, inclusive education and narrative approach.

Hermína Gunnþórsdóttir (PhD) is associate professor at the University of Akureyri, Iceland. Her teaching and research interest is related to inclusive school and education, multiculturalism and education, social justice in education, disability studies, educational policy and practice. She is editor of the Icelandic Journal of Education.

Laure Kloetzer (PhD) is Assistant Professor in Socio-Cultural Psychology at the University of Neuchâtel, Switzerland. Her research interests include learning and development in formal and informal contexts, as well as transforming dialogue and collaboration in professional, educational or other institutional contexts. She is doing citizen science and collaborative research, i.e. research which creates tight collaborations between scientists and other people for social innovation.

Tünde Kovacs Cerović (PhD) is Professor of Educational Psychology and Education Policy at Faculty of Philosophy, Belgrade University. Serbia. She served as Assistant Minister and State Secetary of Education in Serbia and participated in the work of the Roma Education Fund in Budapest. Her recent research and publications address education of Roma, migrants, children living in poverty and inclusive education.

Louise Pagden (EDD) is a senior lecturer at the University of Winchester. She lectures on both undergraduate and post-graduate teacher training courses, as well as post-graduate research courses. Her research interests lie in second language education, education policy and refugee education.

Michelle Proyer (PhD) holds a Tenure Track position in inclusive education at the Centre of Teacher Education and the Department of Education of the University of

Vienna. Her research focuses on disability at the nexus of culture and migration. Currently, she oversees a project for refugee teachers.

Wayne Veck started his teaching career as a teacher of English to students from Afghanistan and Iraq seeking refuge in the UK. He is now Reader in Education at Winchester University, where he is also the Faculty of Education Health and Social Care's Head of Research and Knowledge Exchange. He has published widely about inclusion and exclusion in education.

Dragan Vesić (MSc) is a doctoral student of Ppsychology and a junior researcher at the Institute for Educational Research, Belgrade, Serbia. He is a Secretary General of the Editorial Board of the *Journal of the Institute for Educational Research*. His interest areas are school absenteeism, intercultural education and constructivist approach in therapy and research.

Julie Wharton is a Senior Lecturer in the Faculty of Education, Health and Social Care at the University of Winchester. She is the course leader for the National Award for Special Educational Needs Co-ordination. Her research interests are the language of inclusion and children seeking sanctuary.